THE
FENCE

CONTRIBUTIONS IN SOCIOLOGY

Series Editor: Don Martindale

The Social Dimensions of Mental Illness, Alcoholism, and Drug Dependence
Don Martindale and Edith Martindale

Those People: The Subculture of a Housing Project
Colette Petonnet. Rita Smidt, Translator

Sociology in Israel
Leonard Weller

The Revolutionary Party: Essays in the Sociology of Politics
Feliks Gross

Group Interaction as Therapy: The Use of the Small Group in Corrections
Richard M. Stephenson and Frank R. Scarpitti

Sociology of the Black Experience
Daniel C. Thompson

The Incomplete Adult: Social Class Constraints on Personality Development
Margaret J. Lundberg

Sociology in Australia and New Zealand: Theory and Methods
Cora V. Baldock and Jim Lally

Handbook of Contemporary Developments in World Sociology
Raj P. Mohan and Don Martindale, editors

The New Social Sciences
Baidya Nath Varma, editor

The Population Challenge: A Handbook for Nonspecialists
Johannes Overbeek

Victims of Change: Juvenile Delinquents in American Society
Harold Finestone

THE FENCE

A new look at the world of property theft

MARILYN E. WALSH

Contributions in
Sociology,
Number 21

GREENWOOD PRESS
Westport, Connecticut
London, England

Library of Congress Cataloging in Publication Data

Walsh, Marilyn E
   The fence.

   (Contributions in sociology ; no. 21)
   Bibliography: p.
   Includes index.
   1. Receiving stolen goods—United States.
I. Title.
HV6658.W3   381   76-5266
ISBN 0-8371-8910-1

Library of Congress Catalog Card Number: 76-5266
ISBN: 0-8371-8910-1

First published in 1977

Greenwood Press, Inc.
51 Riverside Avenue, Westport, Connecticut 06880

Printed in the United States of America

To my mother, Catherine Walsh
—for always being there

Contents

LIST OF TABLES   xi

PREFACE   xiii

ACKNOWLEDGMENTS   xv

INTRODUCTION 'In Search of the Contemporary
                Receiver of Stolen Goods   3

   Research Strategy of the Inquiry   7
   Conceptual Parameters of the Inquiry   10
     The Wages and Ways of Organization   10
     An Emphasis on Function   13

1 SOME HISTORY AND FOLKLORE OF FENCING   17

   The Classic Case of Mr. Jonathan Wild   17
   The Life and Times of Jonathan Wild   18
   Wild, The Study   23
   The Importance of Organization   24
   The Importance of Power   25
   The Importance of Property   26
   Peachums, Fagins, Pawnbrokers, and Jews—
     The Folklore of Fencing   27
   The Great Failure of Mr. Jonathan Wild   28
   Wild Transformed   29
   Fagin   32

   The Pawnbroker, the Jew, and the Peddler   33
   Clear and Absent Notions of the Criminal Receiver   35
   Truths and Consequences   37

2 DEMOGRAPHIC CHARACTERISTICS OF PROPERTY
   THEFT PRINCIPALS   39

   Describing the Fence   39
   Old Enough to Be a Fence   42
   The Fence's Other Occupation   45
   The Fence and Arrest Figures   46
   A General Composite of the Fence   49

3 PRODUCTS, PRICES, AND PROMOTIONAL
   CONSIDERATIONS   52

   Defining Some Terms   53
   Products   54
     What's for Sale   54
     That Certain Thief   60
     As Much as the Traffic Will Bear   65
     Something Old and Something New   67
     Whatever There's a Market for   69
   Prices   71
     Paying the Thief   71
     Pricing to Sell   76
   Promotional Considerations   81
     Promotion for the Businessman-Fence   82
     Promoting an Image   83

4 LEGITIMATE FRONTS FOR ILLEGITIMATE
   ENTERPRISE   85

   Business in Its American Setting   85
   A Word About Fronts and Blinds   86
   Legitimate Fronts   87
     The Integrative Front   88
     The Functional-Facilitating Front   92

The Dissonant Front 100
Marketing Indicators in Legitimate Fronts 103
Illegitimacy and Circumstance in the Fencing Trade 106
  Criminal Enterpreneurs 107
  Independents 111
  Employees 113

5 THE RIGHT MAN FOR THE RIGHT JOB:
    FENCING NETWORKS 116
  The Fencing Network 117
  The Kinship Network 119
  The Work-a-Day Network 123
  The "Play" Network 128
  The Network Maze 133
  Theft and the Network Mechanism: An Evaluation 138
    Association 139
    Risk-Taking 140
    Recruitment 141
    Procedural Ratiocination 142
    Selective Skill Diffusion 143
    Information Dissemination 144
  The Network and Its Implications 145

6 THE DECREASING UTILITY OF THE THEFT GAME 147

  The Theft Game 149
    The Theft Game—Type A: Police versus Addict 154
    *The Theft Game—Type B: Police versus Known
      Burglar* 160
    *The Theft Game—Type C: Police versus Good
      Burglar* 164
  The Conventional View of Theft: An Assessment 170
  Property Theft: An Alternative View 174

  EPILOG *A New Look at the World of Property
      Theft and Beyond* 178

  APPENDIX *The Data: Some Notes and Caveats* 180

CONTENTS

NOTES   188

BIBLIOGRAPHY   203

INDEX   207

List of tables

1   Race and Sex Distribution of Fences   40
2   Distribution of White Males Within Subgroups   43
3   Age Distributions of Fences and Burglars at Data Site   44
4   Percentage Age Distributions of Legitimate Self-Employed Managers and Administrators in Wholesale and Retail Trades and of White Male Fences from Sample in These Same Trades   45
5   Distribution of Sample Fences on the Basis of Occupational Affiliations   47
6   Distribution of Burglars on Basis of Occupational Affiliations   48
7   Business Establishments of Fences Arranged in Order of Frequency   49
8   Distribution of Fences Relative to Arrest History   50
9   Distribution of Burglars Relative to Arrest History   51
10   Distribution of Fences by Degree of Product and Product-Line Specialization   56
11   Products and Product Lines Handled by Criminal Receivers in Order of Frequency   57
12   Products and Businesses of the Businessman-Fence   59
13   Product Listings of Fences by Type of Thief   64
14   Number of Fences Dealing with Each Type of Thief   66
15   Number of Fences Specializing in Goods in Each Marketing Class   70

16   Integrative Fronts of the Businessman-Fence   89
17   Segmentation Found in Integrative Fronts on
     the Basis of Clientele   90
18   Functional-Facilitating Fronts of the Businessman-
     Fence   93
19   Functional-Facilitating Fronts and Their Product Lines   95
20   Clienteles Served by Functional-Facilitating Fronts   97
21   Dissonant Fronts of the Businessman-Fence, Their
     Product Lines, and Clienteles   102
22   Primary Vocations of the Criminal Entrepreneur-
     Fence   108
23   Occupational Affiliations, Product Lines, and
     Clienteles of Fences Employed by Others   114
24   Model of the Game Matrix   152
25   The Theft Game—Type A: Police versus Addict   157
26   The Theft Game—Type B: Police versus Known Burglar   163
27   The Theft Game—Type C: Police versus Good Burglar   168
28   The Theft Game—Type D: "We" versus "They"   169

Preface

In any review of U.S. crime statistics, the overwhelming prominence of theft offenses in the total picture is everywhere revealed. Additionally, victimization studies by the National Crime Panel have suggested that approximately three times as many theft events occur as are reported. No crime category is perpetrated as frequently against as wide a range of victims as is theft. Theft becomes, more by its pervasive nature and consistent occurrence than by its drama, this country's number one crime problem.

Perhaps it is the sheer frequency of theft that robs each single crime of its drama. Admittedly, an individual burglary or larceny is rarely as dramatic or as shocking as are most violent crimes. And yet, familiarity with theft events would seem to have obscured the fact that they are serious intrusions on our lives. The theft victim experiences a trauma no less real than the violent crime victim, though perhaps less compelling in its detail. Still, the frequency of theft has inured us somehow, often making it an accepted, albeit unpleasant, fact of modern life—one which rarely startles or enrages us.

The lack of drama associated with theft has tended to make innovative thinking on the subject somewhat difficult. Such is particularly the case with property theft, a large and important subset of theft. Studies on property theft are primarily thief-oriented. The unique, extra dimension inherent in property theft is often ignored. This dimension relates to the fact that stolen property must, in most cases, be converted by the thief to a more useful and relevant medium (cash or drugs, for example). This need to convert goods gives property theft a transfer function and engenders the critically important requirement that at least one other functionary besides the thief be involved in the consummation of the crime. It is this other functionary, the fence or receiver of stolen goods, to whom this inquiry is directed.

Without considering the fence, we are left with a view of property theft which stops at the thief and place of the initial event, and fails to move with the crime to the person of the receiver and the setting in which the initial event is consummated. Official records indicate that property thefts continue to escalate while the rates of solution remain poor and the rates of recovery of stolen goods remain even poorer. When the fence is not considered, we fail to appreciate the drama, complexity, and organized nature of property theft or to understand the severe limitations of most current approaches.

There is, of course, no magic solution to the persistent problem of property theft. It is hoped, however, that this inquiry, by taking a new look at the subject, will describe the problem in such a way that new approaches can be discovered and effective strategies can be developed.

We have lived with property theft a long time without knowing it well at all. Knowing it better may be the first step toward experiencing it less.

Acknowledgments

For one as indebted as I to so many people, these are both the happiest and the hardest pages to write. Happy, because I have had considerable help and encouragement, but hard because I must in a few pages express a degree of gratitude that could fill volumes. I have come to depend on many different people who have seen the manuscript in various stages of development.

To the district attorney's office and the detectives in the Safe and Burglary Squad at the data site, thanks for their assistance and sharing of significant knowledge as well as for their personal interest. I shared a part of their lives and work and was given thereby a research experience rich in concern, in understanding, and in mutual respect that will rarely be matched, I suspect.

To friends and colleagues at the School of Criminal Justice, Albany, New York, who shared and/or burdened under the highs and lows of the original research project; in particular to Jo Ann DeSilva, Harriet Spector, and Mildred MacLain, who helped with the first draft of the manuscript and showed special courage in doing so, many thanks.

To Professor Hans Toch, who more than anyone else has influenced the style of the research herein, a thank you for stimulating me to go "out there" and explore and experience. To Professor Leslie Wilkins, who very particularly and carefully shaped my way of thinking about things, who taught me to ask "how" and not "why," and whose essential intellectual freedom encouraged me to "run it around the block and see if the wheels come off," I owe a special gratitude.

To Professors Duncan Chappell, Michael Hindelang, and Donald Newman, for their patience, support, and encouragement, I thank you. To Professor Newman particularly goes appreciation for his editorial criticism and boundless wit. To Professor Hindelang goes much gratitude for his time and encouragement and for being methodologist, mentor, and friend. To Professor Chappell goes a deep and abiding gratitude for interesting me in fencing, for not knowing the words "can't" and "shouldn't," for letting me grow and take charge, and for being a colleague and friend.

To friends and colleagues in the Law and Justice Study Center go many thanks for listening through these last furious months of excitement and hysteria and to my frets that have accompanied them.

To Roma St. James for her patience through several revisions, editions, and corrections; for making intelligible the pages of scribbled notes that I could hardly read any more; and for believing it was all very important, a very special thank you.

To my husband, Bob, who, after having been the one person who has seen the whole process, remains patient ear and strong shoulder, go a particular love and gratitude for the serenity, understanding, and unfaltering belief that made it more bearable, and for the months of listening, proofreading, and hand holding.

Finally to my mother go love and gratitude for being there; her curiosity, enthusiasm, sensitivity, objectivity, and strength make nothing impossible.

THE
FENCE

Introduction
In search of the contemporary criminal receiver of stolen goods

For more than two centuries, commentators who have looked at property theft have found it necessary to address not only the thief but also the criminal receiver of stolen property. The receiver has been described as a very important actor in property theft and a crucial figure in the support and maintenance of the thief. In 1770, Sir John Fielding, in testimony before the English Parliament, attributed London's increased burglary and robbery rates to the existence of immediate outlets for the proceeds of theft provided by receivers.[1] Patrick Colquhoun, in *A Treatise on the Police of the Metropolis* (1795), was most forceful in his indictment of the receiver.[2]

> In contemplating the characters of all these different classes of delinquents (that is Thieves, Robbers, Cheats and Swindlers), *there can be little hesitation in pronouncing the Receivers to be the most mischievious of the whole; inasmuch as without the aid they afford*, in purchasing and concealing every species of property stolen or fraudulently obtained, *Thieves, Robbers and Swindlers, . . . must quit the trade*, as unproductive and hazardous in the extreme.
>
> *Nothing therefore can be more just than the old observation, "that if there were no Receivers there would be no Thieves".* — *Deprive a thief of a sale and ready market for his goods and he is undone.*

Similarly in 1928, the Association of Grand Jurors of New York County, in its study of the receiving laws of the forty-eight states and Alaska, described the receiver as follows: "He not only furnishes the incentive to crime by providing a market, but he organizes and directs criminals, and very often finances them."[3] More recently, the President's Crime Commission characterized the receiver as one of the two "essential relationships"[4] which the professional criminal must establish in order to successfully survive. In 1968, Jerome Hall, whose analysis of criminal receiving had provided the basis for the Crime Commission's remarks, updated his own work of 1935 and stated: *"It is clear that the criminal receiver is the heart of the theft problem.* Not only large-scale professional theft but also countless thefts by juveniles and occasional offenders depend on the availability of a regular market—and to provide that service is the crucial function of the criminal receiver."[5]

Despite protestations since the eighteenth century regarding the importance of this figure, the criminal receiver (legally defined as one who *"knowingly* possesses—buys, receives or conceals—stolen property, with intent to benefit himself or a person other than an owner thereof or to impede the recovery by an owner thereof"[6]) conveys at best only a faint impression of criminal conduct to most of us. With the exception of literary representations of the receiver—Dickens' Fagin perhaps being the most notable—we really know very little about either the crime or the person of the criminal receiver.

This lack of information about the "fence" (as the criminal receiver is colloquially called) and about criminal receiving generally is particularly surprising in a nation where theft losses each year total billions of dollars, for the criminal receiver has traditionally been associated with the support and facilitation of thievery. Colquhoun, for example, describes the receiver as "affording aid [to the thief] . . . purchasing and concealing" stolen property; the Association of Grand Jurors refer to fences as "furnishing incentives, providing a market, organizing and financing" property theft; and Hall says the fence is "providing a service." The substantial amount of property theft in this society suggests a potentially important part played by the criminal receiver. Hence a long overdue investigation of him, his crime, and his relationship to the thief appears warranted. Such, in effect, is the goal of this study: to investigate contemporary criminal receiving and to describe its principals, processes, and functions. In short, we have been in search of the contemporary receiver.

Because the fence is a relatively unknown crime figure, it is necessary to distinguish our subject of study from others who may come into contact with stolen property. The law limits the parameters of the receiving population by requiring "knowledge" on the part of the criminal receiver. Thus, anyone who unknowingly acquires stolen property is not considered to be in violation of the law. We have accepted this limitation and do not include the "innocent" purchaser of stolen property to be part of our concern.

The thief, however, presents a different problem. By virtue of his activities he often possesses or conceals stolen property. Where criminal receiving is proscribed under a possession statute, thieves can be, and are, arrested for just that. Does that make the thief a criminal receiver? For our purposes, we have said no. The person or persons actively involved in the actual separation of property from an owner are not to be considered criminal receivers unless he or they also perform the tasks associated with the redistribution of the property to a final consumer.

The final consumers of stolen property present problems analogous to those raised by the thief. Someone who knowingly buys stolen property deprives an owner thereof, and hence violates criminal receiving statutes. Here, however, we have adopted the guidelines of Jerome Hall in distinguishing between the "lay" and the "professional" receiver. The lay receiver acquires stolen property for personal consumption. The professional receiver acquires stolen property for the purpose of resale. [7] Although we by no means condone the behavior of lay receivers, *professional* receivers are the basis of this inquiry.

Having stipulated the professional receiver to be the major subject of our concern, it is necessary to decide whether to focus on him as an individual or as a principal in property theft. Clearly the latter has been our interest. Thus we are concerned with the manner in which the receiver "affords aid . . . furnishes incentives . . . provides a market . . . and organizes and finances" property theft—if indeed that is what he does. Although we have seen it as somewhat important to describe the kinds of individuals who are professional criminal receivers, we place greater emphasis on the *crime* of criminal receiving as exhibited through individuals.

Finally, it is necessary to establish a conceptual framework in which to organize and relate the crime of criminal receiving. We have chosen to view information relating to the criminal receiver and his activities within the structure of a "new look" at property theft generally. Thus, criminal receiving is not studied as a separate entity, but rather as a set of persons and activities relating to the theft and to stolen property. For if the criminal receiver is important to property theft, then what we learn about him and his crimes should provide a new and deepened understanding of this crime area.

Having set the above ground rules—that we are studying the activities of those individuals who acquire stolen property for the purpose of resale as they relate to the organization and patterns of property theft existing in society—we are ready to begin our investigation of criminal receiving. "Beginning" is not, however, easy or straightforward when one considers the somewhat illusive and anonymous criminal receiver. We have, therefore, begun by "looking backward," where the fullest account of any receiver is to be found in the life and actions of the eighteenth-century British receiver Jonathan Wild. In order to grasp some of the cultural strands that constitute current notions of the receiver, we have investigated the probable sources of the folklore of criminal receiving. In this way we have attempted to account for the anonymity of this offender and his offense, and the lack of an investigation of either.

We then consider criminal receiving as it is currently exhibited by individuals in one urban area of the United States. Hall's precept has been our guide:[8]

... the only adequate approach to the criminal receiver is that which deals with him as an established participant in the economic life of society.

Thus we have viewed the receiver's established participation in society in an economic or marketing milieu as the intermediary in the flow of property from productive sources (thieves) to consumption ends (customers). It has been instructive and revealing to compare this intermediary with other intermediaries in the economic life of society.

Finally, we have "looked forward" with the aid of game theory to interpret what contemporary criminal receiving tells us about how we respond to property theft and also how we *might* respond to this area of criminal activity. A reexamination of the relationships between the thief and receiver and between the police and both of these figures has provided a new framework, the Stolen Property System (SPS), in which the activities of all these individuals might be better interpreted.

RESEARCH STRATEGY OF THE INQUIRY

Since this inquiry has constituted a search for the contemporary receiver, we must identify how and where he has been sought and found. There would appear to be three available choices or strategies of research. First, a researcher might directly interview fences themselves. This strategy carries two broad implications: (1) that the researcher knows who and where the fences are, and (2) that the fences are willing to cooperate. Neither of these implications is necessarily unfounded or even insurmountable in the breach. A local police department might be able to supply information on who and where fences are.[9] A similar inquiry placed with thieves might yield analogous results. Still another method might be to investigate those persons or places traditionally associated with receiving. Using this approach, a researcher might survey and interview local pawnbrokers and peddlers. Once found, the fence would have to be persuaded to cooperate—an eventuality that is likely to depend on many factors: the nature of the initial contact, the trustworthiness of the researcher, and the general openness of the fence as an individual.

The second strategy a researcher might pursue is to find the contemporary fence as he exists in the eyes of the thief. Again problems of locating and gaining the cooperation of respondents are present but perhaps to a lesser degree than with the fence himself. Any prison will yield a sample of thieves of varying loquacity who are potential information sources. The word "potential" must be stressed, for although a thief may be fairly easily found, he may be less easily persuaded to talk about his fence.

The thief should not be ruled out, however, as a valuable tool in a search for the contemporary fence. He is after all in an excellent position to comment on the receiver's activities, and although his knowledge on the subject may be limited to his specific contacts, the nature of his perspective cannot be found in any other source.

A third research strategy capable of yielding a portrait of the modern fence is the use of official sources—with particular reference to the police. Other agencies in the criminal justice system—the courts and correctional institutions—are not likely to be well-acquainted with the fence. Joseph P. Busch, the late district attorney of Los Angeles County, in questioning before the Senate Small Business Committee noted that statistics on receiving stolen property are misleading since many persons arrested for the offense are really burglars rather than fences. [10] The same situation is also apparent in New York where the specific offense became criminal possession of stolen property in the 1967 revision of the penal law. Many criminal possession arrests in New York reflect burglary arrests rather than the apprehension of receivers of stolen property. Even when arrested and convicted, however, fences are not likely to become prison statistics. District Attorney Busch said, "Generally speaking . . . you would expect that they would [go to jail] . . . [but] as you will hear from some of the receivers that will testify here, they get suspended sentences and fines." [11] Other witnesses before the Senate Committee who were alleged to be receivers testified to not having served time for the offense, although they did admit to having been fined and given probationary sentences.

The search for the contemporary receiver via official agencies, then, revolves around working with the police and not so much with their statistics as with their intelligence materials. This strategy raises the critical question of access to such materials. John Mack, in his work on professional criminals in Great Britain, notes that although "what the police know is patchy and largely inferential, it is also true that the police know a great deal more about crime as a major behavior system than any criminologist can get to know without their help." [12] Here lies a vast untapped resource for criminologists. First because, as Mack suggests, "[t]he successful police detective is apt to be almost as uncommunicative as the able criminal." [13] But perhaps even more important as a barrier to police-assisted research than the tight-lipped detective is what Mack sees as the unwillingness of criminologists to ally themselves with police agencies. He finds criminologists generally reluctant to acknowledge police expertise that might help them find the "able criminal" preferring instead to concentrate on those "caught criminals" who have already been processed by the judicial system and hence reside outside police jurisdiction. Mack suggests that whether the gap between detectives and criminologists is a function of social scientists' biases or because of a lack of rapport with police professionals, it results in the loss of some significant crime information relating primarily to what Mack calls "able criminals."[14] For an understanding of these inaccessible, highly skilled offenders, the police are the single best resource for research. It is this strategy in fact that the present research has employed. The author was most fortunate in being granted access to investigative files on fences by a police department in a northeastern city of the United States. It is from the information contained in those files that the bulk of the material which follows was drawn. (The data are described in detail in Appendix A.)

There are caveats which must be attached surely. For example, "fences known to the police" do not necessarily constitute the entire population of fences operating in and around a particular area. If the police knew all of the offenders committing each crime in the penal code, our crime control efforts would be significantly advanced beyond their present state. Wherever deficiencies and/or omissions in the police files were found they will be noted, discussed and hopefully accounted for. On the whole, however, the police information obtained by the author is thought to be a fairly comprehensive cross section of the twentieth-century fencing industry, albeit in one American city.

In addition to police files, official agencies allowed access to some of the informants used by the local district attorney's Organized Crime Strike Force in a series of fencing prosecutions that were proceeding concurrently with the research project.[15] These informants were burglars who had turned state's evidence—and they provided the researcher with a slightly different perspective than could be obtained from the police alone. Each source in effect served to balance and validate the other and give a richer understanding of the world of the receiver. It should be noted that interviews and association with offenders themselves were limited to the district attorney's informants. To have proceeded otherwise would have put the researcher in a rather precarious and unwarranted position.[16] The choice of the officially assisted research strategy, then, essentially precluded the subsequent use of either of the other strategies discussed above. Just as the researcher who allies himself with the offender does not want to risk that individual's alienation by an association with the police, so research assisted by the police must remain "official" in nature and relinquish associations with the criminal world.

CONCEPTUAL PARAMETERS OF THE INQUIRY

This search for the contemporary receiver has been shaped by one final element about which the reader should be informed—the conceptual parameters under which the author has studied. We have alluded to these earlier, but the underlying assumptions of organization and functionality and their implications must be spelled out.

———————

Consistently, both the popular and scientific tendency is to view the criminal's behaviour as a problem of individual maladjustment, not as a consequence of his participation in social systems. Perhaps it is for this reason that in criminology we have had thousands of studies that have sought some damaging trait in the personalities of individual criminals, but *very few studies of the organizational arrangements among criminals who commit crimes in concert.*[17]

The Wages and Ways of Organization

The first fundamental assumption is that property crime is an *organized* criminal behavior system. That is to say, it is crime committed and facilitated by a rational differentiation of functions and specialties among offenders. We follow the path charted by Cressey in his discussion of criminal organization when he notes that the identification of organizational features "is more a problem of specifying ranges on continua than defining types" such that it becomes proper to say "that some organizations are more organized than others."[18] "Organization in this context," says Cressey, "is equivalent to 'rationality',"[19] and he further sees the influence of the degree of rationality (that is, organization) present as affecting the character of the crimes committed by organized segments of the criminal population. Cressey is careful to distinguish between "organization" referring to rationality and "an organization" in which functional activities are differentiated, although he sees the emergence of greater organization as a function of such role differentiation.

When we call property theft "organized," we refer to Cressey's dual meaning. First, we contend that it is criminal conduct rationally pursued; and then we suggest that it is operationally dominated by criminal organizations displaying a "structure of occupational specialties" resulting in divisions of labor and the differentiation of functional roles among property theft principals.

We are also indebted to McIntosh who has noted the "changes in the organization of thieving"[20] accompanying urbanization and industrialization. McIntosh sees theft as originating in the piracy and banditry of the outlaw as a societal isolate. Once urbanization occurs, the anonymity of urban existence added to the concentration of potential theft victims in trading centers has the effect of transforming theft into a fairly routinized, urban, *craft* activity in which small amounts of property are stolen from a large number of victims. While the livelihood to be gained from such a craft is not likely to be great for each individual thief, the urban situation can support a fair number of thieves in at least a subsistence state. In addition, because each victim loses only a small amount of property as the result of each theft, no large-scale precautions against theft will be taken, allowing a modus vivendi to emerge between the "trade" and the agencies of social control.[21]

Once industrialization occurs, however, McIntosh sees theft changing from craft crime to *project crime* in order to reap the benefits of the larger amounts of property held by a relatively small number of powerful institutional owners. Since such owners will go to great lengths to protect their property, the conflict between thieves and their victims becomes once again overt with frequent innovations in the technology of protection and of thieving. As a result each theft or short series of thefts presents unique problems and becomes a risky project and requires intelligence, work, and planning carried out by an ad hoc team with the relevant skills.[22] Thus, as theft changes to respond to its changing environment, the organizational needs of thieving change too.

McIntosh's characterization of the first of these organizational changes comes close to demonstrating Cressey's thesis. "The market [for stolen property]—the fence—was the first to become a differentiated part of the underworld,"[23] occurring as the craft criminal became comfortably and anonymously ensconced in the urban setting. McIntosh sees the transition from craft to project theft as requiring even more of the "rational differentiation of occupational specialties" which Cressey notes:

> ... the fact that teams have to be recruited and coordinated for specific jobs or series of jobs, that information may need to be specially obtained, and that the takings from each job may need special marketing arrangements has meant that the underworld has become *less homogeneous in its composition and more complex in its structure.*[24]

The search for such heterogeneity and complexity in contemporary property theft becomes the focus of this inquiry once organization is assumed for the activity. Cressey notes that the thief who steals and resells the stolen goods participates "in an organization made up of at least two positions,"[25] though he occupies both of them. At this simplest of levels, then, we must confront the "organization" of property theft; how much more organization are we likely to encounter when both the specialties and the individuals performing them are differentiated? McIntosh concludes that "the underworld now includes many . . . who are not themselves thieves, but who are necessary to the new kind. There is a division of labour within the underworld, and the bonds that tie its members together are no longer those of likeness, as in the craft underworld, but those of difference and complementarity."[26]

Our assumption regarding organization in property theft will greatly affect how we investigate the criminal receiver. The focus will be not on the dimensions of his individual criminality, but rather on the ways in which the "differentiation" and "complementarity" of his role affects the ratiocination, or organizational attributes, of property theft. It will make the fence's organizational characteristics more important than his individual attributes. Finally, it will find us less intrigued by the individual receiver than by the manner in which his individual circumstance defines the nature and scope of his organizational setting. By positing organization as a fundamental part of property theft, we refuse to treat criminality as an individual matter, and like Cressey, we search instead for "evidence about the relationships among criminals [and] about the structure and operations of illicit organizations."[27]

An Emphasis on Function

A second assumption refers to the functional relationship believed to exist between the participants in this crime area, the thief and the fence.[28] The belief that a special relationship exists has consequently affected our inquiry method. The functional relationship between fence and thief is here posited to correspond to the relationship existing between the legitimate marketing mechanism and the legitimate producer of goods. Note that we have not called the fence-thief relationship analogous to the marketer-producer relationship; we have said that they correspond to each other. That is, the relationship between the production and the marketing of goods exhibited in the legitimate marketplace is assumed to be reproduced in the illicit marketplace through the thief-fence interaction.

This is by no means a revolutionary thought. The concept of the fence as the "market" for the thief's goods was evident in Colquhoun[29] and Fielding,[30] and found similar expression in this century in the report of the Association of New York Grand Jurors:[31]

> He [the criminal receiver] not only furnishes the incentive to crime *by providing a market*, but he organizes and directs criminals and very often finances them.

The associated idea that criminal receiving of stolen property consists in the *performance of marketing* functions may be more recent but is not unique to this study. Witness, for example, the following note of Lewis:[32]

> Beyond maintaining a market or consumer analysis, the hustler who is "fencing" must also work out acceptable profit margins in his "retailing" operation. . . . It would indeed be difficult to find in a legitimate economic enterprise endeavors which exceed this hustle in the exercise of sophistication and rationality.

The characterization of the fence's role as that of a marketing mechanism, then, is not new, although we do believe that the corollary to this characterization placing the thief in the production role is unique. Similarly we believe that the extension of the dimensions of the thief-fence relationship according to the marketing framework is somewhat innovative. Reliance on the field of marketing rather than the field of criminology has resulted in a different approach to this relationship. And since we have taken our functional characterization of this relationship quite seriously, its effects will not be subtly felt. Our vocabulary will consist of terms like the "industry," the "trade," the "channel of distribution," and the "market"; such terms as "subculture," "argot," "socialization," and "self-concept," so common to criminological study, are generally not used.

Having seen the subject of our inquiry (the fence) in a marketing role, we have chosen to view his activities and associations with others in this same framework. In this, we might go even further than did Hall saying, "the only adequate approach to *property theft* is that which deals with *it* as an established part of the economic life of society."

One final influence should be explained. It is Radzinowicz who perhaps best expresses this perspective:

> The very attempt to elucidate the causes of crime would be better put aside. The most that can be done is to throw light upon the combination of factors or circumstances associated with crime. Even then it must be recognized that these very factors or circumstances can also be associated with other forms of social maladjustment or indeed *with behavior accepted as normal*.[33]

Apart from organizational and functional assumptions, the author has opted as well to explain the "how" rather than the "why" of criminal receiving. Emphasis is placed clearly on the discovery of "the combination of factors or circumstances" associated with that offense and with property theft generally.

A concentration on organization, functionality, and "factors and circumstances" has led quite naturally to a general lack of emphasis on the personal traits and characteristics of individuals in the theft microcosm. It should be noted that this was not a decision cast in stone from the beginning. On the contrary, early research efforts devoted some attention to the demographic and occupational characteristics of fences and thieves. At the same time, however, two sources of influence were leading the research away from individual characteristics toward more "functional" and "organizational" descriptors.

The first of these emerged from the historical analysis to be described in the following chapter. What the hazy (and often limited) folklore of fencing demonstrated was that attempts to explain the crime in terms of individual careers only succeeded in shrouding the central point that the fence is a *structural* *"given"* in property theft whenever the thief steals to convert rather than to acquire the fruits of his labors. To continue an individualistic account of fencing seemed no more profitable in explaining twentieth-century fencing than had been portraits of Jonathan Wild in describing the eighteenth-century version of the activity.

The second and more important influence was the data itself. As demographic information was analyzed, it became clear that the fence as an individual was not particularly "interesting" scientifically. He was neither pawnbroker nor street peddler. He wasn't a retired thief. He wasn't even confined to the poorer parts of town. Instead he was a 45-55-year-old, white, male businessman. As such, he looked strikingly similar to most managers and administrators in wholesale and retail trades (as described by census statistics) and even more strikingly dissimilar to his partner in crime—the thief.[34] In short, the fence was demographically a very ordinary man; wherein, it was felt, might lie his illusiveness and, perhaps, his success. To pin down his illusive though ordinary nature, focus was shifted to descriptors more relevant to the commercial world of which he appeared so much a part. In this regard, the fence was treated as that individual, or group of individuals, performing the role of market manager in the property theft industry; that is, as the mechanism (a combination of person plus setting) by which property stolen by the thief is disposed of and redistributed. Like legitimate market managers, the fence occupies an intermediary's niche in the movement of property from original owners to new ones. The illegitimate property flow of contemporary theft is shown in Figure 1.

In this schematic the thief is seen to act upon a piece of property by stealing it; the property moves with him until he reaches the fence. The fence buys the property from the thief, performs a set of marketing functions, then redistributes it to a new owner(s).

This shift of focus, describing the fence not as an individual receiver of goods but rather as a functional mechanism important to the commission of property theft, became the central theme of the research, giving rise to the specified parameters described above. It was a focus to which the data related comfortably and within which a more comprehensive description of contemporary property theft was to be discovered.

What follows, then, is both a historical and a contemporary picture of the criminal receiver. The former has largely been an interpretive search of a common history. The latter has been the author's own investigation as revealed largely by police files. It comprises the interest and concern of a dozen detectives and a very professional young burglar—in a sense what *"they"* would like to tell you about fences and fencing. It is not, however, a search that is considered ended, for in finding the fences known to these sources, new questions have been raised and new areas of research have been stimulated.

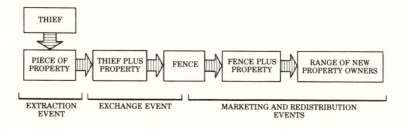

FIGURE 1.   A SCHEMATIC OF PROPERTY THEFT EVENTS

1 | *Some history and folklore of fencing*

THE CLASSIC CASE OF MR. JONATHAN WILD

In order to gain some perspective on our position in relation to the criminal receiver, we have investigated some pertinent history. In doing so we have learned that criminal receiving as an "original offense" has a much shorter history than does the crime of theft itself;[1] that despite protestations of his importance spanning three centuries, the criminal receiver has remained a shadowy and little known figure in the annals of crime;[2] and finally, that the actual role played by the criminal receiver vis-à-vis the thief and the theft of property generally has been little explored.[3] The anonymity enjoyed by the contemporary criminal receiver, then, cannot be assumed to have been derived from current circumstances alone. Instead it is likely to have followed directly from the perspectives brought to property theft and to its principals (the thief and the receiver) over many centuries.

A classic example of the somewhat myopic view taken toward property theft generally and the criminal receiver in particular surrounds the life and activities of the eighteenth-century English receiver Jonathan Wild. This classic case is quite instructive, not for its unique or overdrawn facets (although these elements undoubtedly help it command the attention necessary for it to become classic), but instead because of its representativeness, its ability to clearly elucidate the essential dimensions of the offense, and its analogistic value.

Wild demonstrates both the extraordinary as well as the endemic aspects of criminal receiving, showing us first the incredible breadth and scope which a receiver's activities can span, and at the same time underscoring those elements essential to the crime. The first part of this chapter is devoted to Wild's individual career and the lessons his example teaches; the second part of the chapter considers the folklore of fencing either inspired by Jonathan Wild or emergent in spite of him.

THE LIFE AND TIMES OF JONATHAN WILD

Jonathan Wild first came to official attention in the metropolis of London in 1710 when several creditors to whom he had become obligated brought an action against him.[4] As a result of that action, Wild was committed to the Wood Street Compter[5] as a debtor. The life expectancy of London debtors in this period was hardly envious. Once in the compter they were immediately preyed upon by other prisoners, bailiffs and all manner of officialdom, such that anything of value they had retained on their persons was stolen. In addition they were expected to have funds available for "considerations" to these same persons if they were to enjoy even the meanest necessities of life. It is remarkable to note that Wild managed not only to survive the compter but also to ingratiate himself to enough officials to earn the position of trusty.

When in 1712 an act of Parliament relieving insolvent debtors of their obligations was passed, Wild immediately sought and was granted his freedom. He took up residence in one of the lower districts of the metropolis where he engaged in petty thievery, and also built up a small business of returning lost pocketbooks, diaries, and so forth to their owners. Wild found this latter trade more to his liking since it was significantly less dangerous and more self-determinate than the thief's occupation. Far more persuasive, however, than his own limited experience with the receiving trade was the example set by the then Under City Marshall, Charles Hitchen. Employing the power of his office, combined with liberal helpings of bribery and brutality, Hitchen had become a substantial receiver of stolen goods and taker of thieves. Thief-taking was a practice that included "bribery, blackmail, informing, framing, receiving and theft compounded together by thieves, thief-catchers and the 'authorities'."[6] It had developed following a 1693 statute which provided that any person (or persons) who was instrumental in apprehending a thief and bringing evidence leading to his conviction was worthy of a £ 40 reward.[7] Hitchen and most London officials were engaged in this lucrative endeavor. Wild, intrigued by the entire process and determined to become a part of it, moved in 1713 into a small shop near Cripplegate (Hitchen's main bailiwick) and began a receiving business. Hitchen noticed his new, ambitious competitor and made him his first assistant. For the next year the two maintained a very close association, Wild wielding much of Hitchen's power and authority as the Marshall's "man."

After a while, Wild found Hitchen's methods significantly lacking in finesse and subtlety and decided to launch out on his own in 1714 with the following newspaper item:[8]

> Lost on Friday Evening 19th March last, out of a Compting House in Derham Court in Great Trinity Lane, near Bread Street, a Wast Book and a Day Book; they are of no use to any one but the owner, being posted into a ledger to the day they were lost. Whoever will bring them to Mr. Jonathan Wild over— against Cripplegate—Church, shall have a Guinea Reward and no Questions asked. (*Daily Courant*, 26 May 1714.)

This was the first of hundreds of advertisements that Wild was to place in London newspapers in the next ten years. Wild had learned from the example of Hitchen and other thief takers and receivers that the mistake most often made by the thief's confederate was to take possession of stolen property for cash. He determined that by avoiding actual possession of stolen goods, one could also escape the venue of receiving laws. His practice, then, was to receive of the thief (who was either formally or informally in his employ) only the *particulars* of the theft, at which point he approached the true owner of the property, hat in hand, endeavoring to be of assistance in having his property restored.

Eventually his reputation, even among "the Quality," for services faithfully rendered had become so renowned that owners of stolen or lost property approached him to plead their cases for his assistance. In 1716 he bought a shop in the Old Bailey and dubbed it "Jonathan Wild's Lost Property Office." Many persons, great and small, made daily pilgrimages to his shop in search of news about their missing possessions. At the same time that Wild was currying favor with "the Quality," he was systematically extending his control over the numerous gangs of thieves operating in London. To that end he kept strict account books of the activities of the thieves he was directing. Wild saw not only the lucrative but also the exploitative possibilities of the 1693 thief-taking statute. He was particularly intrigued by its use as a disciplinary measure against recalcitrant thieves. He took pains to publicize his every triumph, dubbing himself the "Thief-Taker General."

Wild realized rather quickly that in order not to be caught in the middle of his own schemes, he had to carefully orchestrate the activities of all those he sought to control. To achieve this end, Wild devised a "system" for the management of his affairs that brought both standardization and accountability to English thievery. He standardized the activities of the various classes of thieves by employing actors to school his operatives in the fine arts of impersonation and deception according to the needs of their varying trades. His bands of pickpockets were taught the dress, language, and manner of "the Quality" so they could mix inconspicuously in theatre crowds and at balls. Highwaymen were taught unintimidating approaches to coaches and traveling parties. All were taught the use of diversionary tactics to avert attention should difficulties arise.

His accountability system was constructed primarily to enhance his control. He divided London and the countryside into districts and assigned particular gangs or individuals to these districts. Often he separated thieves whose loyalties appeared stronger toward each other than to him. Wild had a fairly reliable check system on the "honesty" of his thieves through the loss reports given him by distraught owners. He knew therefore when a thief was trying to hold back some contraband and never failed to note such behavior. In fact there was very little that Wild did not record. He kept a record of productivity for each gang and noted their failures and successes, strengths and weaknesses. He maintained a clear picture of each individual's value to his organization and when the time came to sacrifice someone for the sake of public appearances, he had enough damaging evidence on nearly everyone to do so.

At £40 per head thief-taking was a fairly lucrative occupation, and by the time of his death, Wild was alleged to have brought some 95 souls to the hangman. Despite these circumstances, it seems clear that Wild's thief-taking activity was more a management/public-relations endeavor than a money-making venture. As shall be seen, the extensions Wild made in his empire made his need for thieves greater than his need for money.

Having his affairs in and around the metropolis in satisfactory order, Wild sought new ventures. One of these was a manipulation of the British "transportation" procedure, by which some first offenders and misdemeanants were sent to the new world (primarily North America) for 7 or 14 years rather than hanged. The penalty for premature return was capital, and a reward existed for anyone "discovering" such return. Wild saw in this system a vulnerable supply of operatives over whom he could exercise control and at the same time extend his territorial authority. He cultivated the partnership of the captain of one of the larger "transportation" ships, whereby many transportees never left England or went only as far as Ireland. These individuals then began plying their thieving trades in these new locations. To maintain discipline and earn the gratitude of the countryside, Wild would occasionally "discover" such persons to local officials. "Thief-Taker General of all of Great Britain and Ireland," the title Wild eventually used, became quite appropriate. He was easily more aware of criminal activity in any part of the British Isles than any other person or official agency.

His power had become overwhelming but not without some loss of support. Many officials whom Wild had earlier corrupted were angered by the inroads made into their activities, and much of the populace, suspicious as to the true nature Wild's affairs began to question the beneficence of his "public service." In 1719, Parliament passed the statute 4 George I, C.11, revising the procedures related to the transportation of criminals. It is said that it was Wild's dispute with one of the drafters of this statute that caused the inclusion of sections 5 and 6, which provided that any person who took a reward for the return of stolen goods to the true owner, who did not also bring the thief to justice, could be tried for felony. Because of public and private suspicions surrounding Wild's activities, the true target of the legislation was lost on no one. The 1719 statute became popularly known as "The Jonathan Wild Act"; and it became a frequent diversion of much of the populace to try and predict just when he might be trapped into demise.

Not so easily daunted, Wild merely varied the operations of his Lost

Property Office so as to remain within the law. He no longer published rewards for the return of goods and refused to take any payment for his services. Instead he merely brought owner and unknown persons together and any money that was exchanged was, he made clear, their business. He feigned no further knowledge, proclaimed that he was only trying to help and displayed spirited indignation toward anyone who might suggest that his motives were any other than public service in nature. The fact that the "unknown persons" with whom Wild put owners in contact were his confederates, was not overlooked by most persons, but his operation was just too complex for either the law or the public consciousness to deal with.

For property that was not claimed or reported stolen, Wild developed new outlets. In 1720, he bought a sloop and began a lively smuggling and receiving trade between England and the Continent, taking goods of the English wealthy to their counterparts in Holland and bringing back such commodities as sugar and flour which, because of trade restrictions, were in both short supply and heavy demand in Britain.

Wild seemed unperturbable. He failed to make the mistakes which the drafters of the 1719 statute had anticipated. Instead he carefully tailored his activities to conform to the precise requirements of the law, and although he was systematically incurring the wrath and resentment of an equally corrupt officialdom, his profits (and influence) continued to grow. There appeared no way to stop him or to successfully impugn the unassailable public face he had created for himself.

In 1724, however, Wild began to take himself as seriously as he expected others to do. In that year, completely underestimating the snobbishness of the English quality, he began petitioning (unsuccessfully) the Court of Aldermen for the Freedom of London, that is, for the status of Freeman of the city. Wild apparently felt that his socioeconomic position and his record of public service warranted such recognition. After two petitions failed, he became convinced that what he needed was a dramatic "discovery" on some notorious criminal to force the aldermen to consider him favorably.

The opportunity soon presented itself. Between 1723 and 1724, Jack Sheppard had injected himself into the forefront of London crime. This diminuitive housebreaker was not only skilled and daring, but considered by many to be gallant as well. For Wild, who considered Sheppard a possible threat to his authority, the housebreaker appeared to be just the thief he needed to "take". In June 1724, Wild began a pursuit of Sheppard that was to become an obsession. He finally succeeded in November 1724 when Sheppard was led to Tyburn Tree (the London place of execution in this period).

No round of applause greeted this, Wild's latest accomplishment. Instead, grim and bitter public questioning of the state of justice in Britain was left in the wake of Sheppard's death, and much of the dissatisfaction focused on Wild. He might well have survived even this crisis of confidence, however, had he not begun to behave in some rather uncharacteristic ways.[9] He began, for example, to conduct his receiving activities much more feverishly and recklessly. His closest associates saw in this a certain weakness which they exploited by holding back stolen goods in return for higher prices. This affected Wild's ability to recover items quickly and lost him patrons among the wealthy. He also began to involve himself in the most petty of activities, somehow believing he was impregnable. In 1725 Wild was arrested for shoplifting and for violating sections of the "Jonathan Wild Act." Neither case was very strong; and it was Wild's own foolish and unsolicited statement in open court that hanged him. Wild went to Tyburn in May 1725. The throng that assembled for the occasion was large and angry. Writers who attended the execution noted that not one sympathetic voice was raised in his behalf. Accompanying Wild was the spectre of the many men, women, and children who had, by his whim, preceded him and the awful vision of a man who, impressed by self-conferred authority, had tried to buy with blood what he could not buy with money.

WILD, THE STUDY

It is incredibly tempting to credit the extraordinary career of Jonathan Wild to either individual genius (in which he was not in the least lacking) or to his historical context (in which the lack of an organized police force and the peculiar punishment and reward structure of the British judicial system created obvious exploitative situations). Similarly, because Wild was such a remarkable criminal, it is easy to lose sight of the facts that first, he was at base a receiver, and second, that his whole organization was geared to facilitate that primary enterprise. But if we, possessing an historical perspective, can be tempted into thinking that Wild was something more than a very clever fence, his contemporaries were overwhelmed by that impression. Wild was toppled because he was Wild, and when all the indignation surrounding his death died down, there was little doubt that it was the man and not the machinations that were objected to.

Genius though he was then, and crude though his times were, Wild was successful because he understood three critical ingredients of a successful criminal receiver: organization, power, and property. [10] He rose above his contemporaries because he alone appreciated the careful interweaving necessary among these elements.

THE IMPORTANCE OF ORGANIZATION

Wild brought to his disparate collection of public and private activities an astonishing organizational sophistication that speaks more of the twentieth century than of the eighteenth. His was not an age known for subtle imagery nor for a precision in the functioning of organizational structures. And yet Wild's activities had both of these characteristics. His understanding of the utility of public relations is quite remarkable, and although the media choices of his time were limited, Wild created for press and populace an unassailable image of himself.

At first this may appear neither subtle nor particularly relevant to the contemporary scene, since fencing is acknowledged to be a low-visibility activity anonymously conducted. But to maintain this view is to be hopelessly tied to the subtleties of our own age where image-building is a well-developed process and where legitimacy is a presumption conferred on any activity that conforms to its very superficial trappings. Jerome Hall suggests that we have already been led too far in this direction: [11]

> [Contemporary receivers] have been shrewd enough to devise methods of operation which escaped public notice. They dress their illegal traffic in all the paraphernalia of lawful enterprise ... they are equipped both mentally and financially to take full advantage of the weaknesses in the administrative machine, should prosecution be initiated.

It is, then, the "paraphernalia of lawful enterprise" that allows legitimacy to be presumed. Image creation is likely to be as important an element in the program of the modern fence as it was for Wild, except that our contemporary presumptions and our wholesale acceptance of the Madison Avenue ethos may have made the task today much easier and far less perceptible.

But beyond his understanding of image creation, Wild was a master in the art of precisely fitting together a complex of activities into an integrated whole consistent with that image. In our time, Wild's organizational talent hardly seems prodigious but it must be remembered that few relevant models existed in his age after which to fashion a wholly private business empire. [12]

The level of sophistication Wild brought to the management of his "corporation" must be credited to individual talent. The development of an organization at all was a requirement of the trade. What Wild saw more clearly than any of his contemporaries (and many successors) was the fact that a receiver of stolen property cannot operate in a vacuum. He cannot be only a fence; he must be part of a setting, a structure—an organization with a reality all its own. Jonathan Wild was a success because he submerged himself within the structure and authority of the Lost Property Office and the Thief-Taker Generalship. He saw organization as both the lifeblood and the insulator of the criminal receiver.

In the investigation of the contemporary fence, Wild's case begs for a consideration of the fence's organizational scenario. The numerous organizational models existing today have given the fence some very specific models upon which to fashion an operation. Wild's lesson about *the organizational necessities of criminal receiving* should therefore guide our consideration of the operational setting of the contemporary receiver rather than the uniqueness of his own example.

THE IMPORTANCE OF POWER

In addition to organizational abilities Wild's expert assessment and manipulation of the power structure of society contributed to a successful operation. Wild saw the vacuum that the lack of unified law enforcement created, and was determined to fill that gap himself. Through his thief-taking activities, Wild at any one time easily knew more of what was happening in London's underworld than all the law enforcement bodies in Great Britain combined and this knowledge allowed an even subtler manipulation of the "powers that be," a control over information.

Today's fence does, of course, face organized police forces but the fragmentation that Wild observed has not everywhere improved. The receiver's operations today are not likely to be confined neatly according to law enforcement jurisdictions, and where lack of cooperation exists, it can be manipulated and exploited as surely as during Wild's time. Similarly, just as eighteenth-century English authorities had to depend on Wild for information on the theft scene, so today police forces may rely on the fence to clear stacked-up burglaries. In this way the fence may have acquired a tacit immunity on the basis of information only he can provide.

Wild, however, not only manipulated power; he also exerted it directly, and often brutally. He knew that the key to a complex organizational structure was control. It is tempting to point to the evils of the bounty system and the severity of punishments in Wild's time as being the foundations for his control, but that is to overlook another of the central lessons of his case: *control for the receiver is imperative.* Exactly what the dimensions of the contemporary fence's control mechanisms are is again a point that Wild asks us to consider. Is a subtle form of thief-taking still a part of the receiving trade? Or have the needs of the thief become so urgent and compelling that the fence's control is unquestioned? Wild's age provided him with some rather diabolical disciplinary tools. What analogous tools does today's fence use? Or are such even necessary? Again, we should not look to Wild for the specifics of the contemporary receiver's power. He has merely told us that the ability both to manipulate and exercise power is a necessary element of the trade.

THE IMPORTANCE OF PROPERTY

Having looked at Wild's organizational and control abilities, we turn to the final factor that gave shape and direction to his affairs— the whole question of personal property: its abundance, distribution, and nature. In the eighteenth century personal property tended to be concentrated in the upper classes and was of a distinct and highly individualized nature (snuff boxes, watches, jewelry, etc.). It made, therefore, much more sense to "recover" property for its owner than to receive and resell it as the fence does today.

Though not the most obvious, then, the element of property was perhaps the most critical factor in shaping the specific practices of Wild's enterprise. It is also the factor on which Wild and his successors differ the most. For, unlike Wild, today's fence does not face a situation of highly individualized property owned on a limited scale. Now consumer goods are mass-owned and mass-produced with at best imperceptible differences between them. Today's fence does not have to involve himself in a complicated system of "recovering" property. He is a marketer now, reselling what has originally been bought and sold elsewhere. This is not to say, however, that the contemporary fence need not concern himself with the question of property, for it remains today (as it was for Wild) the one element that will most shape his day to day operation. It is also the one element of criminal receiving that we as twentieth-century consumers best understand. Wild's case isn't necessary to underscore the importance of property to the fence, but it does dramatize the manner in which changes in property ownership and production determine the range of activities that can fall under the heading of "criminal receiving."

Three lessons from the case of Mr. Jonathan Wild are these: (1) the criminal receiver needs an organizational setting in which to operate, (2) the criminal receiver needs mechanisms by which to exercise and manipulate power, and (3) the criminal receiver in shaping his activities is inextricably tied to the existing levels of property ownership and production. We should not expect to find the contemporary fence as unique as Jonathan Wild, but we should be surprised to find that the above three elements are not essential to his operations.

PEACHUMS, FAGINS, PAWNBROKERS, AND JEWS—THE FOLKLORE OF FENCING

No matter how superb and innovative a criminal, Jonathan Wild remains little known today. Given the absolute control which Wild exerted for nearly a decade over British thievery as well as the machinery of British justice, his minute historical niche seems rather curious. Even more curious is the manner in which neither the prominence of his last years nor the notoriety attending his death managed to survive him by even half a century. Wild's obliteration upon death was accomplished even faster than had been his meteoric rise to power and prominence in life.

Our concern here is not, however, that notoriety be long remembered, but rather the process by which it fails to be instructive. Even in his own time the life and actions of Jonathan Wild "taught no lessons, brought no reforms and alleviated no suffering." [13] For example, despite Wild's perfect demonstration of the fence's control over and initiative involvement in thievery, it took England more than a century to make criminal receiving an original offense. [14] If the full and dramatic account of Jonathan Wild left no lasting impression of the fence, neither did the pictures presented by his (mostly literary) successors. Criminal receiving remains today a crime without a criminal. No composite picture attaches to the offense; no household name appears as its personification.

This is indeed an unfortunate circumstance. Criminal characterizations and even caricatures are a useful device for the conceptualization and description of criminal behavior. Without them, not only the behavior but also the proscriptions regarding behavior can remain remote indeed. Unless conceptually identified in the actions or activities of individuals, legal proscriptions are frequently meaningless. In the case of criminal receiving, the lack of suitable characterizations or caricatures has left us without a clear impression of either the fence or his crime. To understand why this is so, we need to look more closely at the following four areas: (1) the descriptive failure of the Wild example, (2) the development of later caricatures of the fence and their difficulties, (3) the received notions of the fence and their origins, (4) the consequences of the criminal receiver's "character" development for the contemporary scene.

THE GREAT FAILURE OF MR. JONATHAN WILD

In the last few years before his death, Jonathan Wild had achieved a prominence that frequently put his name on the lips of both the mighty and the lowly in Britain. It was a dull man indeed who didn't know about the redoubtable Mr. Wild. His name and actions seemed destined to be long engraved on the minds—if not the hearts—of his countrymen. Some curious things occurred, however, upon his death. In death, Jonathan Wild took on an aura even larger than he had acquired in life—an aura that obscured rather than enhanced his memory. His contemporaries, unable to sort out and understand the incredible breadth and scope of his enterprise, satisfied themselves with the all encompassing explanation that Wild was a manifestation of evil incarnate. In this way the details of his organization and rise to power were glossed over and replaced with a few suitably gory anecdotes which lent credence to the "evil man" theory.

The handiwork of the pamphleteers who peddled "biographies" of Wild before and after his death only tended to confirm the popular conclusion. These writers saw that their audiences were interested merely in sensational accounts of especially evil deeds rather than a detailed biographical analysis. Even Daniel DeFoe, who puts himself on record at the beginning of his "biography" as spurning "the several obscure and ridiculous accounts" of Wild,[15] offers no real analysis of those elements which contributed to Wild's rise to overwhelming power. Instead DeFoe reaches the conclusion that Jonathan Wild "is a perfectly new scene."[16] He does acknowledge that both the willingness of the government to reward the detection of criminals and the willingness of owners of lost property to pay for its recovery did seem to "favour" Wild, but refused to see others as equally capable of Wild's manipulations.

DeFoe's interpretation and the popular "evil-incarnate hypothesis" sharply focused public consciousness on Wild; and it was the person Jonathan Wild that attracted horror, hatred, and disgust rather than his activities. "In short", says DeFoe, "there was a kind of an universal rage against him, which nothing but his death could satisfy or put an end to . . . ."[17] In his death the rage was replaced by a universal relief. The issue had found its resolution; there remained little interest in what he had done or how he had managed to come to such notoriety.

WILD TRANSFORMED

Had the transfiguration of Wild stopped at this point he might still have secured a comfortable historical niche—if only as an evil man. The memory of the nefarious Jonathan Wild was to endure long enough, however, to undergo two important literary treatments that were to seal his fate in obscurity. The first of these treatments was by John Gay in *The Beggar's Opera*. First performed in 1726[18] (less than a year after Wild's execution), the play transforms Wild from a man to a symbol.

In *The Beggar's Opera*, Gay sought to expose and parody much of his society's hypocrisy. Using the classical operatic format, he peopled it with the basest elements of society, commenting first on the artificiality and stiltedness of opera and then on the manner in which the populous (through its insatiable curiousity) tended to raise criminals to an "epic" prominence. Most important for us, however, are Gay's portraits of the play's two main characters: Peachum (the receiver and thief taker) and MacHeath (the thief). The parallel between these two individuals and Wild and Jack Sheppard was immediately appreciated by Gay's audience, but what was also recognized was Gay's further parallel between the dynamics of low society and high society. Peachum was obviously more than Jonathan Wild. He was the man of power—greedy, jealous and cruel in the preservation of that power; MacHeath, the man who exploits the public but at the same time is exploited and manipulated by someone more powerful. Gay's characters protest at every turn their similarity to those men of state and of wealth who are generally well-regarded. They shun the label "criminal", seeing their behavior no different from those who accuse them of wrongdoing. Thus, MacHeath, a highway robber, professes to be no different from those robbers of the public in high positions of government, who nevertheless escape punishment.[19] Similarly Peachum identifies himself with the mighty and powerful in society (the legal profession in particular) and fails to understand why he should be labeled a scoundrel while such others operate with impunity.[20] Peachum does see, however, that despite the similar relationship which he and lawyers share with thieves, they are in constant opposition. He explains it this way: "The lawyers are bitter enemies to those in our way [occupation]. They don't care that anybody should get a clandestine livelihood but themselves."[21] *The Beggar's Opera* was sharply criticized and its sequel, *Polly*, was suppressed by the government. Opposition writers, most notable Swift, came to Gay's defense when he was charged with undermining public morality.[22] Two prominent opposition journals, *The Craftsman* and *Common Sense*,

continued the politicization of the MacHeath and Peachum characters. Through MacHeath (or Sheppard) they questioned the justice of
hanging a highwayman for stealing a shilling while merely firing a
minister of state who stole millions. It was in the characters of
Peachum and Wild that the opposition most reveled, for here was the
symbol of arbitrariness, greed, corruption, hypocrisy and cruelty
which to them was the quintessence of the Walpole Government. [23]
Wild became less and less associated with thief taking and receiving;
instead he came to symbolize the corrupt statesman.

The use of Wild for political and moral satire was culminated in
1743 with Henry Fielding's novel bearing Wild's name. [24] The events
which Fielding recounts are so far from the particulars of Wild's life
that no one mistook it for a new "biography." Instead Fielding sought
to carry to an extreme the politician-criminal metaphor by placing it
in an ethical context. The novel focuses on the moral qualities of the
"great man" and the "good man." Wild, the "hero" of the book, is
known throughout as a truly "great" man. He displays those qualities
of "greatness" such as greed, egotism, hypocrisy, and corruption, of
which Fielding notes politicians and statesmen are made.

Fielding's moral point is so obvious that it is almost overdrawn.
Each laurel he places on the "greatness" of Wild becomes a bitter
satire on the moral decay of political leadership and the unfortunate
ethical position of statesmanship. Fielding's concern for a complete
moral revitalization of the seats of power was a valid one, but he was so
determined to teach his own ethics that he obscured completely the
lessons which Wild himself could amply demonstrate.

Wild as receiver and thief taker, provided a superb comment on the
machinery of justice and the duplicity of officialdom. He also presented a stark picture of the wretchedness of the common criminal,
manipulated by the greed of others. Gay, Fielding, and others were,
however, looking for larger, more universal commentaries, for which
they needed an all-encompassing character. They removed Wild from
his own arena to one of government and statesmanship. Here he became not a shadow of himself but a symbol of the decay of others. So
enmeshed did Wild become in the polemics of others that his own
lessons were completely lost. The writers who used Wild protested elo-
quently the injustice of British justice yet failed to attack through him
the specific evils his case brought to the forefront. Thus, men and

women continued to be hanged on false testimony; the government continued to make thief-taking lucrative; and money continued to grease the wheels of justice.

FAGIN

Perhaps the best known literary portrait of a receiver is Fagin in Charles Dickens' *Oliver Twist*.[25] Fagin is described as a "crafty old Jew, a receiver of stolen goods." It is interesting to note that Dickens' considers the "personal," rather than the "professional," description of Fagin more important. Dickens, in other words, does not empha-size the role of the fence in the criminal subculture but rather the wretched and lonely existence of the Jew, the outcast, who is also en-gaged in a criminal endeavor. In his preface, Dickens notes that he has no intention of dressing in palatable tones the misery of the under-world, but instead his moral purpose is to show the reality of such a wretched existence. Thus, though Fagin may have some modest wealth extorted from his bands of youths, he does not revel in it. In-stead Fagin's "enjoyment" of his estate is a rather private and de-mented ritual that he conducts when the boys are asleep and he is sure of being alone. The picture of the receiver incoherently mumbling to himself as he fingers his treasures is a tragic portrait. It is also a sym-pathetic one. As one critic has put it: "Fagin . . . [is] never despised, even though what [he does] is despicable."[26] Instead he is treated ambivalently throughout the novel.

For example, perhaps the most enduring facet of Fagin's character, apart from greed, is his role as a corrupter of youth. And yet, Dickens' description of life in Fagin's "school" fares considerably well next to his description of Oliver's existence at the poor house where he "asked for more." Fagin's boys are not hungry though the life he demands of them may make each meal he feeds them their last. Neither are the youths he employs likely to have fared better without Fagin. Like him, they are outcasts first, before being *outlaws* as well. In Fagin's case at least, Dickens does not imply in this a causal statement, but the issue is not so clear with the children. *Oliver Twist*, published in install-ments between 1837 and 1839, was a topical work coming three years after the 1834 revision of the English Poor Law. The human conse-quences of the legal embodiment of Malthusian philosophy was part of what Dickens was questioning, as were many others. In 1850, as a journalist and editor he made a clearer statement: [27]

> Ought the misdeeds of the parents to be visited on their innocent children? Should pauper and outcast infants be neglected so as to become pests to Society . . . ? Common sense asks, does the state desire good citizens or bad?

We are not given the information necessary to attribute Fagin's "bad citizenship" to a neglected childhood, nor even to his outcast heritage. Dickens' stronger concern with Fagin is a rather complex "crime does not pay" statement in which for even Fagin, the "man of means," life in the criminal world is a demented, cruel, and lonely existence.

Between the lines of the involved plot, Dickens does manage, however, to say a few things about the role of the fence vis-à-vis the thief. He is portrayed as both the tutor and the protector of the thief; as the initiator of the thief's criminal behavior; and as the greedy extorter of the lion's share of the thief's profits. Fagin is a powerful figure in his control over the boys and even more invincible in his handling of the murderous housebreaker Sikes. At the same time, however, Fagin is a weak and infected individual, ridden with doubts and suspicions and cowering in the light of day. Dickens leaves us, then, with a picture of the fence as a disgruntled social outcast whose only solution to his own inadequacies is the ability to lord over other unfortunates for whom he makes himself an economic necessity. Far from the glamor and prominence of a Jonathan Wild, Fagin is a grimy man imposing an even grimier existence on those dregs of society over whom he exerts control. It is well to remember this portrait of Fagin, for he more than any other caricature of the fence has endured to provide some fairly interesting contemporary comments.

THE PAWNBROKER, THE JEW, AND THE PEDDLER

The final strand in what might be called the "folklore" of criminal receiving emerges from the activities associated with the pawnbroking trade. On the model of the Italian towns, pawnbrokers like other tradesmen were regulated in the conduct of their business in most of Western Europe by the sixteenth and seventeenth centuries. [28] Though recognized as a trade, pawnbroking was not well-respected.

By 1757 the notoriety, or at least suspicion, of pawnbrokers led in England to their further regulation under the False Pretenses Act. [29]

Sir John Fielding testified before Parliament's Committee of 1770 that despite controls on pawnbrokers there remained other dealers in second-hand merchandise and certain metals who were outlets for stolen goods. Fielding further noted that such persons were primarily Jews and that they provided much of the support for the current thievery problem. Thus began what Colquhoun was later to call "a piece-meal System" [30] of dealing with the area of criminal receiving. Commencing with the Receiving Stolen Goods Act of 1770, Parliament passed a series of laws associating specific tradesmen (dealers in gold, silver, jewelry, second-hand goods, and shipping merchandise) with possible receiving violations.

Colquhoun's *Treatise on the Police of the Metropolis* distinguished the different arenas of the receiving trade and accounted for the involvement of pawnbrokers and Jews. Colquhoun's chapter "On Cheats and Swindlers" delineated that class of "Swindling Pawnbrokers . . . [who] are uniformly receivers of stolen property; and under the cover of their license do much mischief to the Public." [31] He suggested that a uniform licensing system be adopted with the affirmative requirement that a "certificate of character" [32] be produced for those who wished to enter the trade. In this way, Colquhoun contended, the honest pawnbroker would be protected from the negative connotations of the trade.

Colquhoun's discussion of the Jew's involvement in receiving suggests a wider dilemma. He described Jews as active in two different arenas of the trade. First, there were Jews who functioned as low-level receivers often operating through the bribery of servants or dock workers. [33] Second, he noted a different class of Jews who acted as outlets for other receivers and were responsible for the concealment and transportation of stolen goods both in and out of London as well as in and out of the country. [34] Colquhoun acknowledged, however, that the barring of Jews from apprenticeships in many trades just about forced them to find livelihoods in such "nefarious practices" [35] —a situation he suggested be eliminated. However, a report of "The Society for the Suppression of Mendicity," published in *The Quarterly Review* in 1839, reveals that Colquhoun's suggestion was not taken. The *Review* clearly and indiscriminately attributes a large part of Britain's crime problem to Jews: [36]

A Jew seldom thieves, but is worse than a thief; he encourages others to thieve. In every town there is a Jew, either resident or tramping; sure to be a Jew within forty-eight hours in the town, somehow or other. If a robbery is effected, the property is hid till a Jew is found, and a bargain is then made.

Dickens' portrayal, then, of Fagin as a crafty old Jewish receiver was immediately understood and appreciated by an audience that generally associated Jews with the criminal subculture.

The report also classified peddlers, gypsies, and itinerant merchants in general as persons who maintained criminals and made their crimes profitable.[37] By 1871, the English Parliament had enacted a law regulating the activities of these individuals as well. This statute was the forerunner of the peddlers' and solicitors' licensing procedures which today are found in nearly every British and American municipality. Britain's legal experience with, and conventional wisdom regarding, pawnbrokers, peddlers, and itinerants was replicated in America.

These American manifestations of the British experience with the above types of individuals, combined with the literary folklore discussed earlier, form the basis for current notions about fences. How these very different strands of legend, literature, and law have intermingled and become confused is our next topic for consideration.

CLEAR AND ABSENT NOTIONS OF THE CRIMINAL RECEIVER

Of the three components in the fence's folklore, it is the legendary strand (dealing with Wild and Sheppard) that can be considered most expeditiously. Despite the fact that John Gay's work saw a more recent revival through Brecht and Weill in *The Three Penny Opera*,[38] it is unlikely that the underlying dramatic conflict between the Sheppard-hero and Wild-villain can be appreciated at all today. Both Gay and Fielding were addressing specific audiences whose understanding of their satiric devices and political comments was immediate. Such understanding is beyond a contemporary audience. Attendance by the author at a recent performance of *The Beggar's Opera* illustrated this point. Billed as the "first musical comedy ever presented on the British stage," it was enjoyed as such, but somewhere the political and moral controversies were lost. Similarly irretrievable is the "legend" of Wild as a whole. Neither Wild the man, nor the symbol, nor the politician, nor the "great" one, lives today. He is a part of the folklore lost to history, contributing nothing to the contemporary norm.

Not so with Fagin, however. Fagin has survived the passage of time to breathe some life into the contemporary fence. This is curious in a way since Dickens' development of him as a receiver is secondary to his personality development. Nevertheless, a judge was heard, in the recent sentencing of a man for criminal receiving, to call that man "a Fagin."[39] The fact that neither the defendant nor the details of his case in any way resembled Dickens' character is not as important as is the judge's use of "Fagin" as a generic term. The use of "Fagin" implies a sinister and contuminous connotation. "Fagin" was obviously the worst name the judge felt could properly be used to characterize the defendant.

Fagin's influence has appeared elsewhere on the contemporary scene. Police files at the data site revealed a more appropriate use of the name in characterizing a young female fence who directs the activities of thieves 12-15 years old. "X is a female Fagin" wrote the police; and the fact that she is an American Indian as well seems to make the parallel consistent in a true Dickensian manner. Even the "social outcast" dimension is present. In this American city, then, Fagin still contributes to our notions of the contemporary fence.

But if Fagin has a contemporary meaning, the occupations of pawnbroker, junk and second-hand dealer, and peddler have some more generalized connotations. A study of fencing—once understood—rarely fails to elicit the comment: "Oh, you mean like the pawnbroker?" Regardless of widespread regulation of that industry, then, conventional wisdom continues to endow pawnbrokers with a certain wiliness. Though a decent occupation, pawnbroking generally isn't regarded as one of the more respected in American society. Based as it is on the economic exigencies of others (a dimension not limited to pawnbroking, but of heightened visibility), the industry is rarely found but in the dirtiest, oldest, and poorest sections of an American city. It may be that its location alone engenders doubts as to its respectability. The details of life in the "inner city" have always remained suspect to the majority of the population that neither

experiences nor understands them. Some have even termed existence
in that netherland "subcultural"[40] which may immediately suggest a
retardation in the development of cultural values and norms. The
pawnbroker, though not necessarily a part of that existence, remains
proximate enough to it to acquire some of its "notoriety."

We cannot leave the contemporary notions of the fence without one
final portrait, growing out of the British peddler strand of receiving
folklore. Consider a man standing on New York's Times Square.
You've probably seen him, or someone like him. His suit is worn out
and he may have seven or eight watches on his arm. He may also have
a tattered, velveteen-covered board with a varied assortment of costume (or is it?) jewelry decorating it. And his prices are outrageously
"reasonable"! To most of us, he is the fence—or at the very least a con
man. In any case, we assume he did not get his wares "decently" or
"legally," for he doesn't dispose of them in that manner. Of all our
contemporary notions of the criminal receiver, it is his presence that
remains most persuasive, most enduring, and, perhaps, most endearing.

TRUTHS AND CONSEQUENCES

"Endearing." It seems so appropriate in this case. There is nothing
horrifying or despicable about the man on Times Square. He *is* endearing, despite our suspicions of the illegitimacies that attend his
trade. He does not threaten us, and even if he is a fence, the conse-
quences of his behavior seem remote indeed. We may be heard to say,
"Where's the harm?"

Analogous impressions attach to other types of criminal receivers.
The pawnbroker is held in check by laws and licensing procedures.
Junk and second-hand businesses may be bothersome but are similarly accounted for. We are left, then, with a Fagin; and here the first
blush of horror begins to show. An initiator of youthful crime is never
condoned, which is probably why Fagin has survived as so clear and
dastardly an impression.

With the exception of someone who encourages neighborhood children to steal hubcaps, however, the odd assortment of personnages
conventionally associated with criminal receiving could not raise a
solid round of moral indignation at a convention of saints. Our no-

tions of a fence leave us with the impression of a casual and intermittant criminal—who is, and then isn't, doing something illegal, but who in any case is confined to that side of town which has little consequence or concern for most of us. To the extent that such harmless notions of the criminal receiver are correct, then our complacency is well founded and criminal receiving will continue to be a crime in search of a criminal. To the extent that our notions are wrong, however, we will have seriously misjudged both the importance and the power of the fence and our ability to keep him in check. This error will affect not only the crime of criminal receiving but the course of theft as well.

2 | *Demographic characteristics of property theft principals*

While the clear emphasis of this study is on the criminal receiver as a *marketing mechanism*, it is important to present the characteristics of the individuals in the sample studied. This is particularly true with regard to how sample receivers compared with others demographically and occupationally similarly situated as well as with the other major actor in the property theft industry, the thief. What follows, then, is a presentation of sample fences as described by the factors of race, sex, and age; by occupational classification; and by familiarity with the criminal justice system (as evidenced by arrest records); as well as some comparisons between the fence and the thief and the fence and the legitimate market manager at the data site on some of these same dimensions.

DESCRIBING THE FENCE

Table 1 lists sample fences by race and sex. As can be seen, the fencing industry at the data site was populated overwhelmingly by white males, followed at a distant second by black males, and finally by all females, each female grouping being the smallest category. This demographic pattern for the fencing trade was most interesting when compared with that present at the data site in the census occupational category most analogous to fencing, the category of "managers and administrators (except farm)."[1] The legitimate marketing system at the data site, for example, shows the same dominance of white males, but a somewhat different breadkown with regard to other parts of Table 1. In the legitimate economy at the data site, white females performing similar roles outnumber black males in managerial and administrative occupations approximately 13 to 1 and their non-white counterparts approximately 24 to 1.[2]

TABLE 1: RACE AND SEX DISTRIBUTION OF FENCES (N=114)[a]

RACE	SEX	
	MALE	FEMALE
White	101	3
Non-white	7	3

[a]The author, after having excluded those individuals about whom sufficient information could not be obtained, derived a sample of 115 fences from police files. Still many of the files remained incomplete for certain variables such as age, race, arrest record, or occupation. The primary reason for incomplete demographic information apparently results from the fact that many fences have never been arrested and police therefore lack the opportunity to acquire such data. The N for each table relating to fences can, therefore, be expected to vary.

Some individual dimensions of the fencing trade at the data site accounted for the particular proportional representations of race and sex subgroups in the sample. First, the involvement of women in fencing appeared to derive more often from a personal commitment than a commercial one. Thus, all but one of the women represented in the sample owed her association with the trade to the theft career of an important male in her life, either a brother or son, for example. Given this personal dimension of involvement characteristic of the female fence subgroups, one would not expect the prominence of women fences to approximate their presence in analogous roles in the legitimate economy where involvement is due more often from entrepreneurial desires rather than personal commitments.

Second, the theft industry at the data site generally did not appear to lodge considerable confidence in women as equal partners in crime. Thus women were not only poorly represented in the fence sample, but also largely absent from the population of thieves. A random sample of 100 burglars, for example, yielded only five women all of whom displayed records of involvement in thefts in ancillary roles, for example, as drivers, look outs, or accessories after the theft.

Finally, the small but proportionately surprising number of non-whites in the sample was accounted for in part by the nature of the research site. The city which was studied is one of deep ethnic biases and even deeper racial ones. These biases reach out into the world of crime as well. There are, for example, many white fences who refuse to deal with non-whites under any circumstances, leaving an important vacuum in the property theft arena for the non-white addict and straight burglar. To some extent, then, some non-white fences may be seizing an opportunity which only the particular brand of racial prejudice found at the data site has afforded them. Also accounting for the relatively large proportion of non-whites performing the fencing role is a phenomenon characteristic of all large cities—the movement of white residential and commercial interests from inner-city areas. When the inner-city area of the research site was plotted, all but one of the non-white fences was located within it. Nineteen white fencing outlets were also located in this area but only eight of these dealt with non-white thieves. Non-white fences, it would seem, have been granted entrepreneurial opportunities wrought not only by outright racial prejudice but also by more subtle racial attitudes which have changed their neighborhoods, shrinking the number of white businesses present to answer the area's demand for fencing services as well as for goods and services generally.[3]

Since white males made up the largest subgroup of the sample, this segment was further subdivided (as shown in Table 2). As can be seen, most white male fences were found to be businessmen (some 66 percent of this segment) of either the "most respected" type (those who preside over well-known, successful enterprises at the data site) or of the "marginal" variety (smaller businesses ranging from less successful to barely surviving in nature). For this latter group, fencing may be the means by which solvency is maintained at all. Estimates are that one-third of all small enterprises go out of business within two years of operation and that 50 percent fail within three years.[4] Most of the small businessmen fences identified here, however, had been in business more than five years and were long-standing, neighborhood institutions. Although there was no way to validate this hypothesis, it is suggested that given the normal failure rate for this class of enterprise, involvement in fencing may have been the key to preventing business failure.

The third subgroup of white male fences was a particularly interesting one. We called it the "illegal entrepreneur" group (representing 13 percent of the segment) and it was comprised of those individuals connected in some direct way to the criminal superstructure existent at the data site. Most of these individuals were fairly successful businessmen but their successes were within an entirely illegitimate economic setting, that is, as loansharks, enforcers, or gambling racketeers. For these individuals fencing appeared to be just another enterprise in a varied and totally illegal business portfolio.

The success of the illegal entrepreneur is hardly matched by the burglar-fence subgroup, which was comprised of theft offenders attempting to make a career jump to the fencing trade. Although this group was a small one, it was of particular interest, since it represented perhaps the least successful group of fences in the entire sample.

The final subgroup of white males was really a catch-all category including primarily independent entrepreneurs and those who were employees of others.[5]

OLD ENOUGH TO BE A FENCE

Table 3 lists the age distributions of the sample fences and burglars. The comparison in age of these two theft principals was striking. On

TABLE 2: DISTRIBUTION OF WHITE MALES WITHIN SUBGROUPS (N=101)[a]

WHITE MALE SUBGROUP	NUMBERS
Most respected businessman	29
Marginal businessman	37
Illegal entrepreneur	13
Burglar-fence	9
Other (employees, independents)	13

[a]The N is derived from Table 1.

the basis of median ages the fence at 46.5 years was 18 years older than his partner in crime, the thief, whose median age was 28 years. The age distributions were even more revealing and interesting for what they told us about the careers of burglary and fencing. Another look at Table 3 reveals that while the number of burglars peaks in the late twenties, the population tails off after age 30. Burglary, then, would appear to be a career with large entry possibilities but little staying power for most individuals—a transitory occupation from which individuals move on to other things. The near normal distribution of age for fences, however, suggests an entirely different pattern. It suggests that fencing is a fairly stable career to which individuals gravitate and remain. And while burglary may be the young man's oyster shell, fencing appears to be neither the young man's game nor the old man's folly, but rather the middle-aged man's stock-in-trade.

But if the fence did not compare well with the thief chronologically, he did bear resemblance to his legitimate counterparts—that is, to managers and administrators in the legitimate economic system. The median age of male managers and administrators (except farm) at the

TABLE 3:   AGE DISTRIBUTIONS OF FENCES[a] AND BURGLARS[b]
           AT DATA SITE

AGE BRACKETS	NUMBER OF FENCES	NUMBER OF BURGLARS
under 16	0	0
16-20	1	7
21-25	5	26
26-30	5	33
31-35	8	11
36-40	11	13
41-45	16	4
46-50	15	6
51-55	16	0
56-60	8	0
61-65	7	0
66-70	4	8
over 70	0	0
	Median age - 46.5 years	Median age - 28 years

[a]Based upon an N of 91, reflecting those members of the sample for whom age data were available.

[b]Based upon a random sample of 100 burglars, from police files.

data site was 45.0 years according to census statistics. The comparable figure for females was 48.1 years. In addition, when the white male subgroup of fences in wholesale and retail trades was compared with their legitimate counterparts performing managerial roles in wholesale and retail trades strikingly similar age distributions were discovered. Table 4 presents this comparison.

While the fence, then, appeared too old to be a thief, he did display the requisite age to perform administrative and management functions in the legitimate economic system. This was precisely the type of

TABLE 4: PERCENTAGE AGE DISTRIBUTIONS OF LEGITIMATE
SELF-EMPLOYED MANAGERS AND ADMINISTRATORS IN
WHOLESALE AND RETAIL TRADES[a] AND OF WHITE
MALE FENCES FROM SAMPLE[b] IN THESE SAME TRADES

AGE BRACKETS	PERCENTAGE OF LEGITIMATE MGRS	PERCENTAGE OF WHITE MALE FENCES
16-17	.5	--
18-19	--	--
20-24	3	--
25-29	5	--
30-34	6	8
35-44	20.5	24
45-54	27	40
55-59	14	18
60-64	13	5
65 & over	--	--

[a]U.S. Department of Commerce, Bureau of Census, Characteristics of the Population, vol. 1, New York, pt. 34, sec. 2, Table 174. Percentages derived from the appropriate subgroup in Table 174.

[b]Based upon an N of 38 representing that subgroup in the sample.

role that we had imagined for him. To understand how well he was able to perform it, we must next turn to another individual dimension of sample fences—their occupations.

THE FENCE'S OTHER OCCUPATION

Table 5 provides a breakdown of occupational affiliations (either licit or illicit) of members of the fencing sample. The first three subgroups were derived from the Standard Industrial Classification codes while the latter four categories relate specifically to occupational affiliations found in the sample itself. As can be seen, the overwhelming majority of fences were found to own (64 percent) or work for (10 percent) a legitimate business entity (the precise number is 81 out of 110 cases). The fence, then, was generally a legitimate, productive member of society, a status distinguishing him greatly from his associate in crime, the thief.

A random sample of burglars in police files yielded the distribution of occupational affiliations found in Table 6. Here the pattern was almost exactly the inverse of that for fences; that is, 78 percent of burglars were *not* known to be gainfully employed while 74 percent of fences were. Similarly while 70 fences were proprietors of legitimate businesses (roughly 64 percent) only four burglars could be so classified (4 percent).

The fence, then, distinguished himself from the thief not only in years but also in business ability and in the possession of gainful employment. He was most likely to be a legitimate proprietor of a business and a more detailed listing of his enterprises read with a normalcy that was disarming. Still, some business ventures appeared frequently enough in the sample to raise questions as to whether there may not be some businesses that are fence-specific, that is, characteristic of the industry generally rather than idiosyncratic to the sample studied. They are presented so the reader may compare them with other available information about fencing operations. Table 7 lists the specific businesses of proprietary fences in the sample in order of frequency, omitting those with a frequency of one.

THE FENCE AND ARREST FIGURES

One final individual analysis was conducted regarding the fence's arrest record. Table 8 presents the findings of this analysis.

It is particularly interesting to compare the arrest records of fences (Table 8) with those of burglars (Table 9). Only two burglars have never been arrested compared with 43 members of the sample of fences. In addition the burglar's arrest history displayed a component of drug-related offenses in one-third of the cases—a dimension totally absent from the sample fences' arrest records. Thirty-five sample burglars were addicts while none of the individuals in the fence sample was known to be. Perhaps the most alarming component of

TABLE 5:   DISTRIBUTION OF SAMPLE FENCES ON THE BASIS
           OF OCCUPATIONAL AFFILIATIONS (N=110)[a]

OCCUPATIONAL AFFILIATION	NUMBER OF FENCES	NUMBER IN SUBGROUP	PROPORTION OF SAMPLE ACCOUNTED FOR BY OCCUPATIONAL AFFILIATION
Business Ownership	70		64%
CMTW business[b]		21	
Retailing Business		40	
Service business	7		
Other (nonprofit, educational, or private corporation)	2		
Employed by Others	11		10%
CMTW business		6	
Retail business		3	
Service business		--	
"Other" business		2	
Illegal Goods & Services Entrepreneur	14[c]		13%
No Outside Business or Occupational Affiliation (retired, welfare, burglar, etc.)	15[d]		13%

[a]Some fences for whom information was incomplete were excluded here.

[b]Construction, manufacturing, transportation, and wholesaling.

[c]Differs from previous N in this category of Table 2 with addition of a non-white illegal entrepreneur.

[d]Includes burglar-fences.

the burglar's arrest record was not related to the use of narcotics, but rather to the use of weapons. The author, in selecting the burglary

TABLE 6: DISTRIBUTION OF BURGLARS ON BASIS OF
          OCCUPATIONAL AFFILIATIONS ($\underline{N}$=100)[a]

OCCUPATIONAL AFFILIATION	NUMBER IN SUBGROUPS	NUMBER OF BURGLARS
Employees of Others		18
Odd jobs	4	
Working for fence[b]	3	
Construction worker	3	
Steel worker	2	
Heavy manufacturing	2	
Railroad worker	1	
Social worker	1	
Cab driver	1	
Bank employee	1	
Proprietors of Business/Self-Employed		4
Plasterer	1	
Junk dealer	1	
Part-owner tavern	1	
Nursing home administrator	1	
Unemployed		78

[a]Same sample as earlier reported.

[b]The author was intrigued to find that in a random sample of burglars selected from police files, three members would be found to work for individuals identified in the fence sample.

sample at random, was surprised by the frequency of weapons' use by individuals at the youthful end of the burglary population spectrum. Many young thieves appeared to reflect an impatience with the slow but carefully planned modus operandi of the successful burglary, preferring instead direct assaults upon individuals and businesses aided by the use of weapons or force rather than stealth. To the extent that the escalation to assaultive crime found in the records of such individuals reflects a more basic change in the standard operating policies of the young thief in general, they may represent a basic change in the theft industry away from burglary and toward robbery.

One final comparison between the arrest records of the fence and the thief is noteworthy at this point, and this is with regard to fre-

TABLE 7: BUSINESS ESTABLISHMENTS OF FENCES ARRANGED IN ORDER OF FREQUENCY ($\underline{N}$-59)[a]

TYPE OF BUSINESS	NUMBER IN SAMPLE
Antique dealer, art appraiser, auctioneer	8
Furniture/appliance stores	7
Restaurants	7
Bars/taverns	6
Light construction/remodeling companies	6
Grocery stores	5
Novelty stores/second-hand merchandising	5
Salvage companies	4
Jewelers/jewelry manufacturing	4
Auto parts/repairs/service stations	3
Moving/trucking companies	2
Pool room/bowling alley	2

[a]Includes all businesses with a frequency greater than one in the sample.

quency of arrest. Of those fences who had been arrested, the median number of arrests was one. The burglar, however, displayed a median arrest rate of six. Thus, not only was the thief more likely than the fence to have been arrested; he was also more likely to have been re-arrested.

A GENERAL COMPOSITE OF THE FENCE

Having looked, then, at some basic demographic, occupational, and arrest characteristics of the fence from the sample, we could paint this rather general picture of that individual: the criminal receiver is a white male in his mid-to late forties who owns and operates a legitimate retail establishment; he probably has not ever been arrested but

TABLE 8: DISTRIBUTION OF FENCES RELATIVE TO ARREST HISTORY ($\underline{N}$=115)[a]

ARREST CATEGORY[b]	NUMBER OF FENCES
No arrests	43
Vehicle and traffic arrests only	3
Theft arrests (includes burglary, larceny, CRSP, auto theft, possession tools)	32[c]
No arrests until the 1971 Strike Force Bust[d]	15
Disorderly person	1
Vice arrests (includes gambling, loan sharking, narcotics, promoting prostitution)	6
Theft plus violent or assaultive arrests (includes assault, robbery, gun charges)	13
Sexual offense arrests	2
Arson	1

[a]Interestingly enough, arrest information was available for the total sample. This issue being particularly important to detectives.

[b]The categories used refer specifically to the situation at the data site in which a special enforcement effort resulted in arrests that otherwise might not have occurred.

[c]This category may slightly ibflate the arrest experience of the fence since the subgroup includes burglar fences.

[d]This category was thought to be important to note for the reason described in note b. If one combines this group with the first two categories, fully 61 out of 115 fences (53%) were found to have no more serious experience with the criminal justice system than that involving a traffic offense.

TABLE 9: DISTRIBUTION OF BURGLARS RELATIVE TO ARREST HISTORY ($\underline{N}$=100)[a]

ARREST CATEGORY	NUMBER OF BURGLARS
No arrests	2
Theft arrests only (includes forgery, B & E,[b] larceny, burglary, CPSP,[c] possession of tools)	28
Theft plus drug-related arrests (includes CPDD,[d] possession of paraphernalia, MHL[e] statutes)	18
Theft plus weapon and assaultive arrests (includes robbery, possession of weapon, assault)	37
Theft, drug-related, plus assaultive arrests	15

[a]Same sample as earlier reported.

[b]Breaking and entering.

[c]Criminal possession of stolen property. This is New York's receiving statute, although many more thieves than fences are arrested under it.

[d]Criminal possession of a dangerous drug.

[e]Mental Health law statute violations are common in the records of addicts.

if he has, his record is likely to show only one such encounter with the criminal justice system (and that as a traffic violator); he looks very much like the totally legitimate manager or business administrator in our society. The fence is to be distinguished greatly, however, from the other primary figure in the stolen property industry at the data site, the thief, since the former is decidedly older (by almost 19 years); has an established business and/or occupation (78 percent of thieves do not); and displays a lesser involvement with the wheels of justice (a median arrest rate of one compared with 6 for the thief).

3 | *Products, prices, and promotional considerations*

An analysis of the individual characteristics of criminal receivers found that the contemporary fence is typically associated with a legitimate business enterprise (in 74 percent of the cases)[1] and most often as an owner and/or operator of such an enterprise (in 64 percent of the sample).[2] All fences are by definition, "businessmen"—that is, they are individuals receiving stolen property for the purpose of resale.[3] As such they provide goods and services to others regardless of whether or not they operate from a traditional commercial establishment. However, we are most interested in the "businessman-fence" (denoting a dual commercial role in both a legitimate and an illegitimate business world), for it is this individual who emerges as the dominant functionary in the distribution sector of the theft industry and as the most interesting and challenging theft offender from a criminological standpoint.

The "businessman-fence" is significant criminologically because of the several "publics" he serves. As a fence he provides much needed disposal services to a criminal population (thieves) and at the same time purveys wanted goods to an array of customers. As a businessman he purveys goods and services to a similar (if not the same) array of customers and at the same time exudes a facade of commercial legitimacy accepted by legitimate business counterparts. The businessman-fence has his feet in two worlds, so to speak—one whose social acceptance is high, the American ideal of being "in business for oneself"; and one whose social acceptance has yet to be demonstrated, namely the realm of illegitimate commerce we shall call, for now, the theft industry.[4] As such the businessman-fence presents the possibility of closing a long-standing analytical gap between what American criminologists have labeled "traditional or street crime"[5] and what they have alternatively called "white-collar" offenses or "occupational crime."[6] The more we know about the criminal receiver (with particular reference to the businessman-fence) and the nature of his decisions regarding his illicit endeavors, the better we can understand the two broad areas of crime which he bridges and the better we can try to deal with the general area of property crime, whether it occurs on the street or is conceived in the executive lounge of a large corporation.

This chapter and the next one discuss the *commercial* characteristics of the contemporary criminal receiver. To do so, we have borrowed the marketing concept, "marketing mix," first introduced by Neil Borden.[7] Marketing mix refers to an integrated set of policies relating to products, prices, distribution, and promotion which a marketing enterprise must develop if it is to succeed and grow.[8] Borden's concept is helpful not only for its ability to succinctly state the range of the decisions a fence as a market manager must make, but also for its presentation of four distinct elements on which it is possible to differentiate between individuals in the fencing trade. In this chapter we will consider the varied policies of the criminal receiver relating to product, price, and promotion; the next chapter considers distribution patterns in the property theft industry.

DEFINING SOME TERMS

Before we analyze the fence's marketing mix, it is important to stress his dual role as middleman in the theft industry. The fence is *both* a buyer and a seller of stolen property and as such faces two distinct markets. The first market consists of theft offenders, the production component of the theft industry, for whom the fence is a customer. But perhaps more important, the criminal receiver also faces this same market as a seller in his own right, offering much needed disposal services for a population in illegal possession of merchandise. The second market consists of those segments of the population,

whether knowledgable or naive, institutional or individual, who purchase stolen property. In this market the fence remains primarily a
purveyor of *goods*. Although the fence can be identified functionally
as both a buyer and a seller, operationally he can be seen facing both
markets in the seller's role.

In order not to confuse these two markets, two different terms shall
be used. Those individuals for whom the fence provides *services* are
identified as his *clients*; while those individuals to whom the fence
purveys *goods* are called his *customers*.[9] It is well to keep both these
markets in mind as we discuss the elements in the fence's market mix.

PRODUCTS

The first element in the marketing mix refers specifically to the
complex interplay of factors that determines the range and depth of a
product line that is to be offered for sale. Obviously the theft industry
does not produce goods in the sense of "creating" them; thus legitimate marketing policies relating to research and development and
product innovation are unnecessary.[10] The theft industry does,
however, produce goods in the sense of "regenerating" them, that is,
goods that already were commercially available and purchased reenter the market as "new" (but stolen) products. The fence, who is
ultimately responsible for negotiating the redistribution of these
goods, must develop some product policy plan. He must consider
(1) the range of products he will handle, (2) from what sources he will
acquire them, (3) in what quantities and/or assortments he will accept
them, (4) in what condition he will agree to receive them, and (5) the
nature of the market to which he plans to sell the goods. These five
considerations are essential to the development of the fence's product
line and, just as important, they also serve as product-centered differ-
entiations between individuals in the fencing industry.

What's for Sale

It would, of course, be nearly impossible for every fence to handle
every type of item generated within the theft industry; and our evidence suggests that few even try to do so. Instead receivers tend to
limit themselves if not to specific products at least to product lines.
For example, while a fence may not limit himself to television sets he

may confine his activities to a broader product area such as entertainment equipment (televisions, stereos, tape decks, radios, and records). Similarly rather than handling only men's suits, a fence may limit himself to the product line clothing. However, some fences do specialize within product areas. No fences in the sample were found to be so specialized as to handle not only one product but also one particular brand. Thus even the one-product fence carries at least a brand assortment of illicit goods.[11]

Table 10 presents a distribution of fences by degree of specialization as measured by number of products or product lines handled.[12] The table clearly shows two strong trends within the fencing industry. One of these is the tendency of fences to specialize along product lines rather than within such lines. Thus fences appear more likely to carry a full line of products rather than specific items from a line. The most frequent case finds the fence limiting his illegal goods to either one or two full lines of products, a pattern found in approximately 59 percent of the sample. The number of fences who handle three or more specific product lines is relatively small; fences designated as generalists, connoting the handling of products so wide-ranging and changeable as to defy specificity, comprise about 6 percent of the sample.[13]

Another trend to be found in Table 10 relates to the product specialization of the fence. Here the dominant tendency is for the receiver to concentrate his activities on but *one* product with a brand assortment. The one-product fence is to be found in 12 percent of the cases, exactly doubling the frequency of the generalist. The fence who carries 2 unrelated products represents only about 4 percent of the sample. The dominance of the one-product fence tends once again to emphasize the apparent preference of the illicit middleman for the product line rather than for individual products; once a fence handles more than one product, he tends to establish a full line rather than add similar or unrelated items.

Table 11 lists in order of their frequency those individual products and product lines handled by criminal receivers. The products and product lines found in Table 11 is consistent with a list of goods reported by classes at a seminar on fencing held by the U.S. Attorney's Office, Northern District of New York, as being those products comprising 90 percent of the losses attributable to theft.[14] The list of goods noted at the seminar included the following: clothing, jewelry,

TABLE 10:   DISTRIBUTION OF FENCES BY DEGREE OF PRODUCT AND
             PRODUCT-LINE SPECIALIZATION ($\underline{N}$=85)[a]

NUMBER OF PRODUCTS HANDLED	NUMBER OF FENCES OPERATING	PERCENTAGE OF FENCES IN CATEGORY
1 product, one brand	0	0
1 product, brand assortment	10	12
2 products, brand assortment	3	4
3 or more products, brand assortment	0	0
NUMBER QF PRODUCTS HANDLED		
1 product line, brand assortment	31	36
2 product lines, brand assortment	19	22
3 product lines, brand assortment	7	8
More than 3 product lines, specified	2	22
Specified as a generalist	5	6
Product information incomplete	8	9

[a]Files on approximately twenty members of the sample did not contain any product information and these individuals were therefore excluded from this table.

tobacco, electrical appliances (household and entertainment), cars/accessories, food, plastics/plastic items, and alcohol. With the exception of goods in the foodstuffs and plastic industries, the fences in the sample appear to conform with the industry as reported at the national level.[15]

If there is any product line on which the fence sample here appears to differ substantially from stolen property arrays reported elsewhere, it would be in the metals area (four members of the sample handled these items, reflecting an interesting departure from the national norm).[16] For the most part, however, the sample individuals showed an affinity for those goods that are leaders in the industry nation-ally.[17] We see from Table 11 that for the one-product fence the most popular items are televisions and cigarettes. For the one-line fence, clothing and jewelry are the most frequent specialities.

TABLE 11: PRODUCTS AND PRODUCT LINES HANDLED BY
CRIMINAL RECEIVERS IN ORDER OF FREQUENCY[a]

SINGLE PRODUCTS	NUMBER OF FENCES HANDLING THE GOOD
Televisions	18
Cigarèttes	6
Stereo sets	5
Tape players	3
Watches	3
Automobiles	1
Cameras	1
Records	1
PRODUCT LINES	
Jewelry	21
Clothing	14
Office equipment	6
Metals	5
Appliances	4
Furniture	4
Furs	4
Liquor	4
Liquor	4
Antiques	2
Coins	2
Men's clothing	2
Power tools	2
Art objects	1
Auto parts	1
Guns	1
Paintings	1
Stamps	1

[a]The product or line is counted each time it appears whether as the whole or only a part of a receiver's trade. The table is based on a sample of 85 fences.

There appears, then, to be a specific "product set" forming the grist of the stolen property mill, even though the industry as a whole reflects an ability to handle a wide-ranging and varied group of products. To what can we attribute the clustering of fences about this certain product set? Surely the degree of specialization demonstrated in but one data site suggests a more than random patterning of behavior; and yet randomness has for some time stood as an explanation for the industry. Conventional wisdom tells us, for example, that the receiver's product line consists of what the thief brings him—the pristine logic of which seems hard to refute. And yet it is difficult to imagine that the disparate collection of individuals in the thief population could possibly yield such a specific and well-defined product set that holds industry-wide not only locally but also nationally. Where, then, is the direction? While it is true that the fence can handle only what is brought to him, "what the thief brings" is subject to far more determination than the simplicity of that phrase implies. "What the thief brings" depends largely upon what the *fence* will take; and what the fence will take depends significantly on his social and economic circumstances.

This is where the businessman-fence emerges once again as a key figure. For the fence without a trade, who works from his home or the street, the limitations on his commerce are great. He will be confined immediately to items low in bulk and volume, transportable by a personal vehicle. With little storage space, his trade will remain hand to mouth; he will buy only fast moving and readily negotiable items; and he will restrict himself to individual products rather than full lines. The stock-in-trade of the tradeless fence found in the sample, consists of cameras, watches, televisions, and light household appliances.

The businessman-fence, on the other hand, finds the constraints placed upon him more useful than limiting. More often than not his legitimate business provides him with a guide by which to determine his illicit trade. Table 12 compares the most frequent products of the businessman-fence with his legitimate business enterprises. With the exception of restauranteurs, bar owners, and light construction contractors, the legitimate occupation of the businessman-fence matches well his illicit product line. Thus of the 21 persons who handle jewelry illegally, 10 (or approximately 50 percent) have a legitimate commerce in the jewelry line (as either jewelers or antique dealers). Of the 18 re-

TABLE 12:   PRODUCTS AND BUSINESSES[a] OF THE
             BUSINESSMAN-FENCE

FENCE'S LEGITIMATE BUSINESS	# OF FENCES WITH BUSINESS	PRODUCTS HANDLED THROUGH BUSINESS
Antique dealer/art appraiser/auctioneer	8	Jewelry, furniture pieces, paintings, objet d' art, antiques generally
Furniture/appliance retailer or wholesaler	7	Televisions, clothing, records cigarettes, furniture, furs, stereos
Restaurants	7	Typewriters, office equipment, televisions
Bars/taverns	6	Clothing, furs, televisions, stereos, jewelry
Remodeling/light construction companies	6	Coins, jewelry, televisions, clothing
Grocery retailers	5	Cigarettes, clothing, televisions, tape decks, whiskey, tools, typewriters
Novelty/variety stores, second-hand merchandising	5	Clothing, watches, televisions, tape decks, cigarettes, men's clothing, jewelry, stamps, auto parts
Salvage companies	4	Metals, metal products, alloys
Jewelry retailers and wholesalers	4	Jewelry
Auto parts/repairs/ service stations	3	Metal goods, televisions, light household appliances
Moving and storage/ trucking companies	2	Furniture, appliances, televisions
Pool room/bowling alley	2	Jewelry, televisions, light household appliances

[a]All legitimate businesses represented in the sample with a
frequency greater than 1 are included in the table.

[b]Denotes all goods handled by each business type but does not
imply that each individual handles all goods found in category.

ceivers known to buy stolen television sets, five are legitimate television retailers and one is a legitimate television wholesaler, representing 33 percent of the illicit television trade found in the sample.

The same pattern is sustained in the clothing and the cigarette lines where 35 percent and 66 percent of the illegal commerce is handled by individuals who have a legitimate trade in these same items. The metals area is perhaps the most dramatic, however, for all of the known fences of metal products are legitimate dealers in such goods.

There are several advantages to doing business in this manner. To begin with, the fence who can mesh his illicit products with legitimate goods can remain fairly safe. A jeweler in possession of jewelry, after all, raises little suspicion; about as little as does the salvage dealer in possession of nickel alloy. By confining one's fencing trade to the legitimate product line, then, the addition of similar items can be made to appear like "business as usual." An additional advantage to a similarity between a legal and illegal inventory is the ability to fill out an otherwise legitimate product line from illegitimate sources.

Another advantage of the legitimate-illegitimate product mix is that it does not necessitate any special storage arrangements, since both products are identical. No secret warehouses are needed; little cloak and dagger is necessary. All is very neat, tidy, and almost mundane. The apparent lesson is: "If you want to handle hot televisions, get yourself a television store."

Not quite. For even if that were very easy—and the capital requirement for such an undertaking is fairly high—you would still need something more than that mere economic position to be a successful receiver. What you need is *communication* with the right illicit sources of supply. [18] Just what these sources are and what influence they have on the product line of the fence is the subject to which we next turn.

That Certain Thief

The fence's "sources of supply," as they were euphemistically called above, are of course thieves; and they can have some constraining influences upon his product line. This may seem a bit contradictory since the argument that the receiver's goods consist simply of "what the thief brings," was disputed earlier. We will stick with our disputation, however, adding this: while it is true that the thief only brings what the fence will take, it is also true that the fence can only demand and expect those goods which the thief is capable of delivering. In other words, the unskilled thief cannot be expected to do the work of the professional; and the fence who is acquainted only with the former individual must content himself with that range of goods appropriate to his stealing abilities. Thus the experience and skill level of the thieves with whom the fence operates place some inherent restrictions on his product line.

The pecking order in the occupation of thievery has been elsewhere studied and anlayzed, most notably by Sutherland, Cameron, Shover, and Maurer.[19] Some of the accepted types of thieves found in the literature include the following: the professional thief, the booster, the snitch, the joyrider, the petty thief, and the cannon.[20] The classification scheme used here is not derived from these sources, however, but from the working definitions used by members of the detective squad with whom this research was done. No doubt the detectives would be surprised to have their classification scheme called such, since it was not consciously so developed, but rather as a shorthand way of communicating information about different classes of burglars. Since their classification of thief "types" is simple and useful, we adopt it here. It is not that the work of the aforementioned authors is rejected or considered invalid, that a new classification is here introduced. In fact some of the types used resemble in no small way those accepted in "the literature." Instead, the detectives' "types" are selected for their appropriateness to this specific research effort, relying as it has so heavily on the work of those police officers.

The detectives characterize the pecking order of thieves as follows:

1. *The good burglar* is the professional thief—that skilled individual reminiscent of Sutherland's Chic Conwell, though with his gentility somewhat tarnished over time. A member of the elite circle of thieves, he has the following hallmarks: he is nearly always a specialist, is generally an older thief but may be in his mid-twenties, works less often than other thieves, uses extensive planning in executing a theft, only selects targets of high value, and rarely carries a weapon. There does exist a subset of good burglars which the police specially designate as "safe men." This group is the most skilled of thieves but remains small and seems to be constantly getting smaller. It is therefore recognized here but henceforth considered within the general "good burglar" classification.[21]

2. *The known burglar* is the less skilled but highly active thief who has established himself over several years, with the police notably, as a consistent thief. His hallmarks are generally: a less than subtle style of entry, volume rather than quality thefts, a substantial arrest record, a low to minimal planning capacity, a high activity level, and the frequent possession of weapons. The longevity in the trade of this thief is shorter than is that of the good burglar often because of extensive imprisonment causing a loss of affiliation with former cohorts, or a movement away from burglary and toward robbery.

3. *The young burglar* is in the process of "becoming" a thief, and is usually between seventeen and twenty-five years old. He is classified as "young" until his behavior or his known associations earn him membership in one of the above groups. The young burglar has few distinctive hallmarks (except age), borrowing from both groups above, but generally the following is true of him: he associates very obviously and constantly with other young thieves, steals a variety of merchandise as the opportunity arises, has an arrest record, has an extremely high activity level, and is often in possession of a weapon.

4. *The juvenile burglar* is rarely encountered by the theft detective, since his behavior is monitored primarily by youth officers. He is distinguished, however, by the following: he is under the age of sixteen, he usually finds counsel and direction from older thieves or fences, he is generally not addicted to drugs, he usually steals low-volume merchandise in his neighborhood, and he often associates in gang settings. The juvenile burglar is another thief in the process of "becoming"; a situation which somewhat saddens and horrifies the seasoned detective. [22]

5. *The booster* is almost the carbon copy of Cameron's description of the professional shoplifter but more often than not is also addicted. He has an extensive record for both larceny and narcotics and depends primarily on quantity rather than quality merchandise thefts.

6. *The junkie* is the addict-thief, generally the least skilled and most active of thieves. The junkie thief has the longest arrest record of any thief. He steals the most available items which rarely are of large unit value, and while very systematic,

exhibits almost no planning in his thefts. He is by far the most hapless, least respected, and least rewarded of thieves.[23]

Given these varied thief types, it is not surprising that they steal different merchandise. The junkie, for example, is highly unlikely to approach a fence, diamonds in hand. Similarly, the good burglar will hardly agree to devoting his not insignificant talent to the theft of such low-unit value items as tape players, toasters, or stereo sets. A fence who is interested in diamonds, then, must know the good burglar; for tape decks, he need know only the addict. "Knowing" in some cases may be a simple function of location.[24] The least mobile thieves are the addict, who cannot stray too far from his connection; the juvenile, who rarely has the means to travel beyond his neighborhood; the young burglar, who often depends on a local fence for tutelage; and though less often, the booster as well who looks for a convenient drop for merchandise.

For these types of theft offenders the neighborhood fence can be at once a refuge and a last resort. He may often occupy a monopoly position by virtue of his location, but this advantage is at the same time balanced by the limited range of goods which the neighborhood thief can deliver. The fence who deals with the more mobile thief will not need to rely on proximity to attract business, but he will be no less dependent on the skills of the thieves who know him for the *choice* of a product line.

This is perhaps the key to the fence's product line with reference to the thief. For unless he is a generalist, the fence *can and will choose* a product line from among the goods which his bevy of thieves can deliver. The thief does not choose for him, but rather limits his options.

Table 13 lists those items chosen by receivers known to deal with different types of thieves.[25] Though not mutually exclusive lists, there exist differences in product lines between those fences who deal with each type of thief. Even when similar types of products are yielded by different classes of thieves, they are likely to differ in quality and value. Hence the jewelry stolen by the good and the known burglar are often different in nature, with the former looking for large gemstones and the latter for bracelets, brooches, and the like.

A sample of 100 burglars taken from police files yielded the following proportional estimates for the various thief types: good burglars, 7

TABLE 13:   PRODUCT LISTINGS OF FENCES BY TYPE OF THIEF

TYPE OF THIEF	PRODUCTS HANDLED BY FENCES DEALING WITH THIS THIEF
Good burglar	Jewelry, furs, paintings, guns, coins, art objects, antiques, watches
Known burglar	Office equipment, metals, televisions, liquor, jewelry, furniture, cigarettes
Young burglar	Televisions, stereos, jewelry, household goods, office equipment, tools
Boosters	Clothing, watches, furs, tape decks, cigarettes
Junkies	Televisions, clothing, cigarettes, records, tape decks, liquor, office equipment, household appliances, cameras, stereos

percent of the sample; known burglars, 39 percent; young burglars, 20 percent; boosters, 5 percent; and junkies, 29 percent.[26] This breakdown is interesting when compared with Table 14, in which the number of fences dealing with each type of thief is shown. What is important about the breakdown of fencing units here is the manner in which the number of fences servicing each group of thieves fails to correlate with the proportion of that type of thief present in the theft population. Thus although good burglars are estimated to comprise only 7 percent of the theft population, they are serviced by the same number of receivers as that found for addicts who number 29 percent of the burglary population. On the other hand, the known burglar, who is by far the most common member of the theft population, has almost half the number of fences to do business with as does the good burglar. Part of the explanation for this fencing array lies in the value and volume of goods "produced" by each type of thief. Thus the good burglar who yields high-value merchandise though not necessarily in great volume will attract many fences for whom a single transaction can be very lucrative. The addict is much more active but his goods are generally of low unit value. He will attract a good number of fences but not nearly as many in proportion to his numbers. This is because a fence cannot depend solely on the products of a single addict; he will rely instead on the goods of many. The known burglar produces goods of intermediate value (as compared with the other two thieves) but he will do so very often in a volume manner. It is the storage and transportation requirements of such volume trade that is thought to account for the relative paucity of fences dealing with the known burglar.

In Table 14, then, we have a picture of an industry that arranges itself in a rather rational and efficient manner in order to respond to the disparate array of its sources of supply and to the nature of the goods they "produce."

As Much As the Traffic Will Bear

Perhaps one of the more fascinating of the fence's product decisions relates to the volume of goods he will accept both over time and per transaction. Decisions relating to size and assortment of "orders" are easier to resolve since they depend for the most part on two main factors: (1) the social and economic setting in which the receiver plies his trade and (2) the sources of supply with whom he is associated.

The setting of the receiver cannot be stressed too much as a significant influence on the product he handles. The street fence, for example, whose storage and transportation resources consist of his two hands or the trunk of a car must limit the number of goods received per transaction. This fence will also reduce the complexity of his operation by concentrating exclusively on one product at a time, eliminating any real assortment problem. Hence, of the ten members of the sample known to be one-product fences, half are unaffiliated with any legitimate business establishment. The businessman-fence who generally maintains his own storage facilities can comfortably handle much larger individual deliveries, as well as a wider assortment of goods. This is why this type of fence is more often found handling full product lines rather than individual products.

The fence's partner (the thief) may often determine the size of each transaction. The addict, for example, rarely engages in volume thefts; he steals only as much property in an outing as will pay for his drug needs. The fence who deals with addicts, then, cannot expect to receive more than one or two products per thief per transaction. On a completely different level but exhibiting a similar pattern of behavior

TABLE 14:   NUMBER OF FENCES DEALING WITH EACH TYPE OF THIEF (N=90)[a]

TYPE OF THIEF	NUMBER OF FENCES KNOWN TO DEAL WITH SUCH INDIVIDUALS[b]
Good burglar	28
Known burglar	15
Young burglar	16
Booster	11
Junkie	28
Other[c]	8

[a]Many sample members were not linked to any particular thief type and are therefore omitted from the table.

[b]The total number of fences for each group does not represent exclusive dealings with that type of thief. Instead where fences are known to deal with more than one type of thief they are counted in each category separately.

[c]This category includes juveniles and such special police designations as "mob burglars" and "black junkies," the latter indicating the special significance attached to race by many in the fencing industry. Since many fences refuse to deal with blacks of any thief class, those who do so are specially noted by detectives.

is the good burglar. This thief, specializing in items of high unit value, will not generally commit thefts yielding large quantities of merchandise. The fence who handles the largest transactions and the widest assortments deals with the young burglar, the known burglar, and the booster, for it is through their combination of skills that large-volume theft can be successfully perpetrated. Hence this fence is generally the one found to have the greatest short-run storage capacity.

But even the ownership of luxurious storage facilities does not dictate the maintenance of a huge stolen property inventory. This is particularly true where a businessman-fence is involved, for his legitimate buying arrangements may preclude the establishment of too large an illicit inventory, lest his failure to reorder should incur the ill will and/or suspicion of a legal supply source. For the fence, then, "what the traffic will bear" often has less to do with his own avariciousness and more to do with some very practical business considerations.

Something Old and Something New

Not all the stolen property is new and in perfect condition, and this situation can present the receiver with some further product decisions to make.

The handling of used merchandise is particularly suited to certain legitimate trades such as the second-hand general merchandise outlet, the "trading post" type of retail establishment, and the auction house. The data sample yields twelve members known to engage legitimately in such businesses; and it is not surprising to find that the illicit trade of these individuals centers upon the receiving of used goods obtained chiefly from private residences. Most common among the items handled in these outlets are televisions, stereos, clothing, and light household products. The predominant thief involved is the addict.

The market in antiques is technically, of course, a used merchandise trade, although it has some significantly different connotations. Nevertheless an antique business is not precluded legitimately from carrying items whose "antique" designation remains many years away. Even the legitimate range of products appropriately handled by the antique dealer, therefore, has a somewhat amorphous definition. This may be why the antique dealer is so prominent a figure in the fencing industry, numbering eight members of the sample. The illicit commerce of these receivers represents a further outlet for used goods in the theft industry, chiefly for the good burglar and the young burglar. Property stolen from private residences such as jewelry, coin and gun collections, silver pieces,[27] art works, and various "objets d'art" is the primary illegal product line of these receivers.

A final outlet for used merchandise in the fencing industry is the small-time, hand-to-mouth street fence. This individual, supplied chiefly by addicts and juveniles, will often receive used merchandise, since local neighborhood residents are the normal targets of these thieves. The street fence will accept used merchandise since he can obtain it extremely cheaply, marking his prices to the thief downward because of its "distressed" condition.

It is hard to think of this latter receiver as incurring any special obligations as a result of dealing in used products; rather his major preoccupation must always be a precaution against being arrested. The situation is very much different for the businessman-fence who handles used merchandise through his own retail outlet, however, where local commercial codes often require the keeping of records for every transaction involving such merchandise. [28]

An additional precaution that must be taken in dealing with used merchandise is the possibility that the victim will discover and identify his own property in the fence's possession. Unless an item is particularly unique, ingeniously marked or serialized (*and* a record so kept), the likelihood of this happening is almost nonexistent but nevertheless it could produce an unwanted visibility for the fence vis-à-vis police agencies. [29] To guard against this situation, fences maintain a stock of "John Doe alibis" which, after studying numerous police files, read like a set of canned messages. "A guy came in here, looked decent enough, said he'd hit some hard times and wondered, could I use these candlesticks. They were in good condition so I gave him $20. See, here's the card here. John Smith, that was what he said his name was."

The decision to handle new merchandise must take into consideration the same sorts of questions as that involving used goods, but the situation is somewhat more amorphous. A legitimate dealer in new merchandise does not have the same possibility of day-to-day accountability to official sources as does the second-hand merchant. The businessman-fence, for example, who meshes his legal and illegal product line may have to engage in some creative bookkeeping to survive an audit, but he does not incur the affirmative obligation of daily record-keeping faced by a dealer in used merchandise.

The precautions involved in handling new goods are also surprisingly minimal. Inventory record-keeping by legitimate business concerns is hardly prodigious in terms of generating and preserving the individual identity of single items or groups of items. Large wholesalers and even manufacturer's distribution centers have been found unable to positively identify as theirs, merchandise recovered by enforcement authorities.[30] The mass-produced nature of many new products handled by the fencing industry makes them nearly impossible to trace without a standardized and consistently used serialization system. Most new products, then, have for all intents and purposes no identity, making the fence's job somewhat easier.

Fences who deal in new merchandise fall roughly into two groups: small- to medium-sized receivers dealing almost exclusively with boosters and specializing generally in clothing (16 such individuals are represented in the sample); and the medium- to large-scale cargo and warehouse theft receiving operations, supplied primarily by the known burglar (10 such operations are represented in the sample). While other types of fences may handle new merchandise, it is not with the consistency or volume accounted for by these two main groups.

Whatever There's a Market for

Perhaps the darkest corner of the theft industry is that concerning the nature and scope of the demand for its products. Demand forecasting even in the legitimate business system is often frightfully imprecise—as the makers of the Edsel soon learned. An analysis of the demand for stolen property is clearly beyond the scope of this study. Nevertheless a great deal of general information can be gained about this market by looking closely at the fence's product line. The receiver must, after all, remain close to the pulse of his market. He cannot afford to accept goods that are unsalable or must be stored indefinitely. Losses due to unmarketable goods can rarely be recouped. Even if he is a legitimate businessman, the receiver cannot easily charge off his fencing losses on his tax return. Instead the fence's illicit trade must be profitable. In order for it to be so, he must be able to sell all or most of the illegitimate goods he takes in. In other words, he must know "what there's a market for." Demand is perhaps the single most important determinant of the fence's product line. By studying his product line carefully, we can logically expect to learn something about that demand.

In Table 15, the products handled by criminal receivers in the sample have been classified according to standard categories used by

TABLE 15:   NUMBER OF FENCES SPECIALIZING IN GOODS
IN EACH MARKETING CLASS ($\underline{N}$=85)

PRODUCT CLASSIFICATIONS	NUMBER OF FENCES HANDLING TYPE OF GOOD
Consumer Goods	
Convenience goods	4
Shopping goods	37
Specialty goods	19
Consumer goods generalist	14[a]
User Goods	11

[a]Does not necessarily connote a generalist type operation, but rather the crossing of product classifications in the same product line.

marketers;[31] and the number of fences dealing in each type of good is calculated. Some interesting clues about the fencing industry's conception of the market it faces are revealed. To begin with, the market for property stolen perceived by sample fences is dominated by consumer goods.[32] Those fences handling consumer goods in all categories outnumber their user goods counterparts more than six to one. Second, the concentration of fences in the shopping goods category suggests that those products for which consumers are traditionally willing to expend a comparative shopping effort are also those which are most readily salable through the illicit marketing system of the fence. Third, the rather miniscule segment handling convenience goods suggests that where the consumer is not willing to expend an extra effort in the acquisition of goods, the fence is unlikely to do so either. And finally, the fairly substantial energies devoted by fences to the procurement of specialty goods indicates that the demand for such products is dependable, and the meeting of that demand, lucrative.

PRICES

The most speculated-about element in the fence's marketing mix relates to his pricing policy. Conventional wisdom with regard to this policy can be summed up in one sentence: "The fence is cheap," that is, the fence prices his goods so that they are significantly cheaper than the normal market price. Often ignored in a consideration of the pricing of stolen property, though capable of rendering the same conclusion, is the fact that the criminal receiver has not one but two pricing policies: one with respect to the purchase of illicit goods; and one with respect to their sale. Before drawing any monolithic conclusions here, then, it would be well to look at the two distinct situations in which the receiver's price policies are formulated and discover what limitations and/or guidelines they impose.

Paying the Thief

The first situation in which a receiver must make pricing decisions is in his transactions with the thief. It will be remembered that in our earlier characterization of this relationship, we indicated that the fence is more than a buyer of the thief's product; he is a *seller* of services as well. This added dimension of the fence's position vis-à-vis the thief makes him the more dominant member of the relationship, since the disposal service offered by the fence is critical to the thief. In confronting the thief, then, the fence assumes the role of price-maker rather than price-taker. This does not mean that the prices the fence pays for stolen property are set precisely and invariably. Instead a range of market values exists within which bargaining can take place, with the determination of an exact price influenced by one or all of the following factors: (1) the type of thief involved, (2) a desire to guide the stealing behavior of the thief, and (3) the competitive state of the industry.

While all thieves require the disposal services of the fence in order to convert stolen property to a more negotiable and useful medium, neither the urgency nor the immediacy of that need is identical for all. The addict, for example, confronts the fence with the most urgent and immediate of needs. He must make a connection for his supply of narcotics and must have a negotiable medium with which to obtain it. [33] This places the addict in a less than favorable bargaining position relative to the fence—a situation they both appreciate. Thus the price placed on stolen property where the addict is concerned is low indeed, or conversely put, the price of fencing services is extremely high, reflected in the minimal rewards he can expect from his theft activities. The young burglar faces some similar problems with regard to the pricing of stolen property. His inexperience and generally un-initiated status make him vulnerable to gouging by the fence in the ex-change transaction. Thus the general rule of the fence in dealing with thieves of these types was found to be a 10 percent return on the retail value of the merchandise. Some of the specific exchange rates found in this segment of the fencing trade are: sports coat, $7; $600 stereo console = $65; 6 color television sets and 4 stereos = $225. [34]

It is the good burglar who, by careful planning and forethought, can exact the most favorable prices for his products. His self-confi-dence will make him less apprehensive about reaching an immediate agreement for the exchange of stolen property; his sophistication for the intricacies of the transaction process will enable him to better evaluate the offers made. The inherent value of the merchandise in which the good burglar is dealing will make his "paycheck" large in absolute terms when compared with that of the lesser skilled thief, but that does not necessarily mean that the good burglar negotiates with-in a range of prices approximating the legitimate market value of the product. Instead the fence's rule of thumb when dealing with the good burglar was found generally to be from 30 to 50 percent of the whole-sale price. The use of the wholesale pricing schedule in this segment of the fencing trade reflects the greater sophistication of the negotiating parties with the legitimate price structure. Some sample exchange rates for good burglars were furs valued at $5,000 retail, fenced for $1,200; jewelry valued at $25,000 retail, yielded a $5,600 return (ap-proximately 50 percent of wholesale); a $7,000 antiqued lampshade yielded $1,500. [35]

The second factor influencing the price quoted to the thief relates to the fence's desire to *specifically* guide that individual's theft activities. The fence always has implicit influence in this regard through a ma-nipulation of pricing on different items, but his desire for a particular product or set of products may cause him to set up a "standard price" in order to insure a steady flow of said merchandise over a given period of time. The introduction of a standard-price buying arrangement is, as might be expected, very positively responded to in the theft microcosm. This is because it interjects an element of certainty into the exchange transaction which the thief rarely finds in dealings with the fence. It tells the thief not only what to steal, but also how much to steal in order to earn a specific monetary goal. This is particularly helpful to the addict who has a specific need. The standard pricing quotation was found most often in that segment of the fencing industry dealing with the addict and the booster. It was interesting to note that nearly all of the standard price policies found in the sample were set in the middle to upper price ranges for the groups of thieves involved.

Why, one may ask, would a fence quote a higher than average price for products that he could undoubtedly acquire more cheaply? The answer to this question relates to the third factor influencing the fence's price to the thief, that of the competitive state of the industry. In fact, the influence of competition in the fencing trade has almost classic implications. Those fences who face a significant number of competitors (that is, other fences handling the same goods) must in certain instances price to beat competition in order to increase their share of the market. If a fence has a particular need for a large supply of one or two products *and* a large number of competitors, he will *for a time* price above the average level to fulfill that need. A good example of pricing to beat competition was found in the sample in the person of a fence servicing addicts. This individual had obviously acquired an immediate need for tape decks, for while the street rate for the product was $15, he was quoting a price of $20. This action yielded the following interlude between police officers and an addict:

(Police Activity Report)

We stopped Al (a junkie) on   Street; he had a tape deck in his possession. Said it was only the second one he stole. Mentioned as buying them was Mr.   . Al says everybody's going to him since he's paying $20 and everyone else is only paying $15.

It should be noted that this type of competitive pricing is generally temporary and short-lived. There is significant pressure within the industry to maintain low-level prices. Collusion is not unknown within the fencing industry, and the most frequent examples of collusive practice were found in that segment of the industry dealing with the good burglar. The sophistication of this type of thief may be the reason why this segment of the trade joins together to enforce a given price structure. An interview with Greg, a professional thief, [36] produced this chilling tale of collusion and its enforcement in the fencing industry:

Finding himself in possession of a truckload of stolen furs, Greg, unused to handling property in such volume sought to make a quick deal. He approached a fence with whom he had had satisfactory dealings previously only to find that this individual, appreciating his predicament, was bent on taking some advantage of it. Unwilling to let his efforts go so cheaply, Greg began to survey other fences to see if he couldn't negotiate a more equitable bargain. It was then that he discovered that, as he put it, "the word had gone out," that is, other fences had been alerted to the prior claim placed upon the merchandise by the original fence, and, knowing the exigencies of Greg's situation, had agreed to uphold the territorial rights of their fellow fence. Knowing he could not expect a fair price nor even the original price at the data site (since there would undoubtedly be a "penalty" fee assessed him by the first fence), he took the furs to another large metropolitan area and sold them. On his return, the local industry's displeasure with having been scorned met him, in the person of two "enforcers." He was beaten and the money he had acquired for the furs was taken from him.

The ability to exert control over the pricing behavior of competitors or at least to ensure their loyalty to a given price structure is an important influence on a fence's pricing policy. In effect it allows a fence to neutralize the effects of competition even where the number of competing units might suggest that a lively and varied pricing policy should obtain.

Not all fences, of course, face a highly competitive industry structure in terms of numbers of competitors. Often a fence will have, in effect, a monopoly, generated not by his collusion with others, but rather by the particular inexperience or special needs of the thief. The monopoly may only be a temporary one, but while it lasts the fence can literally extort property from thieves at the lowest prices. Those thieves most likely to fall prey to the monopolistic fence are the booster, the young burglar, and the known burglar. The situation most often faced by the booster is one in which the fence has a monopoly based on location. By maintaining either a business or a "drop" (a temporary storage facility for stolen property) in close proximity to the booster's working area, the fence provides that individual with an extremely convenient place to divest himself of merchandise. Because of this the booster's daily haul can consist of several "shopping trips" and the security of his theft activities can be enhanced by the short distances he needs to transport the goods. The fence, knowing the value of this convenient location, will not let his services be taken lightly. This will be reflected in the minimum prices he will offer to the booster. Unless the booster has other not too distant outlets for his goods or can shift his working area to one where competition has a more favorable effect for him, he will be locked into a relationship with the monopolistic fence that is unlikely to improve.

The young burglar can generate a different type of monopoly for a fence, a monopoly borne of his inexperience. A characteristic trait of the fledgling thief is his unfamiliarity with the fencing industry. He is likely to know only one or two fences and hence will be very constrained in his theft activities by the products they handle and by their prices. The fence, realizing the thief has little or no option to a deal with him, does not have to be generous toward the young thief. This does not mean, of course, that he will take undue advantage of an apprentice thief, for he may have reason enough not to discourage the efforts of this protégé. [37]

Perhaps the fence's main limitation in his ability to exploit an inexperienced thief is the realization that his monopoly position may be short-lived. Continued association with other thieves and acquaintances with older thieves will familiarize him quickly with the ways and means of thievery, including a working knowledge of the broad reaches of the fencing industry. For the young thief in the process of "becoming," the number and range of fences he comes to know will have a significant impact on his future. This is why information about fencing is a reliable bench mark against which the young burglar's career development can be charted. It is also why increases in his information set with regard to fencing will be noted not only by his fence but also by the police. As long as the young burglar remains uninitiated, however, the fence retains the ability to exact from him a monopolistic tariff for his receiving services.

The known burglar, although somewhat familiar with the fencing industry, can generate a monopoly for the fence which is based on inferior skills. Characterized by a distinct lack of innovation, skill, or initiative, this type of burglar will often rely on the fence to plan his theft activities. In doing so, he assumes an indentured-like status vis-à-vis the receiver. His reliance on the fence for information and/or direction in the perpetration of thefts will make the prices he receives less than competitive.[38] In addition the known burglar has generally passed the point in time where he could have made the associations necessary to acquire new skills,[39] making him unlikely to improve as a thief. His dependence on the fence is likely to continue indefinitely, rendering the fence's monopoly almost complete.

The fence's pricing policy then is determined by the nature of his source of supply, his desire at any time to strictly influence that source, and the competitive pressures he must respond to in negotiating transactions with that source. Once the receiver has his products, he is faced with a new set of pricing decisions—the amount to charge his customers.

Pricing to Sell

This second pricing policy significantly differs from the first price determination. This new situation places the fence as seller in what is essentially a "buyer's market," competing with other illegitimate purveyors and legitimate dealers for a finite number of customers. It is generally assumed that the fence's answer to such competition is a unilateral one—to sell all his goods very cheaply. Given how cheaply his merchandise is acquired, we might be tempted to agree with this assumption since we know he can undercut legitimate dealers and still profit. Information from the data sample, however, suggests that the selling price structure of the fence is more than a simple and unilateral mark down from the normal market price. In fact, fences appear to respond closely to some specific marketing considerations in setting their prices.

In studying the available information on the pricing policies of the fences in the sample, it was interesting to discover how well they conformed to the rules of thumb developed by marketers with regard to product classifications in consumer and user markets. In the convenience goods field, for example, where stabilization pricing, (that is, the following of a price leader or the industry norm) is prevalent, the receiver was generally found to be precisely in step with his legitimate counterparts. Perhaps the best example of convenience goods pricing by the fence comes from two grocers buying cigarettes for $2/carton. Their selling price for these cigarettes was $5.50 per carton, or 55c per pack—the normal retail price. Lest it is thought that this was a rather insignificant fencing operation, it should be noted that at the time the two were arrested they were in possession of $3,100 worth of stolen cigarettes.

"Skim-the-cream pricing," the rule of thumb marketers use in the specialty goods area, appears to be used as well by the illicit marketer of specialty products. Undoubtedly many specialty good fences were additionally attracted to the normal premium pricing structure of their professions because of their desire to maintain a public image of themselves as bona fide and respected merchants. This was particularly true of jewelers and antique dealers in the sample who appeared to retain the 100 percent to 200 percent mark up, a norm in those trades, regardless of the prices they had paid for goods. What was particularly interesting was the manner in which the "legitimacy" of goods as reflected in their prices was reestablished by fences, even when dealing with one another. The example most striking to the author relates to two transactions involving a pearl necklace. The necklace had been bought originally from a rather luckless thief for $20. When the original fence sold it to another receiver, however, the price tag was $260! Both fences in this case were jewelry dealers capable of evaluating the true value of the necklace; hence their exchange took on the connotation of a fairly "legitimate" transaction between professionals. The following tale found in the police files shows the "legitimizing" of a product through pricing happening at the final exchange with the customer.

A photo-optical analyzer valued at $1,375 new was sold to a fence for an unreported sum. She being rather unfamiliar with its worth or use sold it to a more specialized fence for $150. The second receiver checked it over and as a legitimate dealer in photographic equipment sold it to a local university at the normal price for a used analyzer depreciated over two years (its age). The price was $975. [40]

The shopping goods area in which product line proliferation and a mixed bag of pricing policies are the norm in the legitimate marketing system shows a similar pattern in the fencing industry. For example, it was impossible to find a uniform price for a television set among fences at the data site. The problem is complicated by the fact that there are so many sizes and styles of televisions on the market and often exact descriptions of those available from fences are not disclosed in police reports. Nevertheless a sampling of prices revealed the following: a used television, $30; a new 21-inch black and white portable, $80; a 19-inch portable, $60; plus assorted unconfirmed reports of new televisions being sold at prices from $75 to $175 depending on the style and size. The only comparison made between the fence's price and the legitimate price made by the police was in the case of the 19-inch portable. Sold for $60, its theft report value was placed at $91, approximately a 1/3 mark off from the regular legitimate price. Although it becomes extremely tenuous to draw conclusions from this one example, the specific mark down used is potentially significant when compared to a rather consistent pricing policy found in another segment of the illicit shopping goods market.

In the sample, the pricing of new clothing by fences yielded the most consistent pattern found for any shopping good. In nearly every case, clothing was sold by the fence at a straight mark down from the regular retail price. Generally the mark down was from 30 to 50 percent but several fences sold clothing at exactly one-third the retail price. Throughout the trade in clothing "a one-third principle" appeared to be operating. The fence who was buying clothing from boosters at one-third of the store price, sold it to his customers at one-third off, obviously seeing the equity of a three-way split, although his profit margin was, of course, a clean 100 percent.[41] The consistency of the pricing pattern for clothing was so striking that one is led to wonder whether similar consistent pricing policies holding across other product classifications might have been in evidence had more complete information been available for other shopping goods handled by the fence. Nevertheless, it should be obvious that it is the shopping goods field in which the "bargains" so often ascribed to the fencing trade will be found. This is not unique, since shopping goods in the legitimate marketing system yield "bargains" to consumers. The fence, then, like his legitimate counterparts, appears to be competitive price-wise only when necessary.

The fences in the user goods marketing segment represent a small portion of the sample and very little pricing information was available about them. Given our knowledge about the industrial sector in which pricing to meet and/or beat competition, combined with a plethora of trade and cash discounting plans, are most prevalent, it is probably accurate to postulate that the user goods fence is a worthy adversary for his legitimate counterparts.

One final marketing consideration for the fence's selling price policy is the setting in which his goods are sold. Market studies have often found a correlation made by consumers between price and quality. [42] A particular phenomenon noted by marketers is the "expected price," that is, a consumer estimate of appropriate price. Thus, many goods are expected to be priced within certain narrow limits and when such expectations are not met, the consumer is alienated and will often postpone or cancel a purchase decision. Generally this alienation may be thought to come from prices above expectations, but the phenomenon can occur as well from pricing at *less*-than-expected levels. When merchandise is priced very cheaply the quality of the merchandise may be questioned; the consumer may carefully examine the merchandise to see if it is satisfactory.

An important influence on the consumer's "expected price" level is where the purchasing decision is made. In a discount house, the consumer expects to find relatively cheap prices in the dry goods and wearing apparel lines, and expects store-brand appliances and other goods priced below name brands in the same product lines; he may even come to expect a break on brand-name products. When expectations are met, the consumer will buy, but when prices are either higher or lower than expected, the consumer may go to a more traditional retailer. The consumer who shops in a "better" department store has a similar but higher range of price expectations. He does not expect to find products in this setting that are "cut-rate" in either quality *or* price; that is not why he goes there. Instead, the consumer expects to pay for quality merchandise as well as for the sense of well-being that shopping there may create.

Setting, then, is a critical factor that must be accounted for in any pricing policy. The fencing trade is not made an exception to this rule. The receiver who sells an illicit product in his own retail outlet must price it in such a way that it conforms to the overall image of the store. With a dual pricing structure, the businessman-fence may not be able to move either line of goods successfully, since it will be unclear to consumers whether he is a nice guy offering them "bargains" or a bad guy gouging them with junk. It becomes, then, as unreasonable for the jeweler-fence to carry a cut-rate line of stolen gems and not expect it to reflect on all his merchandise, as for the second-hand generalist fence to introduce a line of new television sets to his store at normal prices and not expect his customers to respond suspiciously. As it happens, neither is likely to even make the experiment. None of the jewelers in the sample are of the "bargain basement" variety and the respect with which they are regarded in the community suggests that none of their business practices would add to such a perception of them. Similarly, the second-hand merchandisers in the sample displayed a consistent pricing pattern whether the goods they were selling were new or used.

Perhaps the most interesting and deceptive problem of setting in the fencing trade is that faced by the peddler-type fence. The overwhelming impression he creates is one of illegitimacy. This has the effect of keeping his prices fairly low since he must be able, in one price offer, to incur the favor and meet the expectations of his customer. He needs the former to avoid detection and arrest; he needs the latter to quickly consummate an agreement. If his price is too high he may lose not only a sale but also his freedom. If his price is too low, he may be taken advantage of, by being forced to come down even more in price. A "knowledgeable" customer can always bargain him down to an extremely favorable price, but what may not be immediately apparent is the fact that it is this same "knowledgeable" customer that the peddler fence can most readily deceive. Herein lies the second general effect of the peddler's setting. The sheer illicitness of his setting enables the peddler fence to dispose of some worthless merchandise at a significant profit. Once the greed of a customer takes over, his own perceptions of the situation will make him more interested in striking a bargain than in inspecting the quality of the merchandise at issue. This ruse is not merely the fence's game but is played by many others trading on the peddler-fence's setting. [43]

From the information generated at the data site, it is clear that we cannot agree with a monolithic view of the fence's price policy. We must appreciate first the disparate situations in which each of his pricing policies is made; second, the varied persons to which those policies must be tailored; and finally, the competitive conditions with which those policies must successfully deal. In addition, we have found that the fence in not unilateral in his pricing decisions. Instead he is cheap when he must be and dear when he can be; generous when he needs something and exploitative when he does not; competitive when it is reasonable to be so and collusive when it is not. And yet the fence's varied and often surprising pricing policies bring to the world of theft a consistency and a direction that makes the activity both profitable and efficient. It is difficult to imagine that the monolithic and unilateral pricing policy we have conceived for him could work as well.

PROMOTIONAL CONSIDERATIONS

The development in a nation's economy from that characterized by a cottage-based to that of a mass-production-based, industrial sector generates considerable and far-reaching changes. Not the least of these changes is the tremendous increase in output of goods and services, commodities which must be marketed if the economy is to survive and grow. The common aphorism in marketing, "nothing happens until somebody sells something," becomes a watch word as increased production threatens to outstrip, or at least spread thin, effective demand. Mass production creates a need for mass promotion, changing the basic relationship between buyer and seller.

The interaction between general economic development and property crime makes it important to think of the fencing industry in a similar developmental context. Consider MacIntosh's characterization of theft as moving from craft crime to project crime,[44] going hand in hand with a shift in economic base and in patterns of property holding. Noting her description of the emergence of the criminal receiver when the need for a functional division of labor occurs in theft, we can once again understand the critical connection to be made between increased production and the redistribution function. As we survey what is estimated to be a multi-billion dollar theft industry with a growth rate of 180 percent over the decade of the 1960s,[45] our characterization of it must be of a mass-production industry; and our concern must be for its promotional component. "Nothing happens until somebody sells something" is as true for an illicit economy as it is for a legitimate one, and that "somebody" in the theft industry is the criminal receiver. When we investigated the life and actions of Mr. Jonathan Wild, we were seeing the promotional strategies of the fence as he syndicated and presided over a craft industry. When we investigate the contemporary fence, we must look for the promotional strategies necessary for the organization and ratiocination of a mass-output industry characterized by both craft and project crime.

It is difficult, using official files and data, to discover precisely the fence's promotional package. We can, however, develop some appreciation for the degree of effort he need devote to promotion by returning again to the marketing considerations suggested by his product line.

Promotion for the Businessman-Fence

Looking at the product line of the businessman-fence meshing a legal and illicit product line, it is significant to note that the most dominant kinds of goods he handles (shopping and specialty) require very different promotional efforts. Fences who handle shopping goods (by far the largest segment of the industry), for example, can rely on the manufacturers of those products to do much of their promotion for them. Thus, television manufacturers advertise extensively in the media, generally have a warranty program for which they take responsibility, employ the use of regional service and repair centers, and distribute informative brochures and display materials to local retailers. A businessman-fence handling an RCA television set, then, does not really need to "sell" it, but merely to complete a transaction. This is as true for the legal product as it is for the illegal one. [46]

The situation is somewhat different for the businessman-fence in the specialty goods field. The antique dealer, for example, must develop his own promotional program to fit the particular type of customers he serves. He knows that his trade has pre-sold his product line in a generic sense (that is, antiques have a well-defined market) but the job of selling his *particular* line of products will depend upon his own efforts. He must decide on a guarantee program, the extent to which he will extend credit, provide specialized appraisal services, and advertise his presence.

The businessman-fence who handles convenience goods has the least promotional worries. His illicit line has been so intensively presold that it will sell itself; he need only ring up the cash register. It is perhaps interesting in this regard to note the small size of the sample engaged in a convenience good trade. This may indicate that promotion is not considered to be such an undue burden that it will influence fences in a determination of their product lines.

User goods face the most knowledgeable and utilitarian market confronting any seller; they must, then, have a promotional package that can flexibly and readily adapt the product to the customer's needs, both in terms of assortment and service options. It may be the critical importance of personal selling in the user goods field that accounts for the fact that the segment of the fencing sample engaged in the handling of metal products are all also legitimate sellers of the merchandise they receive illicitly. In any case the promotional package of these businessmen-fences will not differ significantly from that which they have developed through their legitimate commercial roles.

Promoting an Image

Perhaps the most important promotional decision for the fence (businessman or not) whose illicit goods are not consonant with his status or circumstance concerns the image he will project. Will he pass himself off as a legitimate purveyor of said goods or will he trade on an illicit image? Very little information could be generated regarding this segment of the industry and its promotional handiwork, although several potential explanations are offered for the reader's consideration.

First, it should be recognized that this segment of the industry is composed of the following types of fencing units: the illegal entrepreneur, [47] the businessman-fence handling an illicit line distinct from his legitimate commerce, the peddling fence, the small-time fence operating from a residence, and the burglar. The stock and trade of all these receivers is primarily products in the shopping goods category. This is thought to be potentially significant since many of these goods are extensively pre-sold in the legitimate environment. That is why we conclude that the fence's image rather than his product is subject to the most promotional effort in this segment of the industry.

Second, a clear breakdown can be made of the several types of fences to be found in this part of the industry. The three latter types, for example, appear to have made a very definite choice as to the legality of the image they wish to promote. Indeed, they trade on the very illicit nature of their "business": the peddler depends on his transience for protection, the residential fence on the good will he engenders with his neighbors, and the burglar on the maintenance of further illicit contacts as customers.

The other two types of fences found in this segment of the industry (that is, the businessman handling goods distinct from his licit line and the illegal entrepreneur) present a much hazier picture to the observer. To begin with, it is the businessman-fence in this segment who is most likely to handle large volumes of stolen property. It becomes especially intriguing then to guess at the nature of the image he projects to his customers. One might posit that given the volume of goods he is able to consistently generate, he could probably successfully represent himself as a legitimate purveyor of said merchandise in the appropriate marketplace.[48] At the same time, however, the well-financed quality of such receiving operations of businessman-fences suggests that they can operate purely on the principle of the well-greased palm, maintaining an illicit image with their customers, not all of whom may be willing participants.

One final promotional strategy, involving blackmail and/or extortion, ranging from the subtle to the less so, is thought to be a distinct possibility as an operating procedure employed by fences in the illegal entrepreneur segment of the receiving trade for the development and promotion of their illicit commerce.[49] The range of individuals over whom the illicit entrepreneur maintains a manipulable rein makes this promotional strategy not only feasible but also effective.

Promotional considerations are an important component of any fence's marketing program. What distinguishes fences from one another, however, is the extent to which promotional efforts center on the receiver's product or on his image. An essential fact of promotion is the extent to which products are pre-sold in the legitimate marketplace. Important as well is the anonymity characteristically associated with the selling function in our society. Both of these qualities of the legitimate commercial establishment permit the intrusion of the illicit marketing man by allowing him to exploit and trade on its not insignificant promotional achievements.

4 | *Legitimate fronts for illegitimate enterprise*

Having reviewed policies regarding products, prices, and promotion made by the fence, we must discuss one final component of his marketing program—the channel of distribution used. The one factor found to most influence the structure of the fence's channel of distribution is his "business" status—that is, the receiver's affiliation with a business enterprise, whether legitimate or not. This factor is what marketers call the "place" element of the marketing mix. It is the businessman-fence who generates the most information regarding distribution channels in the theft industry, since his well-defined "front" contributes to channel stability over time. Both the criminal entrepreneur and the unaffiliated fence demonstrate greater channel variability. Most of this chapter, then, is devoted to the business of the businessman-fence, although some concluding notes relate to his "illegitimate" counterparts.

BUSINESS IN ITS AMERICAN SETTING

The entrepreneur and the private business enterprise he builds are somewhat idealized institutions on the American scene. The history of the American business, therefore, has seen it become the repository of the hopes and dreams of many citizens; of the life savings of the venturesome but luckless, and of the family fortunes of the highly successful risk-takers. It is not without some temerity, therefore, that Americans can look on the business enterprise as something more than the composite of a history of high-minded hopes and cherished beliefs; or, to consider the possibility of its having become as well a veil for the machinations of the unscrupulous.

Business enterprise in the United States accrues a tremendous amount of legitimacy to those who participate in it, doing so with little question as to motives or ends. For those whose ends are less than noble, it becomes a rather simple and obvious step to gather around themselves the accoutrements of the business venture and manipulate them to their own purpose; or, alternatively, to take a pre-existing business operation and shape it to accomplish both legitimate and illegitimate goals.

Publicity surrounding certain scandals and the work of commentators and researchers have made Americans recognize this transformation in business relationships.[1] In learning more about this process, the criminal receiver of stolen property is a very good object lesson. For, to a large proportion of individuals in the fencing industry, the business enterprise and the profession of businessman are the stock in trade. Both are the "legitimate" means to illegitimate ends.

A WORD ABOUT FRONTS AND BLINDS

The fence's business fronts have been little explored. This situation is due primarily to the lack of analysis about fences in general, but also to the failure of commentators to place criminals in anything but illicit settings. Thus conventional wisdom has been allowed to maintain the fence in a street corner milieu or at best in the fringes of a quasi-legitimate pawnbroking trade. The ease with which such explanations have gone unchallenged has made it difficult to confront the far more characteristic pattern of the receiver as affiliated with legitimate business endeavors.

Even writers who acknowledge the "legitimate" settings of crime figures, however, tend to stumble into another pitfall in dealing with the criminal businessman, that of conceptually equating the *front* with the *blind*. In other words, legitimate endeavors of the offender are interpreted exclusively as a ruse behind which illicit activities can be undertaken. Klockars' recent work suggests, for example, that while the fence's legitimate business rarely constitutes a blind to the police, it most certainly serves as a blind (or a convenient rationalizing factor) for the public who "might be offended by a criminal in its presence."[2] What a discussion like this often fails to account for is the possibility that the front can serve more than the unitary function of deception. In some cases it may represent a simple desire for legitimate status, with little attempt to dupe. Deception may not even be necessary where all the relevant participants in the activities of the front are completely knowledgeable and supportive. Even more important, however, is the situation in which the front represents the predominant vocation of an individual whose illicit sideline is less important to him. Many business endeavors, then, may simply be a convenient and efficient way to manage one's affairs whether those affairs be entirely respectable, partly so, or completely illicit.

The term used here in discussing the fence's business is the "legitimate front." It has been chosen because it is thought to embody some appreciation for the *different* functions and ends which a legitimate business endeavor can serve. Where the blinding or deceptive function of the fence's business is dominant, it will be so noted, but where other more important interests appear to be accomplished through the front, they will be recognized and discussed. The term "legitimate front," then, identifies the functional contribution of a business endeavor to *both* legitimate and illegitimate goals—a significant departure from the usual interpretation given the front. It is hoped that the use of this term will yield some appreciation for the fact that criminal activity *not only shapes, but also is shaped by* the legitimate setting through which it is undertaken.

LEGITIMATE FRONTS

One of the most interesting findings in the data sample was the discovery of the criminal receiver in 64 percent of the cases as owner/operator of a permanent, legitimate business enterprise.[3] This segment of the fencing industry, the businessman-fence, projects a rather glaring rebuttal to the fly-by-night image that has often characterized the trade. It was the permanency and the stability of many of these business enterprises that generated a reevaluation of the term "front." Some businesses owned by fences represent substantial financial investments, making it difficult to conceive of them as mere blinds erected to cover up illicit activities. An analysis of the nature of the businesses represented in the sample and their relationship to the illicit trade engaged in by their owners, eventually yielded the following tripartite classification of the businessman-fence's legitimate fronts:

1. The integrative front.
2. The functional-facilitating front.
3. The dissonant front.

The nature of a receiver's legitimate front helped determine the specific channel of distribution for stolen property. The type of front served as an organizing principle around which the whole of the businessman-fence's marketing program revolved. Finally, the legitimate front helped to explain the importance of fencing endeavors in a businessman-fence's total business portfolio.

The Integrative Front

The integrative front is a legitimate business enterprise operated by the criminal receiver through which stolen property is distributed directly to customers. This type of front has two main characteristics: (1) a short and direct channel of distribution (Producer → Retailer or Wholesaler → Customer); and (2) an illicit product line that either matches or closely coincides with the legitimately marketed line. It is this latter characteristic—meshing two product lines—that makes the short distribution channel possible. Integrative fronts are the most frequent type of business operated by the businessman-fence, occurring in 48 percent of the cases.

The integrative front is typically a retail business concern, although of the 34 businesses so classified, nine are in wholesaling or user goods trades. This latter segment, for example, absorbs salvage dealers, jewelry manufacturers, an antique wholesaler, a coin/stamp clearing house, and an electronics supply company. The retailing fence is most representative of an integrative front, however, with the antique dealer, the furniture and appliance dealer, the jeweler and the secondhand goods merchandiser appearing most frequently in this segment. A full list of businesses identified as integrative fronts is found in Table 16.

TABLE 16:   INTEGRATIVE FRONTS OF THE BUSINESSMAN-FENCE
($\underline{N}$=34)

CATEGORIES OF BUSINESS FRONTS	TOTAL FOR FRONT	TOTAL FOR CLASSIFICATION CODE
CMTW Concerns[a]		9
Salvage company	4	
Jewelry manufacturing and wholesaling	2	
Antique wholesaler	1	
Coin and stamp clearinghouse	1	
Electronics equipment wholesaler	1	
Retailing Concerns		25
Furniture and appliance dealer	6	
Second hand/novelty merchandising	6	
Grocery retailer	3	
Retial jeweler	2	
Tool rental retailer	1	
Service Enterprises		0

[a]Construction, manufacturing, transportation, and wholesaling businesses.

The businesses in Table 16 represent a wide spectrum of entrepreneurship ranging from a rather marginal second-hand goods dealer (found in an inner city area) to a very successful and well-respected jeweler (in the central business district). This range of business enterprises is reflected further in the clientele served by the integrative front. Table 17, for example, shows the segmentation within integrative fronts based on the clientele served.

The matches are fairly obvious—the jeweler dealing with the thief most likely to come into the possession of quality jewelry, the good burglar; the appliance or second-hand dealer handling the toasters and stereos of the addict or young burglar. The known burglar is nearly absent from the clientele of the retail integrative front, but he is the predominant thief supplying the integrative wholesaler. Accounting

TABLE 17: SEGMENTATION FOUND IN INTEGRATIVE FRONTS ON THE BASIS OF CLIENTELE

INTEGRATIVE FRONTS	CLIENTELE SERVED				
	GOOD BURGLAR	KNOWN BURGLAR	YOUNG BURGLAR	ADDICT	BOOSTER
Wholesalers					
Salvage companies		X			
Jewelry manufacturing	X				
Antique whole-saling		X			
Coin and stamp whole-saling	X				
Electronics equipment wholesaling		X	X		
Retailers					
Furniture/appliance retailer	X		X	X	
Antique retailer	X		X		
SEcond hand/novelty merchandising				X	X
Groceries retailer			X	X	
Jewelry retailer	X				

for this distinct difference in clientele is the difference in transaction capacity between the retail and wholesale integrative front. Thus the salvage yard or the warehousing facilities of the wholesale enterprise can absorb stolen property in large lot sizes, that is quantity thefts. The thief most typically stealing in quantity is the known burglar, hence the match. It is the small-scale theft of the addict and the good burglar, however, that allows the retailing fence in this group to operate integratively. Were he to begin dealing in larger lot sizes, he would be required to seek outlets other than his own for stolen property.

One might ask whether this might not be practicable for this group of receivers since the profit margins they realize on illicit merchandise far surpass those earned on legitimate goods. Curiously enough, the fence operating an integrative front is unlikely to do so. This is because of one final characteristic of this type of front: the fact that its trade is nearly always at least half legal and in some cases is predominantly so.[4] The integrative front, then, is doing a legitimate business above and beyond whatever illicit operations are being conducted; and the receiver in this situation demonstrates a bona fide commitment to this legal enterprise. That is why he limits himself to an illicit product line that will complement the legal one, and why he generally will make his pricing of stolen goods consistent with the image projected by the legitimate business. The integrative front exhibits a business portfolio dominated by the legal trade, with fencing representing either a bonus type of investment or a means for maintaining the solvency of the legitimate business. It is this quality of the integrative front which seriously calls into question the usual interpretation of the legitimate interests of the offender. This type of front is clearly more than a blind erected for the purpose of engaging in criminal activity. Instead it represents a legitimate career choice made by an individual who finds it practicable and profitable to supplement his income through illegal means.

Of course, the most intriguing question suggested by the integrative front is: Why is it that all merchants do not engage in fencing activities to supplement their legitimate business interests? Beyond questions of personal integrity, two factors seem to contribute to the acquisition of an illicit trade. They are location and knowledgeable contact with actual or potential thieves. We have earlier noted the importance of location in determining a receiver's clientele. It appears that the presence of numerous illicit sources of supply in the entrepreneur's immediate environment makes the establishment of a fencing trade particularly easy and inviting. Thus the merchant in a high-crime or high-drug-using neighborhood would have little difficulty in establishing himself as a fence.[5] In fact, he may use the fencing trade as a kind of insurance against theft, choosing to service rather than secure himself against the criminal elements of the neighborhood.[6] Second, the failure rate of businesses in such areas is likely to be higher than elsewhere, so fencing may be a convenient way of surviving in an occupation. This may be particularly true of the minority entrepreneur. The most successful black businesses in the inner city area of the data site were in service trades (beauty shops, for example) with retailers and manufacturers falling a distant second and third.[7] Included among the integrative fronts found in the sample were the retail businesses of four black fences, suggesting that the survival motive may be especially apt. The businessman-fence whose legitimate enterprise is made marginal by location, then, may try to exploit that same environment to his advantage.

The second factor that contributes to an involvement in fencing is a knowledgeable contact with thieves. Although the specific patterns of such contacts are dealt with more expansively in the next chapter, it should be noted here that such associations are not regarded as causal in nature vis-à-vis the fencing enterprise. Instead it is the businessman who is likely to initiate the contact, offering services to those he knows are, or can be encouraged to become, thieves. Such personal awareness of available sources of stolen property, combined with the prospect of a high rate of return on one's investment, appear to additionally account for the emergence of the integrative front in the fencing industry.

We can summarize the characteristics of the integrative fencing front, then, as follows:

1. It distributes stolen property directly to the customer, having a Producer → Retailer or Wholesaler → Customer channel.

2. Its product line is designed to converge with the dominant legitimate line.

3. It reflects a business portfolio in which the legitimate trade either dominates or shares an equal status with the illicit operation.

The Functional-Facilitating Front

A functional-facilitating front is a legitimate business enterprise operated by a criminal receiver through which stolen property is acquired but *not* distributed. The two main characteristics of the functional-facilitating front are: (1) an indirect channel of distribution to the customer, and (2) a product line inconsistent with the legitimate enterprise. The failure of the illicit line to match the legal product line obviates the use of the front for the purpose of direct distribution[8] of stolen property, although the functional-facilitating front does provide some distinct advantages with regard to the production, ownership, inventory, and transit activities necessary in a distribution channel. Table 18 contains a listing of those concerns in the sample classified as functional-facilitating fronts. From it, a very clear appreciation for the distinctiveness of this type of front can be gleaned.

Perhaps the most striking quality shared by all facilitative fronts is the product-service mesh found in the legitimate product line. Nearly all of the businesses found in Table 18 distribute not merely goods, but either goods on which some service has been performed or the service itself. Thus the restauranteur is not selling food but prepared meals; the bar owner is not dispensing liquor but measured quantities and assortments of that commodity; and the construction contractor is providing not only building materials, but also the labor required to assemble such materials into a specific product. Even though then, the facilitative front is typically a retail concern (as was the case with the integrative front), it is a retailing outlet selling a commodity *plus*. This "plus" is the inherent and inseparable service

TABLE 18: FUNCTIONAL-FACILITATING FRONTS OF THE BUSINESSMAN-FENCE (N=27)

BUSINESS FRONTS	TOTAL FOR FRONT	TOTAL FOR CLASSIFICATION CODE
CMTW[a]		6
Light construction company	1	
Auto parts wholesaler	1	
Restaurant/bar equipment wholesaler	1	
Cab company	1	
Hauling and storage company	2	
Retailing		14
Restauranteur	7	
Bars/tavern owner	6	
Grocery retailer	1	
Services		7
Garage/gas station	3	
Pool room/bowling alley	2	
Dog breeding/grooming	1	
Barber	1	

[a]Construction, manufacturing, transportation, and wholesaling businesses.

which becomes part of the retail product. The peculiar nature of services[9] is that they are "produced" and "sold" simultaneously, making them "un-stealable" for resale purposes.[10] Hence, we should not be surprised to find that the illicit product line of the fence who owns a service or service-oriented business will not coincide with his legitimate line. What may be surprising, however, is to find that even where "stealable" products that are important to the rendering of services or the "production" of service-intensive goods do exist, the businessman-fence with a functional-facilitating front is unlikely to handle them. Thus, none of the restauranteurs in the sample were found to deal illicitly in food stuffs; no bartenders received stolen liquor; no building contractors were found to handle lumber, hardware merchandise, or building tools. This is not to say that such fencing arrangements are inconceivable, but only that they were not found at the data site.[11] Instead fences owning functional-facilitating fronts tend to concentrate on illicit lines of goods quite distinct from their legitimate commerce.

Table 19 gives some idea of the inconsistency between the facilitative front and its illicit product line. The products handled by these fronts are inconsistent not only with the legitimate line but also with the market segments and patterns displayed by the legitimate business. For example, the restauranteur whose legitimate commerce is in a consumer marketplace may handle office equipment illicitly, a line suggesting an industrial market. Similarly, the building contractor, whose legitimate market is fairly distinctly defined, may deal in such widely marketable products as tape decks and liquor. If, then, the functional-facilitating front offers no guidelines for the determination of the product line to be handled illegitimately, to what does it owe its name?

The answer lies in the instrumental rather than the definitional boundaries of the functional-facilitating front. A business front is facilitative not because it defines specific products or arrangements as appropriate but because it is instrumental in making certain types of business arrangements possible. Thus the functional-facilitating front is one that contributes to criminal receiving as an endeavor, regardless of the particular products received. This means that the illicit commerce of the businessman-fence is not so divorced from his legitimate trade as his line of stolen property might imply. Instead the

TABLE 19: FUNCTIONAL-FACILITATING FRONTS AND THEIR PRODUCT LINES

CATEGORY OF BUSINESS	PRODUCT LINES[b]
CMTW[a]	
Light construction	Tape decks, liquor, office equipment
Auto parts wholesaler	Metals
Restaurant/bar equipment wholesaler	liquor, office equipment
Cab company	Tape decks, clothing
Hauling/storage company	Furniture/appliances
Retailing	
Restaurants	Any new merchandise, office equipment
Bars/taverns	Furs, clothing, televisions, stereos, jewelry
Grocery store	Clothing, televisions, liquor
Services	
Gas station/car repair	Televisions, men's clothing
Poolroom/bowling alley	Jewelry, televisions, household appliances
Dog grooming/breeding	Televisions, liquor
Barber	Cigarettes

[a]Construction, manufacturing, transportation, and wholesaling businesses.

[b]Where more than one business appears in each category, product lines reflect the activities of the category as a whole and does not imply that each receiver handles all of the items listed.

legitimate business front becomes critical in facilitating the organization and the stability of the illegitimate endeavor. Functional-facilitating fronts help the fencing trade in three separate contexts: (1) the establishment and maintenance of a clientele, (2) the generation of theft information, and (3) the facilitation of the actual reception of merchandise.

The functional-facilitating front is characterized generally by more than a passing acquaintance with its clientele. In fact this type of business front exhibits the social services dimension of the criminal receiver. Functional-facilitating fronts are particularly susceptible to the establishment of more than business relationships with thieves. Restaurants and bars, for example, provide social sanctuaries where burglars can meet, recruit associates, and make plans in relative safety. Like the bowling alley or pool hall, they also provide recreational opportunities in familiar and relatively secure settings. In addition, with the exception of the restaurant equipment wholesaler, all of the functional-facilitating fronts found in the sample are businesses with normally changeable employment pools. This is particularly true of the light construction and restaurant trades. It becomes possible, therefore, for the receiver to provide the thief with the employment opportunity he may need for parole purposes. This segment of the industry is especially known for such practices. Thus of nine thieves discovered working for fences at the time of the sample, six were in functional-facilitating fronts. The thief may not actually work for the receiver (legitimately at least) but if he does so, it is generally for a limited period. Instead he is often listed on an employee roster for the parole officer's benefit. What makes such arrangements particularly plausible is the number of good and known burglars who maintain either union membership or other employment credentials in building trades (nine such individuals were noted in the sample data). [12]

The ability to provide the thief with social and employment opportunities is an important asset of the functional-facilitating front. It establishes a continuity in supply sources and helps to expand clientele through the referral grapevine in the theft population. The fence, then, may not handle property stolen by all of the thieves who patronize his restaurant, but their knowledge of him often makes him a recommended buyer for their friends. The extension of employment opportunities seems to carry with it certain territorial privileges for the fence. Thus the thief employed by the businessman-fence owes him the fruits of a requisite number of "scores." When such temporary relationships are seen as mutually beneficial, they may develop into permanent ones.

Table 20 lists the clientele served by functional-facilitating fronts. As can be seen, the typical suppliers for these fencing operations are the known burglar, the young burglar, and the addict. Functional-facilitating fronts segment into two groups on the basis of clientele served. The first group consists primarily of receivers in retailing (particularly bars) and service businesses who maintain outlets for the products stolen by addicts and young thieves. Fencing through these fronts tends to remain small in scale and even allows for word-of-mouth distribution through knowledgeable customers and patrons. The second group, located primarily in the restaurant and some CMTW[13] trades, services the known burglar and sometimes the

TABLE 20: CLIENTELES SERVED BY FUNCTIONAL-FACILITATING FRONTS

CATEGORY OF BUSINESS	CLIENTELE SERVED				
	GOOD BURGLAR	KNOWN BURGLAR	YOUNG BURGLAR	ADDICT	BOOSTER
CMTW[a]					
Light construction				X	
Auto parts wholesaler		X			X
Cab company				X	
Hauling/storage company		X		X	
Retailing					
Restaurants		X	X	X	
Bars/taverns		X	X	X	
Grocery retailer				X	
Services					
Gas station/car repair			X		
Pool room/bowling alley			X	X	
Dog grooming/breeding		X			
Barber		X			

[a]Construction, manufacturing, transportation, and wholesaling businesses.

young burglar. These fronts typically deal in quantity theft and require a more sophisticated distribution network. The good burglar is all but absent from association with functional-facilitating fronts. The reason for this, it would seem, is that the functional-facilitating front relies on the type of theft that a good burglar would consider either too worthless (in terms of quality) or too large (in terms of volume). Additionally, the functional-facilitating front often requires a continual working relationship with the fence— something the good burglar does not usually establish. [14] For thieves in this segment, however, such a relationship can be very important indeed. How and why it is important relates to the information that the functional-facilitating front can obtain.

The service factor in most facilitative fronts enables the business-owners to acquire more information about customers than do product-centered enterprises. This is because the service to be rendered either requires the customer to spend a substantial amount of time at the seller's establishment or vice versa. For example, the difference in time spent eating a meal at a restaurant and making a purchase in a department store is obvious. Simply making dinner reservations indicates one's movements for an evening. Functional-facilitating fronts, then, generate information about the routines and/or well-being of their customers—information important to the commission of a crime. The sharing of such information with thieves appears to be a prevalent arrangement in this segment of the fencing industry. It is what is known as providing the "set-up." Set-ups are especially helpful to the inexperienced or minimally skilled thief, and particularly handy for the receiver in strictly determining the goods he will handle.

One final characteristic of this type of front serves to make them particularly facilitative to the criminal receiving trade and that is with regard to the degree of flexibility and covertness by which stolen property can be received. Many functional-facilitating fronts have expanded business hours, not common in general merchandise outlets, thus giving the thief a perfectly legitimate reason for being there. They also have separate delivery entrances and storage areas where goods can be conveniently dropped or reviewed by the fence for purchase. Functional-facilitating fronts in the CMTW trades have many transit facilities, vehicles particularly, in which stolen property can be transported covertly. Frequent comings and goings are characteristic of such establishments, making the movement of stolen property in and out unnoticeable.

Functional-facilitating fronts, then, offer numerous options for the reception, assembly, and dispersal of stolen goods. Because of the volume of trade engaged in by many merchants in this segment of the fencing industry, it is unlikely that the illicit merchandise is distributed locally. Instead a distant indirect channel, necessitating a commercial self-representation by the receiver (or his surrogates) that differs significantly from that by which he is known at the data site, is probably the norm. We say "probably" because this is generally where the trail provided by official sources ends. Only rarely does the provincialism of a local policing unit allow for the generation of information relating to crime initiated in its jurisdiction but continued outside its borders. More typically, once stolen property is thought to have left the immediate police bailiwick it is considered irretrievable and investigation tapers off. Although no specific information about the eventual destination of much of the property handled by the functional-facilitating front can be given, some further characteristics of these businesses growing out of the discussion above, can be noted.

First, the functional-facilitating front will generally be capable of handling a wider range of products than the integrative front. This is because few, if any, items are defined by the nature of the legitimate enterprise as being more or less risky. Instead the front serves to facilitate the reception of any item deemed salable by the fence.

Second, since the functional-facilitating front does not allow for direct distribution of stolen property (except on a limited scale) it will generally indicate the existence of a longer and more carefully coordinated channel of distribution than is common in integrative fronts. Distribution by the functional-facilitating front is also more likely to be nonlocal and involve some further intermediary(ies).

Finally, the functional-facilitating front, because of the nature of the relationship it engenders with the thief, will generally indicate a business portfolio in which the legitimate endeavors of the receiver are of secondary importance. Instead the major commitment of the fence is to his illicit trade even though the maintenance and health of the legitimate business is critical to the criminal endeavor. Here the front can be seen operating as an instrumentality, as a tool of the illicit trade, much as the celluloid strip or the pass-key is the tool of the

thief. This does not rob the legitimate business endeavor of its separate, commercial integrity, just as the crow bar can be put to both
legal and illegal uses by the burglar. It does, however, change the
emphasis, direction, and scope of that business.

The major descriptors of the functional-facilitating front can be
summarized as follows:

1. It has a wide ranging product line inconsistent with that of
the legitimate business.

2. Its channel of distribution is typically long, indirect, and
often not local.

3. It reflects a business portfolio in which the illicit commerce takes precedence over the legal trade.

4. It is generally observed in services trades or in businesses
dominated by service-intensive product lines.

The Dissonant Front

A dissonant front is a legitimate business operated by a criminal receiver and kept *completely independent* of his illicit trade. There is
something entirely inexplicable about the businessman-fence who
owns the dissonant front. One is almost tempted to label this category
"miscellaneous" except that the pattern of illicit enterprise is so consistent. Dissonance, or incongruity, arises from two sources in fronts
of this type: (1) from the utter legitimacy, respectability, and success
of the firms found in this category; and (2) from the similarity of their
high value product lines.

All of the businesses classified as dissonant fronts fall into a most-
respected businessman category[15] of the larger businessman-fence
segment of the industry. All are successful businesses in their own
right, needing no bailing out financially through illicit means. And all
are run with no reference to the illicit trade of their owners. Unlike
other fronts that perform integrative or facilitative functions for the
receiver, the dissonant front remains a totally separate entity. It is
only rarely used for storage activities relating to the illegal commerce;
and transactions involving stolen goods never occur on its premises.
Instead the businessman-fence operates on a personal level, meeting
thieves in bars or in quasi-public places and keeping in touch by telephone.[16] Both the clientele and the product line of this fence are re-

strictive; he deals only with the good burglar for high-value items. Volume trade is neither the hallmark nor the desire of the theft industry in this segment.

The dissonant front, then, might be called the receiver's "other business." It is his public identity; and it offers little hint of the existence of further commercial endeavors that might identify him as something other than a successful legitimate businessman. Criminal receiving remains a significant but invisible part of an otherwise legitimate business portfolio. Perhaps here the legal endeavor comes closest to performing the function of a blind. It is a blind, however, not in an operational sense, but rather in a cognitive one. That is, the receiver does not conduct his illegal commerce behind the structure or under the auspices of his legitimate business, but in the safety and security of a respectable public identity. Like all businessmen-fences, he is different things to different publics, but here the disparities are segregated into totally different arenas.

Table 21 depicts the dissonant front, along with the criminal clientele and illicit product line of its owner. Profitability per unit handled and individual expertise appear to guide the product choices of fences in this category. Thus the art school in this segment does not deal integratively in paintings but rather handles them because of familiarity with and the ability to evaluate the product. [17]

Although details about the final distribution of goods by these fences is scant, a long and complex channel is indicated. All are known to travel extensively or to employ surrogates for that purpose. At least one, the gentleman farmer/golf course owner, is known to maintain an identity as a jewelry salesman on trips to Dallas, Chicago and Los Angeles, suggesting the employment of a dual identity as a legitimized distribution pattern in this segment. Also suspected as contributing to the distribution channel of these fences are links, although entirely *sub-rosa*, with larger criminal superstructures, whose intermediaries and transit facilities can be utilized. Detectives, for example, question the original financing of the legitimate businesses of many of these fences. The police use as supporting evidence of such suspicions, the private associations of receivers in this group with persons reputed to be key figures in a criminal underworld. They see many of the dissonant fronts as the "underworld gone public" and very, very "legit." The author was not completely convinced of the

TABLE 21: DISSONANT FRONTS OF THE BUSINESSMAN-FENCE,
THEIR PRODUCT LINES, AND CLIENTELES ($\underline{N}$=9)

CATEGORY OF BUSINESS	CATEGORY TOTAL	TOTAL FOR FRONT	PRODUCT LINE	CLIENTELE SERVED
CMTW[a]	6			
Light construction		4	Jewelry, coins	Good burglar
Medical supplies wholesaler		2	Jewelry	Good burglar
Retailing	1			
Carpeting company		1	Clothing, furs	Good burglar, known burglar
Services	0			
Other	2			
Art school/gallery		1	Art objects	Good burglar
Golf course/ gentleman farmer		1	Jewelry	Good burglar

[a]Construction, manufacturing, transportation, and wholesaling businesses.

validity of this hypothesis, although the rapid and unexplained move-ment of some high-value merchandise from the data site did suggest that something more than independent businessmen was at work. A set of paintings stolen from a local art gallery, for example, literally disappeared from the area, surfaced briefly in Italy, and is alleged now to be somewhere in Germany.

The main characteristics of the dissonant front are summarized below.

    1. It is generally a very successful legitimate business enter-prise.

    2. It is rarely touched by the illicit commerce of its owner.

    3. It dominates a legitimate business portfolio whose illegiti-mate component remains totally invisible.

    4. It neither defines nor contributes to the distribution chan-nel for stolen property.

5. Receiving of stolen goods by owners of dissonant fronts is personalized and distribution is indirect through what are believed to be long, well-coordinated, and nonlocal channels.

MARKETING INDICATORS IN LEGITIMATE FRONTS

Now that we have described each of the three types of legitimate fronts found at the data site, we can describe the general marketing pattern of each and the manner in which they differ from each other. In doing so, we will compare legitimate fronts on the basis of the following marketing indicators: product line, clientele, length of channel, type of inventory functioning, transit needs, and contactual complexity.[18]

Of all the legitimate fronts, the integrative one has the most restrictive product line. This is because the legal endeavor defines only those products that are congruent with the legal line as being appropriate. Thus, while the integrative segment of the businessman-fence group may as a whole handle a variety of products, each fence will constrain his illicit purchases to a narrow range of goods. Fencing operations associated with the dissonant front display a different sort of restrictiveness with regard to the choice of an illicit product line. Here nearly the entire segment of the industry confines itself to a commerce in low-bulk, high-value items, particularly jewelry. Since the legal enterprise is maintained independent of the illegal one, it offers few constraints. Instead the personalized nature of fencing in this segment appears to define as appropriate those items which display a high profitability rate and yet can be concealed and transported on the person. Theoretically, fences owning dissonant fronts should be able to handle nearly every sort of product, but it appears to be the desire of these receivers to segregate and maintain the integrity of their dual endeavors as distinct entities which tends to limit the product line substantially. Restrictiveness here, then, is by choice while in the integrative front it is by perceived necessity. The functional-facilitating front displays the most varied product line of any legitimate front. This is because the facilitating elements present in the legitimate enterprise can serve equally well no matter what product(s) is being handled. Add to this the substantial commitment made to the illicit endeavor by the fence with this type of front, and few constraints imposed by the legal line will be entertained.

On the variable of product line, then, legitimate fronts range from the restrictiveness defined by legal business interests of the integrative front, to the expansiveness engendered by the commitment to fencing of the functional-facilitating front, and back to a restrictiveness based on profitability per unit of property of the dissonant front.

Legitimate fronts are also distinguished from each other on the basis of the clientele served. The integrative front, encompassing the widest range of entrepreneurial talent, serves the most representative cross-section of the theft population, from the addict through the good burglar. The functional-facilitating front, on the other hand, tends to concentrate its efforts on the volume thefts of known and young burglars, often assisting in the expeditious commission of such thefts. Dissonant fronts deal almost exclusively with the good burglar showing the greatest restrictiveness in clientele of any legitimate front. On the variable of clientele, legitimate fronts lie on a continuum, ranging from a saturation servicing by the integrative front to the exclusive associations of the dissonant front, with the functional-facilitating front occupying the middle range.

The length and nature of the channel of distribution also serves as a differentiating characteristic in the marketing patterns of legitimate fronts. The integrative front displays the shortest and most direct distribution channel. Though dominated by a retail trade, both user and consumer markets are reached by the synthesis of the legitimate and illegitimate lines at the sale point, with few if any intermediaries involved. Thus the pattern is nearly always from Thief → Fence → Customer.

By contrast the functional-facilitating front reflects the longest and most indirect distribution channel. This is because of the inconsistencies generated by service-intensive businesses handling product-intensive goods. Similarly distribution complexity is derived from the volume handled by most functional-facilitating fronts which suggests that although consumer goods are involved, they are destined for intermediate user markets. The channel pattern reflected by the functional-facilitating front can be envisioned as follows: Thief → Fence → Illicit intermediary → Legal intermediary → Retailer → Consumer.

The dissonant front appears to steer a middle, though dual, course with respect to the channel of distribution. While the channel here is thought to be longer than that of the integrative front, it may not display as much indirectness as is characteristic of the functional-facilitating front. This is primarily because the fence in this segment seems to divorce himself from his legal enterprise, and to assume a new, legitimate role in a different setting. Thus, one pattern of distribution noted for this segment is: Thief → Fence → Fence in a new role → Customer. Alternatively, intermediaries supplied by a criminal superstructure or cultivated personally by the fence may be employed, making the pattern more like this: Thief → Fence → Quasi-legitimate connection → Customer. Both functional-facilitating and dissonant fronts appear to destine their illicit lines for user markets, while the integrative front meets the customer directly.

The type of inventory system used may be speculative, where the fence buys goods in anticipation of future sales; or postponed, where the fence receives an order for goods first and then acquires them. The transit needs of the fencing operation concern how loads will be assembled, sorted, and monitored at several points. Both the inventory system used and the transit needs affect the nature of the distribution channel represented by legitimate fronts. A speculative inventory system designed to meet local market demand will serve to keep the integrative front's channel both simple and direct. Since the illicit property rarely moves out of the local area, there is no need for transit sorts or intermediate inventory and assembly activities. Intermediaries are kept to a minimum and the distributive function is accomplished solely by the businessman-fence.

The functional-facilitating front generally taps distant markets, making some sort of transit functionary imperative. In addition, this type of front displays the most common use of a postponed inventory system (engendered by the "set-up"), suggesting that a well-coordinated set of activities must be performed in the transit function to ensure rapid distribution on demand.[19] It is likely, then, that the receiver associated with the functional-facilitating front performs assembly activities and arranges for transit services, with sorting and dispersion activities being relegated to later intermediaries in the channel. A typical pattern might be as follows: Fences (assembly and transit) → Criminal (or knowledgable) Intermediary (intransit sort) → Legal intermediary (distribution to retail outlets).

The fence associated with the dissonant front also seeks distant markets for his illicit merchandise but its bulk and/or volume is generally smaller than that handled by the functional-facilitating front. Hence transit activities and extensive assembly and sorting of goods are unnecessary. Instead this type of receiver can function much like the integrative fence except that his speculative inventory is designed to meet the needs of distant customers. It is only when a particular notoriety or volume of goods is involved that the services of the intermediary (often criminal) need be rendered.

The final variable contributing to the marketing patterns of legitimate fronts is the degree of contactual complexity involved in each, that is, the degree to which specific markets must be cultivated. Here again the legitimate fronts appear to lie on a continuum ranging from the simplicity of the integrative front which uses the same targets for both its legal and illegal products, to the complicated set of relationships that the functional-facilitating front must develop to market a line of products completely inconsistent with its legal trade. Both the postponed inventory system and the use of transit intermediaries by this latter type of receiver suggest that a sophisticated contactual functioning is the key to such an operation. Fences associated with dissonant fronts occupy the middle range on the contactual complexity continuum, tending toward simplicity as the need for the services of others increases.

A brief summary of the marketing patterns for each type of legitimate front, based on the six variables discussed above, is:

The Integrative Front: a restrictive product line; distributed through a short, simple, and direct channel to a local market; designed to service a representative cross-section of the theft population.

The Functional-Facilitating Front: a widely varied product line; distributed through a long, complicated, and indirect channel to distant markets; designed to service the thief stealing in volume.

The Dissonant Front: a restrictive product line of high unit value items; distributed through a long channel of intermediate complexity and directness to a distant market; designed to serve primarily the good burglar.

ILLEGITIMACY AND CIRCUMSTANCE IN THE FENCING TRADE

Up to now we have confined our attention to the businessman-fence and the commercial accoutrements of his style of criminal receiving. In doing so we have left unaccounted for approximately one-third of the fencing sample whose receiving activities are not organized within the context of legitimate business ownership. This latter segment of the sample can be broken down into three groups: criminal entrepreneurs, independents, and employees. Lacking the integrative, facilitative, or respectability benefits yielded by the legitimate front, fences in this segment display a different—and often innovative—approach to illicit entrepreneurship. Their manipulation of the circumstances in their environment makes their style of receiving both interesting and intriguing.

Criminal Entrepreneurs

Table 22 depicts the *primary* vocations of the criminal entrepreneurs represented in the sample. These individuals, then, engage in at least two illegal trades: one which is their major source of income, the other which is criminal receiving. The extent and continuity of their fencing activities differ substantially within the group as a whole. Bookmakers, for example, may engage in fencing as an ongoing second venture conducted within the structural framework of their betting parlors. The narcotics dealer in the sample displays a somewhat different integration of fencing as an important sidelight of his major illicit endeavor. He uses a barter system—he receives stolen property from addicts in exchange for narcotics.[20]

These individuals reflect a continual, ongoing interest in the receiving trade as a sideline. This is hardly true of all criminal entrepreneurs, however. Loansharks in the sample, for instance, maintain an intermittent fencing trade in which they permit debts to be settled through the proceeds of theft. In these cases, the loanshark acts as a criminal intermediary, getting his cut from a theft without actually receiving any of the merchandise. Instead he will arrange its transfer to others in the fencing industry, most notably those associated with the functional-facilitating front. The loanshark becomes, then, a broker-type of illicit middleman, facilitating the distribution activities in the theft industry without assuming ownership functions and while still maintaining his major interests in the illegitimate economic system.

The two enforcers/labor racketeers demonstrate a similar margin-

TABLE 22:   PRIMARY VOCATIONS OF THE CRIMINAL
            ENTREPRENEUR-FENCE ($\underline{N}$=14)

PRIMARY VOCATIONS[a]	NUMBER OF CRIMINAL ENTREPRENEURS
Bookmaking	3
Narcotics traffic	1
Pimping	1
Loansharking	2
Enforcer/labor racketeering	2
Syndicated gambling/racketeering	3
Hood	2

[a]The thief is excluded from this listing since his major
criminal vocation is considered to be operational rather than
entrepreneurial in nature.

ality of interest in criminal receiving, but its overtones are substantially different from that of the money lender. As collection agents for
loansharks or gambling racketeers, they often represent an extortion-
ist-type of criminal receiving which can be particularly disruptive to
the theft industry, not to mention the burglar. Such activity is generally independent entrepreneurship on the part of the enforcer, necessitating the entry of mediators in the theft microcosm to desensitize
such situations.

An interview with Greg provided a rare glimpse at the mechanics
operating in the extortion situation. Greg and three associates had
successfully executed a residence burglary, netting a substantial
amount of expensive jewelry, one item in particular being an $8,000
bracelet watch. A few days after the theft the following series of events
evolved: [21]

A local enforcer in the area decided he wanted the bracelet.
Determining who had stolen it, he and two associates proceeded

to the apartment of the youngest of the thieves involved and took him "for a ride," explaining that the thieves and the bracelet would be expected to appear the following day at a private club in the city so that he might bargain for the purchase of the bracelet. When the thief returned from his ride, he called Greg and explained the situation. Smelling a shake-down, Greg got in touch with the bodyguard of one of the big-time syndicate men in the city. He offered to sell the bracelet to the latter individual at an extremely low price and asked for help. It was given.

The next morning only the bodyguard and Greg made the appointment at the private club. On entering, it was obvious that Greg's evaluation of the situation had been accurate. There sat the enforcer with nearly ten others waiting for the burglars. The appearance of the bodyguard startled them. This latter individual said only three words, "Joe's getting it," and the whole charade was over. Greg and the body guard left and that was the end of the affair. Joe did get the bracelet at a later date, but that was not all. Greg and his associates, in an effort to show their extreme appreciation for the protection given, took some of the loose diamonds from the theft, and commissioned a friendly jeweler to make a pair of initial rings for Joe and his wife.

Apart from depicting some of the human drama existing in the criminal world, Greg's experience demonstrates the power of the illegitimate status in both exploiting and mediating the disposition of stolen property. Joe, and others like him, are only the most marginal of criminal receivers, and yet their status could make them inescapable destinations for many products of the vulnerable burglar. Joe could as easily have extorted the bracelet as paid for it, but his position as a major power broker required a policing of the illicit entrepreneurship of others. Since the activities of the enforcer in this case were deemed inappropriate, it was the thief who was supported. Needless to say, although the criminal receiving of the enforcer and the major racketeer is extremely intermittent and marginal, it represents a significant force shaping the conduct of even the most professional of thieves. Were fencing to become a major sideline for such individuals, the theft industry as we now know it would be substantially changed.

One final type of criminal entrepreneur is found in Table 22 and that is the sort of individual identified as the hood. The term "hood" is often used generically by police to label all criminal entrepreneurs, but here it represents a floating illegitimate status. Generally, the hood is an older member of a criminal superstructure whose operating days are about over, but who maintains an important illegitimate status, somewhat analogous to that of a pensioner in the legitimate employment world. Since he has neither worked at any legitimate employment for any length of time, nor is near the normal retirement age in the legitimate society, he is granted a sort of license to establish a new and less active set of criminal endeavors as an entrepreneur rather than as an operative.

Individuals in this situation tend to float around the criminal social structure picking up whatever action they can, and criminal receiving is one such activity. They come to fencing equipped to their advantage in two ways: (1) their identification with a large and powerful superstructure gives them a "moral imperative" in dealing with the young and inexperienced thief and (2) their long association with significant figures in the superstructure gives them substantial information about and acquaintance with the "right connections" for the disposal of stolen property. The hood will not be supported by the superstructure indefinitely, but rather he is given the opportunity to get his feet on the ground. Once the support is withdrawn, the entrepreneurship of the hood often declines.

Nevertheless, the hood is distinctly more successful in his fencing ventures than is the unaffiliated thief. [22] The sample yielded nine thieves known to engage in fencing activities, including two safe men, three good burglars, three known burglars, and one young burglar. None of these individuals successfully operates as a fence; instead each continues to support himself as an active burglar.

This is particularly true of the older thieves in this segment. At age 44, Tom, like many older thieves, constantly tells detectives that he's "just too old" to keep working; and there is more than a grain of truth in these protestations. He has attempted to move into the receiving trade much as the hood does, in an "elder statesman" kind of role, but his lack of a close affiliation with sources of power and support is quite disabling. In addition, Tom, like many successful thieves, has managed to save very little in capital reserves from the substantial amounts he has earned through his career. With no capital, Tom cannot "purchase" even a minimal front behind which to carry on a receiving trade. [23] Neither can he rely on the protection of a large organization to help him get an entrepreneurial head start or to insulate him from police harassment.

Even a thief of the sophistication of Tom, therefore, tends to have only a brief and disasterous association with fencing. His visibility as a burglar combined with insubstantial financial backing make the career shift almost insurmountable.

Fencing by the criminal entrepreneur, then, takes on some very different connotations and introduces more variety than that generated by the businessman-fence. And yet if information relating to the specific distributional destinations of goods handled by the legitimate front is patchy and incomplete, it remains even more scarce with regard to the criminal entrepreneur. The alleged involvement of many of these persons in "organized crime" imbues their fencing activities with the same sort of illusive quality used to describe most of this group's illicit endeavors. [24] Since receiving remains a sideline for the criminal entrepreneur, however, the volume of the industry's trade accounted for by this segment is rather small. Instead its contactual services (as well as some transit functions) to the businessman-fence appear to be its more significant overall contribution to the theft industry.

Independents

The independent criminal receiver must be credited with the most heroic and innovative entrepreneurship in the fencing trade. Having neither the benefit of a legitimate business front, nor the backing and support of an illegitimate organizational structure, the independent manages to fashion a fencing trade that in a few cases at least is remarkably successful. The six individuals identified in the sample as independents are a rare collection, ranging from the mother of three burglars, officially listed as receiving welfare payments; to the retired black man who maintains a virtual monopoly position in the receiving of property stolen by the good black burglar. This segment of the industry also includes a father and son team of peddler fences, a formally adjudged habitual criminal, and an unemployed factory worker.

Perhaps the two most successful and intriguing independents are Jack, the habitual criminal, and Jerry, the factory worker. Jack was an

independent even while he was accumulating an impressive arrest record (ranging from grand theft, to narcotics sales, to firearms violations, to the fraudulent sale of liquor), with both local and federal authorities in at least four states. After having been arrested and convicted 45 times in New York alone, he was officially adjudged in 1963 to
be a habitual criminal. A successful appeal put him back on the street,
and at age 47, he left behind the vagaries of the hustling life to specialize in the receiving of stolen property. Contributing to his ability to
make the shift was a respected and admired reputation built up over
26 years. It was this reputation that won him the friendship of many of
the better burglars at the data site, most of whom were quite willing to
let him handle their stolen property. They knew he was clever, had
contacts in nearly every adjacent state, and could probably offer them
some useful advice in their own activities. Jack began aggressively,
meeting burglars at their favorite night spots to negotiate transactions
before other fences could be approached. This personal style is still a
hallmark of his operation. He rarely deals with any thief but the good
burglar or safe man, making an association with him somewhat of a
status symbol. He works as an agent basically, assembling property he
knows to be negotiable with his connections in other cities. Without
knowing precisely the scope or income received from his trade, we can
label it as enormously successful in at least one regard. In spite of his
high visibility, Jack has yet to be arrested since he began his fencing
operation!

Jerry, 54 years old, used to be a factory worker, an occupation to
which he is unlikely to return. He was arrested once nearly 30 years
ago for a robbery, attempted rape, and sodomy, a case that was later
no billed. A few years later he was picked up on a lewd act charge for
which he spent 30 days in the county jail. It is not known whether he
lost or quit his job at this point, but he began to surface several years
later as a criminal receiver in the stories of addicts and informants. As
a result of this trade, Jerry has tallied only one arrest, a case later dis-
missed. Authorities had a wire tap on him for over three months,
giving a rare inside view of his operation.

Jerry's fencing trade is organized and multivaried in scope. Con-
ducting most of his business by phone, his contacts are each given
separate times in the day to call. Both buyers and sellers call; and
Jerry, in the true broker's tradition, can usually match up their needs.

Though it is unlikely that many of his associates are known to one another, Jerry's code names for each are familiar to all. Thus, "Robin Hood," the name given to an outlet in a nearby city, is familiar to "Rocky," a young thief at the data site, although it is quite unlikely that they will ever meet. Most of Jerry's trade is in new merchandise, being supplied primarily by boosters and addicts. If and when Jerry has a buyer, a van is dispatched to transport the goods from one contact to the other. Often Jerry never even sees the merchandise. One of the few stringent requirements which he maintains is that his contacts indicate whether goods are "local" or not. Jerry is careful to spread stolen property over a geographically dispersed market, making its distributional path more difficult to trace.

As the reader may have already realized, it is not until we reach the independent receiver that we really confront the *full-time fence*, who, without any other visible means of support, appears to make a decent livelihood from the trade. Often it is mere circumstance that renders these operations successful, but it is surely circumstance that has been shaped carefully and cleverly into a rare brand of private entrepreneurship.

Employees

The final segment of the fencing sample whose illicit commerce we have yet to explore is the group of employee-receivers found at the data site. While the status of these individuals as gainfully employed makes them comparable to the businessman-fence, their lack of a legitimate front of their own often causes them to reflect some interesting fencing patterns. Table 23 summarizes the occupations, product lines, and clienteles of employee fences.

Though the specific products handled by employee fences do not represent a significant departure from those carried in the rest of the industry, this segment appears to display a disproportionate number of generalized lines. Thus, the city employee and the heavy industry engineer, distributing goods to knowledgeable customers through a "store" in their homes, have little constraints placed upon their product lines.

It is perhaps interesting to note that five of the eleven individuals listed in Table 23 operate their illicit commerce from their homes,

TABLE 23: OCCUPATIONAL AFFILIATIONS, PRODUCT LINES, AND
           CLIENTELES OF FENCES EMPLOYED BY OTHERS (N=11)

OCCUPATIONAL AFFILIATION	PRODUCT LINE	CLIENTELE SERVED
CMTW[a]		
Lab worker, manufacturing company	Clothing, watches	Boosters
Cab dispatcher	Tape decks, clothing	Addicts
Clothing salesman	Clothing	Boosters
Engineer, heavy manufacturer	Generalist	Boosters
Truck driver	Autos	Unknown
Truck driver	Generalist	Addicts
Retailing		
Furniture store employees	Clothing	Boosters
Automobile salesman	Generalist	Addicts
Pharmacist	Generalist	Young burglars
Other		
Municipal zoo employee	Cigarettes, televisions, jewelry	Addicts
City employee	Generalist	Addicts

[a]Construction, manufacturing, transportation, and wholesaling trades.

residences in the suburbs quietly removed from their legitimate jobs in the city—the location also of the sources of their illegal merchandise. Their trade is small in scale with a set of customers generated by word-of-mouth contacts. Only three members of this segment (the lab worker, the zoo employee, and a trucker) can be said to participate in fencing operations of any substantial size, and these endeavors are in partnership with others.

Generally the fencing trade of the employee fence is a small, residential, word-of-mouth operation, and it is only when the employee associates with others that the commerce assumes any significant size. In this regard, the employee fence displays a less successful degree of entrepreneurship than does the independent and this is in spite of what appear to be the distinctly meager circumstances of the latter individual.

We have attempted in the preceding pages to demonstrate the varied patterns of trade in the fencing industry which grow out of the substantial status, power, and legitimacy differentials reflected by the members of the fencing sample. If one had to rate the significance of each of the groups of fences, one might, on the basis of the challenges they place upon law enforcement and the proportion of fencing trade they represent, order them as follows:

1. The legitimate front which probably accounts for the greatest volume in the distribution of stolen property.
2. The independent who remains a significant and full time distribution channel.
3. The criminal entrepreneur, whose real debut in the fencing scene in a major role has yet to happen.
4. The employee, who may be the most familiar but still the least significant fence as far as volume is concerned.

5 | *The right man for the right job: fencing networks*

Although we have alluded to the presence of structured and continuous relationships existing among thieves, fences, and other fences, a full development of the theft network has been postponed until now. This was done for two reasons: first, in order to familiarize the reader with the varied types of persons populating the burglary and receiving trades; and second, in order to introduce the structural patterns and functional requirements of the theft industry before dealing with the individual relationships shaping those patterns or fulfilling those requirements.

We focus on the particular groupings of individuals in the sample theft industry, their qualities, and their organizing principles. It is not known how characteristic are the relationships herein described, since very little analysis of group activities among adult offenders has preceded the present research.[1] Most analyses of collective criminal behavior describes the group (or gang) behavior of the juvenile or the highly structured activities associated with "organized crime." The existence, nature, formality, and sociability of offender groupings lying between these two types of criminal conduct remain little explored—a vast gulf indeed. While the discussion following does not purport to fill this gap, it does attempt to shed some light on adult offender relationships relating to the theft and disposal of stolen property.

We begin with the generation of the term "fencing network" and the considerations involved in its choice. Next we describe the nature of the different networks observed at the data site, both as to their divergent characteristics and as to their purposes. This is followed by a discussion of the network linkage system, how and when it occurs. Finally, we conclude with an evaluation of the fencing network, the contributions it makes to the theft industry, the advantages/disadvantages it offers to its respective members, and the criminological implications flowing from it.

THE FENCING NETWORK

The use of the term "network" in the social sciences has generally come to signify the communicational component of otherwise associated clusters of individuals, that is, of the formal or informal group, of the organization or institution, which has emerged for other purposes or ends. The network facilitates the achievement of said ends by providing the linkages needed for the transmission and reception of messages.

The term "network," however, has never remained limited to a communicational context; instead it has come to signify the smaller, unbounded groupings of individuals observed within larger groups, organizations, and so forth.[2] Hence the introduction of the term "social network"[3] as a "set of social relationships for which there is no common boundary."[4] Stebbins,[5] who sees the social network as a subjective construct based on the predispositional characteristics of interpersonal relationships, feels that it may help account for the patterns of distribution of values, attitudes, and information in a society. He determines to place the social network in its situational context where it can be observed, he maintains, "to modify culturally expected behavior."[6] The similarities between Stebbins' subjective social network construct and the criminologist's concept of the modifying influences of the "subculture" are striking indeed.[7] But the similarities in conceptual development of the two constructs does not end here. Wolfe presents a very useful taxonomy of social network concepts in which both the holistic and egocentric perspectives from which they have been studied are represented. The social network, says Wolfe, is a "model in which links are seen as relating persons in social situations,"[8] but such links have more than a monolithic nature. Instead what can be observed are "limited networks" (sets) that are extracts of the total network, based on some criterion applicable throughout the whole network. Wolfe enumerates five such limited networks (sets): [9]

1. *The personal set:* a network limited to the links of one person. This set comprises the egocentric perspective from which a network can be viewed.

2. *The action set:* a network limited to links purposefully created for a specific end.

3. *The role system set:* a network limited to links involved in an organized role system or group.

4. *The categorical set:* a network limited to links involving a type of person.

5. *The field set:* a network limited to links with a certain content (for example, political or economic).

Sets 2 through 5 represent a holistic perspective on the social network since they focus on the *total structure* of the links involved rather than on the relationships of a single individual. Both the categorical and the field set display remarkable analogistic characteristics with regard to the subcultural construct. Thus the unspecified "criminal subculture" can be thought of as a field set in Wolfe's terms, that is, as a network limited to links with a criminal content; while the "drug subculture" can be described as a categorical set, a network limited to links involving a type of person, here the drug user. And yet the network construct appears capable of embracing a wider range of relationships (linkages) than does the subculture concept. It appears much more competent, for example, in dealing with interpersonal linkages that are *not* crime related even though they may exist between criminals.

It is this quality of the network construct—that is, its capacity to conceptualize and account for a wide range of interpersonal links—that has influenced its choice here for the description of groupings within a metropolitan theft industry. For, as shall be seen, the networks exhibited at the data site reflect contents, purposes, and goals more varied than those of the criminal conspiracy or than those often attributed to the criminal subculture. The interpersonal associations to be described herein are more than mutual rationalizing or orienting mechanisms emerging between persons engaged in socially unaccepted behaviors. As such, they often find their origins in other than criminal contexts and serve ends which reflect, although they may not entirely emulate, socially accepted values.

The network concept has not been completely ignored by the criminologist. Mack, for example, in his discussion of the "community" of full time criminals, stresses the lack of importance of territorial location in determining an offender's colleagues. The criminal community, says Mack, "is no longer a place, but a *system of social relationships and functions*,"[10] and while there may remain "delinquent neighborhoods" (that is, areas known to produce disproportionate numbers of delinquents as compared with other areas), there are no longer "criminal areas," in the territorial sense. Instead the full time miscreant lives in a neutral neighborhood linked to others like himself through a *network structure* rather than through spatial proximity. The use of the network concept, then, is not without precedent in criminological study; and it is Mack's conception of the network as a *system* of social relationships and functions that is adopted here. What we try to describe are those systems of relationships and functions that develop between persons engaged as either producers or marketers in the theft and disposal of stolen property. We call these systems "fencing networks," not because the efficient disposal of stolen property is their chief or only end, but rather because they find their organization and their most critical links dominated by the person of the criminal receiver.

The data site has yielded three distinct types of fencing networks: the kinship network, the work-a-day network, and the "play" network.

THE KINSHIP NETWORK

We define kinship network as a set of links dominated by and organizationally tied to the familial relationship between a criminal receiver and at least one other theft-associated person. The kinship network, then, can be viewed as an egocentric grouping, or a "personal set" in Wolfe's terms, except that it is *dominated by*, rather than being limited to, the links of one individual. The origin of these links is not found in an illicit context but rather in the highly cherished kinship group which serves as the webbing to the basic social fiber of American life. Generally the kinship network evolves around a link between a fence and a thief, both of the same immediate family. Thus, we can observe kinship networks dominated by the father to son(s) linkage, the mother to child linkage, the sister to brother or brother to brother linkage, and the uncle to nephew linkage, with the former individual in each case occupying the role of the fence.

The kinship link exists, of course, prior to and independent of the joint or separate criminal endeavors of the individuals involved. What contributes to the kinship fencing network is the importance of the familial tie in generating other links in a group. Thus, the father-fence becomes linked to other thieves through their association with the son-thief. Even if the son does not fence his goods with his father, his contemporaries are quite likely to do so. The familial bond may remain no more than that but it will generate links of a somewhat different order. There is a progressive nature to the kinship fencing network, then, in which one familial link gives rise to several others which give origin to several more. The progression is not infinite, however. Instead it is limited by an awareness of the same kinship link that generates the network in the first place. Thus linkages will not be formed that involve persons unaware of the kinship relationship and the kinship fencing network will only expand within the limits of familiarity with the original, ineffable tie.

It should be stressed again that the kinship tie does not have to possess a criminal content to generate further links, that is, parties to the link do not have to engage in criminal commerce. Nevertheless, the kinship fencing network depends on the connotations of familiarity implied by the kinship bond. "Because John is Sam's father and I am Sam's contemporary, John will be responsive and open to my needs for his services." John is expected to be approachable—even fair perhaps—but above all, John is "familiar." And familiarity, particularly for the young or the unskilled thief, carries with it important safety features. Thus, membership in kinship fencing networks is especially prevalent among young burglars, where familiarity enables the young thief to gain the confidence he will need later when he relies on other less familiar and more "professionally" bound links.

The fence-thief kinship tie is not the only pattern found in kinship fencing networks. Two other types of familial bonds were observed at the data site to generate groupings in the theft microcosm. The first of these kinship ties links the fence with a family member as a partner or as performing either "set-up" or disposal services. Thus, the father-fence may use the business of his son for the distribution of stolen goods; or the brother of the receiver may in the course of his legitimate employment provide set-up information important to the commission of a theft.[11] The most interesting manifestation of a link between the fence and other theft-associated persons involves the case of a receiver as baptism sponsor, that is, as a godfather.[12]

Ritualistic sponsorships associated with sacraments in many religious denominations can generate family-like ties between otherwise unrelated persons. Sponsors at the baptism of a child, then, need not be drawn from a kinship pool but may be chosen from among close friends or neighbors. In the former situation, kinship ties are said to be double-loaded since the parents and godparents become linked not only by prior familial ties, but by a further ritualistic bond that implies both mutual responsibilities and obligations. In the situation where nonrelatives are chosen for ritualistic sponsorships, quasi-kinship bonds are formed between parents and godparents, implying the same sorts of responsibilities and obligations.[13]

The case referred to here (from the fence sample) demonstrates the firmness of such ties and the manner in which their obligations may be met. Carl and Jack (brothers) are fairly successful businessmen-fences. Jack some time ago served as the baptism sponsor to a friend's child, thus linking the two previously unrelated families. Although Jack is known to handle only expensive jewelry illicitly, Carl is known to deal in cheaper items such as watches as well as more expensive gemstones, implying two different markets for his commerce. Carl's activities remain shrouded until it is discovered that some of his cheaper merchandise is being sold by his brother's friend to persons he meets in the course of his employment. It is Jack's quasi-familial ties with this friend that provides Carl with a small-scale, low-visibility outlet for cheaper lines of goods. The friend, displaying an otherwise unblemished record, and having no further ties with persons associated with the theft world, would appear to be obliging some ties made long ago and in a context far removed from the world of theft.[14]

The final type of kinship linkage is what might be called the "big brother syndrome." Although not limited to older siblings, the link-age is distinctly paternalistic in nature, having the effect of attempting to guide the associations made by younger family members in the pursuit of a theft career. Thus, a thief will attempt to limit the associates of his younger brother to the relatives of his own associates. Or, in a very interesting case at the data site, a working trio of young burglars was found to consist of the daughter of a fence, the son of another fence, and the younger brother of a well-known good burglar—a very well-insulated and well-educated trio indeed. Similarly, it was the baptism sponsor of an emerging young burglar at the data site who, as a fence, endeavored to introduce and link up his godchild with some of the more adept thieves with whom he himself was acquainted. The overwhelming desire of these kinship links is to influence the young thief's career pattern by steering him (her) toward "safe" associates, that is, those capable of helping him or at least not unnecessarily jeopardizing him.

Our description of the kinship network does not imply any genetic predispositions to criminality or the existence of any familial monopolies on criminal activity. On the contrary, what the kinship network reflects is the all-encompassing influence of the family group on an individual's life.[15] This is true not only in socially approved contexts such as education and business, but in less approved criminal contexts as well. Thus, we should be no more surprised to find kinship partners in the fencing trade than we are to find family businesses in general; we should be no more intrigued by the fence's son becoming a thief than we are by the doctor's son becoming a dentist; and we should be no more chagrined by the fence's use and abuse of family ties for selfish ends than we are by that same mechanism operating in our own, presumably legitimate, lives. The kinship network did not invent the exploitation of family ties; it merely reflects it. And by doing so, it demonstrates perhaps the simplest and most understandable grouping of individuals in the theft microcosm. It allows for the expression of such approved values as concern for and protection of loved ones as well as for the facilitation and encouragement of criminal endeavors. The kinship network, though simple and mundane, remains the organizing principle around which much of the theft microcosm can be seen to revolve. Although dominated by the membership of the young burglar, kinship networks cut across the whole spectrum of the theft population, generating responsibilities and incurring obligations in variegated patterns. Central to all, however, is the relevant receiver playing the role of the familiar repository for stolen property; of the aggressive seller of illicit merchandise; or of the doting source of the "good connection."

THE WORK-A-DAY NETWORK

The work-a-day network is a set of links dominated by and organizationally tied to a legitimate employer-employee relationship between a fence and at least one burglar. The criminal receiver associated with a work-a-day network is always a businessman-fence, since his employment of the burglar is in a legitimate context (the thief is on the payroll of the legitimate front); the typical thief involved is the known burglar. The degree to which the thief actually functions legitimately remains quite questionable, however, since he is generally considered to be working for the "fence" rather than for the "businessman."

It is the illicit side of their licit link, then, that serves as the cohesive and generative force behind the work-a-day network. It is a link that is both restrictive and binding for the burglar, since it is generally established following a period in which he has been incarcerated and is in need of both financial aid and a "rehabilitative alibi," that is, the need to demonstrate an affinity for "good work habits" in order to keep his parole record clean. The fence who has obliged in this situation can, therefore, require some specified behavioral responses from the thief, responses usually operationalized as a series of thefts or "scores."[16] The obligations of his condition of employment are not of the kind with which the thief is uncomfortable, because the fence, more often than not, has specific scores in mind as well as the necessary information relevant to their commission. For both parties, then, the employment link is very convenient.

A work-a-day network branches out through the known burglar who, by previously established links, forms a work group in order to carry out the expected thefts. The formation of the work group serves to put the fence on record as a currently active buyer and tends to specify the intended product line. This brings other similarly situated thieves, unaffiliated with the original work group but aware of its activities, to the fence, enlarging his sources of supply. The reasons for this are quite interesting and of two orders: first, the activities of a group of thieves is likely to be better known than are those of the solo thief. Second, when new working groups are formed, especially of known burglars, they are generally considered to have been established for at least a series of crimes.[17] This suggests a degree of seriousness to the fence's buying commitment relating to both constancy and volume. When the work group is coupled with the actual "employment" of at least one of the burglars in the legitimate business, the interpretation of the businessman's degree of interest in illicit merchandise is again positive and high. Since the fence is not considered to be a humanitarian, his "favors" for the thief are usually linked to his own particular self-interest. Hiring the parolee is interpreted on the street not as a philanthropic gesture but as an affirmation of a strong demand for stolen property. In some sense, then, the theft population regards the ex-con as does a good proportion of the general population (that is, as an undesirable) and is immediately suspicious of anyone interested in giving him a job. When a known fence does so, the interpretation is considered clear.

A good example of the work-a-day network found at the data site concerns Messers. Brown and Jackson. Between them they own three moving and hauling companies and appear to have become a virtual employment agency for the local parole agency, which remains apparently unaware of their illicit reputations. At any rate, they have a consistent policy of hiring newly released offenders. Because of their legitimate business interests, Brown and Jackson generate a great deal of information about the property holdings of others and are in an excellent position to set up thefts. Their pool of parolees is used as operatives for such events and the thefts often are facilitated further by the use of their trucks for transportation of the stolen property

The cover for these activities remains quite simple. The thief as an employee of the firm has a legitimate reason to operate its transport vehicles. In addition his presence in the warehouse district or the residential sections of the city can generally be given a good explanation as errands can be alleged. Even if he is stopped while transporting stolen goods, Brown and Jackson can protest ignorance and dismay regarding any illegal activity. And yet by using the thief as an employee, the illicit commerce can be kept apart from other employees who may never handle the "tainted" cargoes. It is interesting that only two of Brown and Jackson's offender employees have stayed on permanently. This is probably because the rewards a thief can expect in that situation are minimal indeed. Those who have stayed on are quite marginally skilled individuals whose rewards in any situation would not be expected to be particularly attractive. Nevertheless, Brown and Jackson maintain an ongoing, medium-sized receiving operation sustained by others whose evaluation of the employment link has been interpreted as described above. For the mobile, known burglar, they remain a consistent outlet for furniture and appliance thefts.

A restrictive variation of the work-a-day network consists of what Wolfe might term the "action set," a set of links purposefully established for a specific end. While the work-a-day network remains somewhat ungeneralized and ongoing, the action set exists for only a limited period of time and then is dissolved. The two remain quite similar structurally, however. In the action set, the links between the fence and a group of burglars are in an entirely illegitimate employment context. The burglars are in effect "contracted" by the receiver for a specific set of thefts. In the sample data a salvage dealer illustrates the action network in operation.

Mr. Clark has been a salvage dealer for some time. His illicit commerce in metals is known to some, but he is best known as an outlet for monogrammed silver, etc., taken in residence burglaries. It was an association with Stan, a known burglar, in this latter context that gave rise to an action set. Clark, in questioning Stan regarding his activities, asked if he and his associates might not be interested in "doing some work" for him. The work was to consist of a series of local warehouse thefts of metal alloys. After consulting his associates, Stan told Clark they were interested. Clark provided information relating only to the sources of different alloys and the priorities he attached to each, along with the price he'd be willing to pay. (Although the alloys were generally unused, he quoted scrap prices.) Stan and his three associates did all the rest: they cased the warehouses and provided their own transport vehicles. Clark knew only that he'd be receiving a shipment on a specific night; he never "knew" its source. The action set here lasted for approximately nine months; it was then dissolved as quickly as it had been initiated.

It should be noted that the action set differs from the work-a-day

network not only in longevity of operation, but also in degree of restrictiveness. While the work-a-day network expands to absorb many
disparate sources of stolen goods, the action set remains an exclusive
contract, a buying arrangement that will not generally be extended to
others. Because it draws on already existing work groups and because
it is not dominated by any overt links between the persons involved, it
can often remain temporarily masked from others in the theft microcosm, although it can never remain completely covert. The fence
initiates the action set, then, not as a signal to others, but as a temporal monopoly designed to meet specific needs for a particular type
of merchandise. By stressing the exclusiveness of the arrangement,
the receiver can often dupe the thief into thinking he has a good deal
going, but this remains true only insofar as he is being provided with
some direction to his theft activities. For the known burglar, this may
be enough of an incentive. Stan and his friends, for example, had a
new world opened to them by Mr. Clark. Prior to that time, they had
been engaged in burglaries of lower- and middle-class residences—a
commerce that yielded fairly marginal rewards. Clark may not have
been generous, but his deal was lucrative from their perspective.

Both the work-a-day network and the action set, then, are based on
quasi-contractual employment links between a fence and a thief (or
thieves). As such, both lack the immutable quality of the kinship link;
and yet each manages to give rise to specific and continuous groupings of individuals in the theft microcosm over a given period of time.
The work-a-day network perseveres longer than the action set, and
because it generates an ongoing and somewhat expanded trade, the
work-a-day network generally continues long after the employee link
through which it was initiated has been dissolved. The action set, a
temporally bounded work-a-day network, operates on a restrictive
and limited basis and passes quickly out of existence once its goals
have been met.

While other employment arrangements between fences and thieves,
good burglars in particular, are known to exist at the data site, these
are not seen as network systems. This is because they rarely succeed in
establishing links between the two parties. Instead the good burglar
needing a raison d' être for a particular period of time, will approach
the fence (often in the construction trade) and be given permission to
use the latter's name as an employer. Rarely does the "employment"

consist of anything more; and the "link"—if it can be called that—appears to carry few obligations.

The young burglar generally is absent from the work-a-day network unless or until he has experienced some incarceration. It is difficult to know why this is so, but it is thought that his tendency to flaunt his emergent career and his often flamboyant peer association, until muted by prison experience, is considered inappropriate by the employer-fence. This latter individual is interested in a more faceless employee who can fit in well with the "normalcy" of the legitimate business.

If the young burglar is to be affiliated at all in this sort of network, it will be in an action set. Here, in fact, the prominence of the young burglar is quite typical. The action set provides an excellent learning experience and direction for the young burglar that approximates the internship in legitimate settings. His performance in an action set situation may, in effect, open up further lucrative arrangements with more experienced thieves whom the fence may know or it may shape a modus operandi he will pursue throughout his career.

The fence who deals with the young burglar through an action set must be prepared to offer specific guidance. He may often have to detail a theft for the young thief—a situation he can avoid with both the addict and the known burglar. A fence will do this because by cultivating and training the young burglar he may gain a temporary monopoly over that individual's activities. More importantly, however, it can mean a trading-up in his own commerce to goods for which he previously had no supply sources or which consistently went to other fences. Guidance of the young burglar, though not as common, exists in the theft population as surely as does that individual's exploitation by the fence.

In some sense both the work-a-day network and the action set hark back to the organization of Mr. Jonathan Wild who applied similar links between himself and thieves. Although the work-a-day network has some socially acceptable overtones relating to the employment of the ex-offender, groupings in this context are clearly little more than facilitators of thieving rings.

———————————————

The more profound double sense of "social game" is that not

only [is] the game ... played in society ... but that, with its help, people actually "play society."

Georg Simmel [18]

THE "PLAY" NETWORK

The final grouping observed at the data site consists of what we call the "play" network. "Play" in this context has a special and particular meaning, following the conceptual discussions of Simmel and Mills. [19] Play in their terms embodies that mechanism of group activity which "is clearly and emphatically dissociated from other affairs of the group" and in which "basic issues of the group are presented ... either directly, indirectly or inversely." [20] Not all groups are thought to display the same capabilities for such clear dissociation from group affairs in the form of "play." In fact, the threshold demonstrated by a group in its ability to "leave" itself through the play form is considered to be a function of the "group's capabilities (or resources) for meeting external and internal demands satisfactorily." [21] Effective, integrated groups differ from groups in a state of disintegration and disarray, not only in their threshold for "playing," but also in the nature of the play forms they will display.

It was in the search for some explanatory principle to account for some prevalent and distinct theft microcosm groupings that the play construct described above was adopted. The groupings at issue are those linking the good burglar and the criminal entrepreneur in the quasi-public setting of the private charter club or association. The restrictiveness and insouciant leit motif of such groupings reflected a nature qualitatively distinct from that of other networks or less structured groupings. This distinctiveness was thought to be closely approximated by Simmel's and Mills' concept of "play." We define the play network, then, as a set of links limited primarily to persons identified as good burglars and criminal entrepreneurs and dominated by a recreational or leisure-time setting, almost always a private social club or association. As such the play network becomes an elite grouping in the criminal microcosm, linkage with which is severely constrained. This is because the play network concerns not so much the illicit identity but rather the status attributed to that particular identity. In Wolfe's terms the play network is very much a categorical set, that is, a set of links involving a *type* of person.

The elitism of the play network becomes critical to its interactional activity set since one must have attained a certain level of expertise and effectiveness as a criminal in order to capably "recreate" that identity through the play mechanisms. Mills' description of the play mechanism employed by the most integrated and effective groups helps explain why this is so. Such a mechanism consists of a re-creation of those "characteristics of group processes which have been and are its principal source of effectiveness, gratification and pride." [22] Members of the play network, then, must be able not only to live by their criminal livelihoods but also to consider them gratifying, effective, and a source of pride. Criminal activity must be a resolved issue for them as individuals in order for the group to transcend and recreate it in its "play."

Mack's characterization of the full-time miscreant's criminal activities as his "profession" becomes particularly apt for the members of play networks. [23] Crime *is* their profession; they are proud of it, financially comfortable from it, and comfortable in identifying recreationally with it. In addition, others engaged in less skilled or less successful criminal livelihoods can recognize the status of such individuals and perceive the differences between themselves and the members of the play set.

Status within the theft microcosm is determined by one's skills, one's work habits, and one's financial state. And just as members of more legitimate professions will tend to rank specialties in that profession in similar hierarchical order, [24] so the theft operative can recognize not only his place on a crime status ladder, but the place of his betters. Members of play networks are at the top of that ladder. They have attained a status level within a socially unaccepted profession that offers them the capability to support a setting in which society at large and most segments of the theft industry in particular can be defined as "outsiders." The security and self-assuredness of the play network's members allows that setting to be formally drawn, highly visible, and even officially sanctioned by the very society in which their activities are disapproved. [25]

The play network centers its activities around the private social club at which its members congregate rather intermittently from the late afternoon to early morning hours. No obligations exist requiring appearances at the club and no scheduled meeting times are involved. It is a place to go and relax. Thefts are not planned there and neither is the club used for the storage of stolen property. It is *not* a sanctuary, in other words; nor is it a hiding place. Instead it is a symbol of success, of a comfortable professional status that allows recreation and leisure time. Were the club to degenerate into a hiding place for either stolen property or its members, it would then reflect a disintegration in the network. As Mills observes: "as groups become less able to cope with external and internal demands and as their [threshold for play] becomes lower, there is a tendency for [them to] transform play into problem solving." [26] Persons deemed to need such external support for their criminal activities, then, are defined out of the play network. They operate at a level of effectiveness too low and from a pool of resources too small to support the play threshold of the good burglar and the criminal entrepreneur.

Some distinctive features of the play network demonstrate why such a linkage set will remain exclusive. The first of these is its informational context. Though the club is never a planning place for theft, it is a place where the theft elite can find out about each other's activities and, more importantly, inactivities. Thus the club setting allows for the selection of crime partners as the presently idle are recruited for contemplated scores. Second, the restrictive membership of the club makes such recruitment dependable, since the club includes only those whose expertise is quite interchangeable. Finally, the elitism of the club serves to maintain the aloof status of its members by minimizing even their social interactions with other theft-associated persons. The network tends, therefore, at least for a time, to control the diffusion of skills in the profession by a selective inbreeding in the staffing of work groups. John Mack, who observed the private club phenomenon in his study of Scotland's theft elite, remarked on the analogous tendency among full-time miscreants to move toward what he termed "oligopoly" in carrying out criminal enterprises. [27]

The play network is generally the only grouping in the theft microcosm with which the good burglar will form a link. This is because of its distinctly nonobligatory bind. For the most part, the good thief highly values his independence and security with regard to his theft plans. He sees his bargaining power vis-à-vis the fence as enhanced if he relies only on himself for theft information and execution. Entangling arrangements, like the set up, come too close to slavishness and make one's activities too well known to suit the good burglar. He is proud to be "in business for myself" as one good burglar was heard to say at the data site. Part of the security system of the good thief is the practice of splitting up the proceeds of a theft and selling them to different fences. If several thieves commit a single crime, the security is strengthened if each thief sells his share to a different fence. Greg explained it this way: "the less the fence knows about what you're doing and who you're doing it with, the better off you are." This is probably why the businessman-fence rarely enters the play network and why, as well, the good burglar avoids kinship and work-a-day networks as well as the action set.

Good burglars at the data site were found to work almost always in groups of three or four. Unlike less skilled thieves, however, these groups were everchanging, although members usually were from a distinct pool of talent that existed in the play network. Thus while work groups of young burglars and known burglars displayed constant associations, good burglars appear to float between associations with each other. The thread between good burglars remained outside their criminal endeavors and was observed instead in the exclusivity of their leisure activities.

Bjerstedt [28], in a study of what he calls "preparation, process and product" as three stages in a group's interactional experience, noted that high-status groups tend to more readily share or allocate tasks among their members than do groups of lower status. Although the context of Bjerstedt's work remains decidedly dissimilar from the behavior of the good burglar, [29] his explanation of this *Reihan-Phanomen*, or rotational phenomenon, seems quite interesting here. It would appear that interactions between persons who identify each other as competent and/or talented lends itself to the allocation of a task that often tends to be monopolized by a small few in a group less secure of each other's abilities.

The play network provides the good burglar with a set of links to others of like skill and status, others with whom the joint commission of a theft can be undertaken confidently. The division of labor in the work group of the good burglar is, then, highly developed and can be rotated from person to person with little variation in outcome. The evidence from the data site suggests that it will be rotated. Again the professionalism of the good burglar can be seen in his separation of "work" per se from his other activities. His best or closest friends, as evidenced in the play network, may not always be his work partners— a characteristic much less true of other thieves.

One additional feature of the play network is critical to its members, and the good burglar in particular. This is the inclusion of the criminal entrepreneur in the grouping. Participation in the play network enables the criminal entrepreneur to maintain surveillance over and communicate with members of the theft microcosm. Thus he can be apprised of needs for services that he can facilitate. He can also function through the private club setting as a mediator when, as was noted in the preceding chapter, a possibly disintegrating conflict between the theft industry and the activities of superstructure operatives emerges.

This is particularly helpful to the vulnerable good burglar who needs a somewhat amorphous affiliation with the criminal superstructure to protect him from some of its less genteel elements. The loose affiliation provided by the play network is ideal for both. It allows the entrepreneur's correspondence with and potential power in the theft microcosm to remain sub rosa while entailing minimal obligations for the burglar regarding his theft activity. Without the stability and power introduced by the entrepreneur, the play network loses much of its distinctive nature. It loses an elitism based on criminal status cutting across specialty areas and degenerates instead into a hang-out for thieves.

Settings of this latter type (usually restaurants and bars) are extremely common in the theft world, but they display neither the consistency nor the "play-like" qualities of the groupings described above. As such, they do not constitute real "networks" either, for they fail to conform to the definitional constraint of being systematized social relationships or functions. Instead they are way stations or habitual meeting places where trivial social amenities can be exchanged. For the young burglar they are also places where good burglars can be observed or met, or where the fruits of an illicit livelihood can be flaunted before uninitiated friends. For the known burglar such settings are often the destination of much of his stolen property. For the good burglar such places function as entertainment, as places in which he is known and respected. But these settings, unless they are owned by fences, will vary over time as the theft population (as with the public generally) migrates to new surroundings. Such bars and restaurants appear to establish few significant links with the majority of their burglar clientele, and even if they are fencing establishments as well, they rarely systematize links beyond those associated with the action set.

The play network, then, is the most sophisticated, the most exclusive, and the most stable of groupings to be found in the theft microcosm. It is interesting that we have found these characteristics in the one network type that is least dominated by the role relationship of the fence qua fence to the thief qua thief. This is because the play network is overwhelmed by a symbolic rather than an operational function. In this sense it is designed not to facilitate crime but to facilitate a "body criminal," that is, to recognize and certify the special status of the professional. This is particularly important for the criminal superstructure whose interests in the theft industry remain marginal, but whose desire for moral entrepreneurship in the totality of the crime microcosm is great. The play network becomes, then, a useful mechanism by which the superstructure offers certification and quasi-affiliation to criminal elites who otherwise do not qualify for membership in its ranks.

Thieves and fences (of the criminal entrepreneur type) do meet in the play network, but it is their shared and mutually recognized status levels that allow that "operational" relationship to be transcended, while being reaffirmed. The emphasis in the play network is not on divergence of roles, but rather on the satisfying and rewarding payoffs associated with illicit livelihoods. "Playing" successful and self-assured criminals, members affirm their status as such, displaying little difficulty and even less ambivalence in accepting that identity. Though a very closed network, it is decidedly more liberating for the thief than is either the kinship or the work-a-day linkage. This is undoubtedly because the fence occupying its central, unifying position is the most marginal and least demanding of receivers.

THE NETWORK MAZE

Possibly more important, though much less prevalent, than individual network structures themselves, are links observed between fencing operations. These are always fence-to-fence linkages; and while they are rarely systematized to the point of being labeled supra-networks, they do constitute a unique and interesting set of relationships within the theft industry at the data site. Fences are generally not as cohesive a group, in the sense of knowing and associating with each other, as are thieves. This is particularly true of the businessman-fence who rarely interacts on the basis of his illicit identity with anyone but the thief. Thus the businessman-fence is unlikely to associate with his peers as does the burglar; and even if he knows who they are or is known to them, communication between them is unlikely to be established.

Links between businessman-fences were only observed to emerge where legitimate business links already existed. Hence, antique dealers at the data site appeared to know and communicate commercially and professionally with other antique dealers through normal business channels; and it was this professional link which formed the basis for any criminal link. Such associations were both interesting and expansive as stolen property was observed to shuttle between dealers many miles away. Thus a Canadian antique dealer (and fence) associated with American antique dealers becomes instrumental in both their licit and illicit commerces. Similarly an individual, reported to the author as being a fence in some separate investigations preliminary to the present study, suddenly appeared in the intelligence materials at the data site in that same role. He too is an antique dealer and, although operating his business some 300 miles from the data site, is known and dealt with by members of the fence sample noted here. For this segment of the fencing industry, then, the businessman-fence appeared not only aware of his peers but also involved in double-loading legitimate links with them to facilitate illicit commerce.

The antique trade represented an exceptional linkage system when contrasted with the fencing industry as a whole. Other trades well represented in the sample displayed few, if any, knowledgeable links between businessman-fences. The restauranteurs and appliance dealers, for example, appeared completely unaware of the illegal commerce of their peers. The same was true of the jewelers and bar owners in the sample, who, though they may be acquainted with each other as legitimate merchants demonstrated little further knowledge of each other. Instead a more typical pattern of fence-to-fence linkages made by the businessman-fence are those established with the independent receiver or with the criminal entrepreneur, the latter being the more frequent linkage. An example of each of these types of linkages can perhaps best explain their dynamics.

The independent fence, Jerry, whom we met in the preceding chapter, provides an excellent example of a linkage system between himself and the businessman-fence. Jerry is linked to at least two receivers in the city at the data site and to an undetermined number of others in nearby cities. The bulk of Jerry's operation is in a brokerage setting in which the businessman-fence is linked to others as both buyer and seller. With no business outlet of his own, it is this service to others that keeps Jerry "in business." His relationship with two receivers in the city, one a general merchandise retail outlet and the other a residence used as store, is based on the structure of the action set. For example, the communication of a need for goods by the residence "store" reaches Jerry who in turn communicates that need to others. Jerry's communication of that need in turn activates the action set of another fence to fulfill it.

The general merchandise outlet noted here is the nucleus of a kinship network. When "orders" are received from Jerry, thieves in the network are notified of the required merchandise. The filling of Jerry's orders coexists with other illicit commerce engaged in by the front, so that the network is only reacting to Jerry in an action set format—it is only grouping its members on an intermittent basis for the specific purpose of meeting Jerry's immediate demand. Otherwise the network continues to function within the confines of its somewhat more amorphous kinship dimension.

The same appears to be true of Jerry's other fences who act as sellers. The buyer fences, like the residence "store" noted above, appear to depend on Jerry for goods because they have no particular networks themselves on which to rely. It is through him that the network of one fence can serve the needs of several others. But what is most interesting is that none of Jerry's fences, businessmen or otherwise, seem to know each other, and although they are most definitely linked to each other operationally, they are linked only through Jerry. Given the use of code names in the operation, Jerry's own identity may remain somewhat problematical for some of his partners, but it is assumed that he, at least, knows them all. The anonymity of the fences linked by Jerry is, of course, the key to his continued existence. If they knew each other themselves, there would be no need for Jerry's intermediary services. The reliance on anonymity is the hallmark of many intermediaries throughout the theft industry and may be why links between businessman-fences which do exist remain quite unknown, even to them.

It is the criminal entrepreneur who forges the more identifiable links between himself, the businessman-fence, and other fences. The varied nature of such links is exemplified by an individual at the data site whom we shall call Frank. Frank has an uncanny aptitude for "people brokering," being able to bring together a wide range of individuals through his own egocentric network. His cultivation of the businessman-fence is an excellent example of his considerable talents in this direction. As far as can be determined, Frank is linked to at least three businessman-fences at the data site; a furniture dealer, an antique dealer, and a construction contractor. He has acted in concert or in partnership with each of these individuals in the disposal of stolen merchandise either through their own outlets or through his connections with other criminal entrepreneurs.

Each of these linkages is not anonymously kept from the other parties, however. In fact, all three fences have been known to associate socially with Frank. This is because it is not the secretiveness of links with Frank that is important, but the publicity of those ties. Frank's friendship is in the nature of a recommendation to others. Hence, many of the same thieves deal with the three businessmen-fences noted here, stemming quite naturally from their (the burglars') similar attachments to Frank. The businessmen themselves do not comprise linked fencing operations even though they are aware of each other's affiliation with Frank. Instead each continues his own distinct unit linked to Frank rather than to his counterparts. The reason for this is the fact that Frank's services are somewhat irreplaceable, at least by each other, so that there is little motive for mutual affiliation in the group except through Frank. For example, for the antique dealer Frank is facilitating the transportation of contraband paintings to and from Europe through Canada. Neither the furniture dealer nor the contractor is capable of facilitating this valuable trade so he has little motivation to link himself with them. Similarly, the contractor uses Frank's association as a recommendation, bringing the business of some of the better thieves toward his illicit enterprise. In this endeavor the other two businessmen are in the nature of competitors, giving him no reason to establish working ties with them.

The criminal entrepreneur, then, links fencing operations to himself, but rarely serves as the basis for further linkages between these receiving enterprises. Instead the businessman-fence tends to maintain a distinct fencing operation in a state of at least minimal competition with his peers. This competition is not, however, designed to serve the interests of the supply source in the theft microcosm, but rather to preserve the integrity of the medium-sized fencing unit as the normatively defined stable state for the industry. The criminal superstructure will help maintain this "stable state" by assuming enforcement functions vis-à-vis the thief and also by retaining only marginal involvement in the industry itself. Monopolies are not, it would seem, considered desirable in the fencing industry, except those temporally constructed out of the inexperience or lack of skill of certain thieves. Thus even among those persons who display little knowledge of each other there is tacit obedience to the "going rate" at which stolen property is to be exchanged and mutual recognition and acceptance of the territorial rights of competitors.

Linkages between fencing networks are important, then, in their ability to set a tone for the industry as a whole. They are usually instrumental links connected to the action set or the unique services of the criminal entrepreneur. The absence of more links between fences is an interesting dimension of the theft industry, keeping it moderately competitive while minimizing conflicts arising out of monopolistic activities. It is a strength of the fencing industry that the integrity of the medium-sized firm can be maintained without overt associations between its participants and without affecting the superior position of the receiver vis-à-vis the thief. Without even knowing each other, fences can display a unified front to the thief, based on what they know to be that individual's pressing needs in the exchange situation. Each fence tends to independently carve out his own illicit trade as his circumstances and facilities dictate, rarely undercutting his competitors consciously and if necessary only in response to temporary conditions. The numerous firms in the industry appear to understand

that their best interests are served through a unity of position against
the thief rather than a disunity of goals based on overextended trade
monopolies.

Few fences are believed to know, that is to be actually acquainted
with, the full range of their peers. Instead they display an awareness
that they are but one of many criminal receivers operating in an area
and that certain norms of the trade itself dictate particular ways of
doing business. Beyond that, they only need or want to know each
other when those norms are being violated by others. In this situation,
it is the criminal entrepreneur who can provide such links as well as
the organized retaliatory power necessary to discourage such violations. It would appear that such intervention is rarely necessitated
(only a handful of instances were observed at the data site), reflecting
a high acceptance of the industry norms.

The thief appears to view the fencing trade as more collusive than it
really is since his ability to manipulate its members remains minimal.
What he fails to recognize is that *he* is the real basis for unity of values
held by the fence. Thus the exigencies of the thief will rarely be as ap-
pealing and as persuasive as what the receiver believes to be the trading integrity of his peers.

Overt links between fences remain a minor feature of the industry,
but a sense of "groupness" does nevertheless characterize much of the
behavior of the individual criminal receiver. For this reason the fence
is much more occupied with the course of his own network than with
an association with the network of another. It is his individual network structure, rather than his acquaintance with his peers, that will
dictate the amount of integration and central coordination he can
bring to his illicit commerce and which will, as shall be seen, most
affirmatively shape the workings of the theft industry as a whole.

THEFT AND THE NETWORK MECHANISM: AN EVALUATION

From what has been observed at the data site, the individual
network of the fence is most critical to an understanding of the course
of contemporary theft. With the notable exception of the addict, [30]
most of the thief population appears to be locked in, at least tangen-
tially, to a network structure, making the lone, unaffiliated thief a

true anomaly. As we have seen, fencing networks serve not only a co-ordinating function in the theft microcosm, but also a status-confirm-ing function. Thus even the good burglar who shuns direct guidance in this theft behavior will seek the affiliation of a network for the certi-fication of his expert skills. The network in turn will tend to define a range of work partners for him which will significantly affect his theft activities.

Few thieves engage in theft uninfluenced by the fencing network(s) to which they belong. Networks obviously must offer significant ad-vantages to their participants. In an analysis of the several network structures reflected at the data site, six separate features of networks have been isolated that are deemed to enhance participation in them. These features are: (1) association, (2) risk-taking enhancement, (3) recruitment, (4) procedural ratiocination of theft, (5) selective skill diffusion, and (6) information dissemination.

Association

Few thieves want no contacts with others engaged in similar behav-ior; instead most reflect the need for association with peers. This is clearly not an "out-group" phenomenon. Police, for example, display the same sort of desire for extracurricular association with each other, as do students, carpenters, assembly line workers, and professional people. Goffman's insight into the recognition of similar "virtual social identities" as being the basis on which interpersonal relation-ships are built[31] is really the mechanism at work here. Identity of "identities" is an important grouping mechanism in society at large.

The thief who is interested in an association with others like him-self can find it through the network structure. This is particularly true because of the stratification earlier noted in the clienteles served by different fences. Thus the thief is likely to become acquainted not only with other thieves through the network but also with other thieves very much like himself. The young burglar meets his peer through the fence just as does the good burglar. Such associations serve more than illicit interests, of course, since they fulfill friendship and social needs as well. This is very important for the thief whose hours of activity may not correspond to those of persons in more traditional lines of employ-ment.

Risk-Taking

Peer association provided by the fencing network also contributes
to the enhancement of risk-taking by the individual thief. This can be
extremely important to the longevity of one's career in burglary.
Shover, for example, suggests that even the best of thieves never really
overcomes the sense of tension accompanying the commission of a
theft; he only learns to successfully handle that tension by his association and experiences with others.[32] The fencing network provides
the thief with associates whose risk-taking propensities are similar.
Thus, knowledge of risks successfully taken by peers may encourage a
thief to take additional risks. Conversely, what is too risky for an associate may be defined as too risky for him also.

The direct and lasting influence of the group on individual risk-
taking has been experimentally demonstrated.[33] For the thief, whom
we are told never becomes completely inured to the risks of his occupation, the group experience fostered by the fencing network can be
especially advantageous. In addition, the support given to the risk-
taking of the thief and his associates by the fence as he rewards their
behavior only tends to reinforce a more favorable attitude toward the
risks of the trade. If the fence is a kinship link, the attitude toward risk
can be even more enhanced since a family member is not normally
interpreted as being supportive of truly jeopardizing conduct. This
may explain why the kinship network is observed to be dominated by
the membership of the young burglar who may need the additional
familial assurance that his activities are not foolhardy or irrational.

Of course the receiver does more than bring together relevant risk-
takers. He also enhances their attitudes toward the risks associated
with theft by affirmatively minimizing them. Thus a set-up provided
by the fence serves to minimize the risks of the crime while at the same
time reinforcing the idea among all participants that theft really isn't
as risky as it seems. In fact, the more set-ups participated in by a thief,
the more he may come to underestimate the actual risks inherent in
theft and to overestimate his own skills. Thus, a typical situation was
observed at the data site in which the dissolution of an action set that
had successfully committed a series of burglaries with information
provided by the fence was apprehended soon after the group began
undirected thieving. This happened because they engaged in some
irrational and clearly risky behavior. For example, one group was
apprehended throwing silverware (that they did not want) out their
car window immediately following a residence theft.[34] Clearly their

perceptions of the true risks involved in theft had been somewhat altered by their participation in the fence's action set.

Membership in a network can also, however, minimize the risks associated with arrest and imprisonment. The work-a-day network particularly reflects this feature. This is because the stigma accompanying involvement with the criminal justice system is somewhat reduced by the network. The network minimizes such stigmatizing processes by reintegrating the offender to his previously familiar surroundings. The unaffiliated offender is likely to return from the prison experience lost and alone, his friends and associates whom he left behind having found new work partners. The network thief finds the post-prison situation somewhat different. First, he can get a job with the fence that will offer him a cover for criminal activities; and then he can find an immediate source of partners willing to trade on the set-ups provided by his "employer." Without such support, it would be difficult for a thief to reestablish ties in the theft microcosm, since he himself might be considered too risky. His affiliation with the fence and the possibility of an emerging action set, however, will make him a more attractive theft partner.

Recruitment

Besides creating an associative and risk-enhancing setting for the thief, the fence and his network perform important recruitment functions in the theft microcosm. We have already seen how this is accomplished in the play network and in the post-imprisonment situation, but recruitment needs are more varied than these. Work groups are constantly forming in the theft microcosm as some thieves are imprisoned and other thieves enter or reenter the occupation. The fence becomes a centralized referral agency for such work groups.

Through the action set, for example, the performance of young burglars can be observed and appraised. Noteworthy behavior by a young thief in such a setting can often lead to his recruitment by other groups for additional theft activities. It is in this way that thieves shift to more skilled networks, thus changing their status classification as a thief. The detective, for example, waits for just such moves by the young thief in order to reclassify him as either a known or good burglar. Knowledge gained by the thief in his new setting can also change the character of the network to the extent that he brings other thieves with him.

Perhaps the more important recruiting done by the fencing network, however, is its initiation of the new thief. This is particularly common in the kinship network where the fence's familiarity will encourage the criminal activity of the young friends associated with the kinship link. Thus the father-fence will actively support the criminality of his son and his friends, changing their attitudes toward theft with every exchange transaction. The fence is in a much better position to persuade the uncertain thief, since he can actually reward that individual's criminal behavior, while another thief can only assist or share in it. The successful theft itself, then, is unlikely to be as critical in shaping the perceptions of the novice as is the *successful disposal* of the proceeds of that theft. The "fun" associated with the commission of thefts will wear thin long before the economic rewards accompanying that activity. This, accompanied by the associative and risk-taking dimensions of the fencing network, make the fence an important recruiter for and sustainer of the theft careers of others.

Procedural Ratiocination

Perhaps the greatest contribution of the fencing network for all participants is the clear direction it gives theft. Through the network the fence can specify the property he wants as well as how and when he would like it. If he does nothing more, the theft has already become a directed activity for the thief. His targets will be narrowed to those capable of yielding such merchandise and a schedule for the "production" of those goods will be introduced. If the fence also includes information relevant to the theft or actually plans and sets it up, theft becomes a completely integrated behavior system. The thief will have few decisions to make in such a situation; in effect, he merely has to follow the directions given.

It is important to note that the directing of theft by the fence is not only advantageous to the thief. It is also important to the fence who can better plan his marketing program in the certainty that he will be receiving the type of goods he wants. But the network does more than this. It ratiocinates theft by prescribing a certain chronology and a given eventuality to the crime. That is, each step in the theft of a piece of property becomes predicted on some understanding of the step to follow.

For example, suppose the fence has enunciated a need for television sets. The thief begins his activity with a given goal, that is a television. He seeks a theft target capable of yielding a television, and once he gets it he knows exactly how and where to dispose of the merchandise. The crime event becomes extremely deterministic. Without the procedural guidance of the network, the thief must depend on an instinct as to the exchangeability of a property item; some inkling of where it can be exchanged; and his own initiative in getting it there. Nothing is certain in the procedures he follows, particularly the certainty of reward. On the other hand, all is certain with the network structure, allowing the crime to flow smoothly to its predetermined end. Each person knows what he's doing, when, and how; and in many cases, how much he will receive for so performing. Proceduralizing theft removes much of its mystery and uncertainty, a feature of the network especially comforting to the young and inexperienced thief.

Selective Skill Diffusion

The network is particularly important in combining the skills of its individual members. Associations made through the network structure contribute to the expertise of the thief. Unless he is a particularly talented person, the thief will rarely attain theft skills on his own. Instead he must learn from the experiences and techniques of others. The network can provide the tutelage experience for the thief by helping him make contacts with others. It can also constrain him by limiting his contacts to only those skills exhibited by the network's membership. The diffusion of skills, then, is very much determined by the exclusivity of the fencing network. Association with the good burglar is only likely to occur if the thief can manage to affiliate himself with a network through which that individual is known to move. This means that the thief must be associated with the good burglar through either a kinship link (for example, as his brother), or through a link with that individual's fencing outlet. In the former case, the kinship ties are likely to generate the kinds of learning experience necessary to improve skills. In the latter case, a link with the fence is likely to recommend the young thief to the more experienced thief as part of a work set, where such skills can be taught. The thief who displays neither of these links to the good burglar is unlikely to gain the skills necessary to enter that status group. This is why the restrictiveness of the burglar's initial network affiliations are so critical to his career development.

The neighborhood fence, for example, may be very convenient, but he can also be extremely limiting in terms of the contacts to be made within his network. At the same time, the less familiar fence can be the source of important associations. Part of the difference relates to the regard in which the fence is held throughout the theft microcosm, either because of the size or quality of the thefts he generates or because of the type of goods he handles. The neighborhood fence is unlikely to be known outside his bailiwick so that association with him, no matter how competent, will not recommend the thief to more significant personnages in the industry. Other fences may be well known for their attention to detail in the commission of a theft or their generation of the "big score." To be a member of such a network can have important referral benefits for the new thief.

Kinship and locational proximity to such fences appear to be the important determinants of such initial associations. But there are other variables. Race, for example, is an important barrier to network membership at the data site, giving the moderately skilled black burglar little opportunity to improve on those skills by association with good (mostly white) burglars. Instead his career development will depend on an awareness of and an ability to enter the network of the one black fence operating in the city known to service the closely knit group of good black burglars. Ethnicity can also play a role in the opportunities for association with certain fencing networks.

Skills, then, are not equally diffused throughout the theft microcosm. Instead they tend to be concentrated within network structures whose entry opportunities are in many cases severely limited.

Information Dissemination

One of the great advantages of network affiliation is the opportunity to be made privy to its pool of information. The network contains information relative to skills and work partners as well as specific information relating to the commission of thefts. Alone, a thief could not possibly hope to generate the same amount of information as the network can. Each of its members monitors possible theft targets as well as the behavior of the police. By centralizing all of this information in the fencing unit, it can be carefully reviewed and transmitted to relevant network members.

It should be noted that the network is capable also of enforcing the loyalty of its members through the selective withholding of information. Thus, the recalcitrant thief can be isolated from the ongoing activities of the network, a situation unlikely to enhance his theft endeavors. Networks generally try to mask the activities of their members by transmitting "noise" to outsiders. In this way it is hoped that the intricacies of the network will escape the uninitiated and the security of the membership can be maintained. Nevertheless, the activities of groupings in the theft microcosm never succeed in going unnoticed; and the network itself will fail to resist the temptation of taking credit for the "big score," well done.

With the many features offered by the network it is not surprising that most thieves find it both advantageous and necessary to become so affiliated. The network serves as both an insulator and an isolator for the thief. It insulates him from the solitary, highly risky theft activities of the lone thief by offering him association with others capable of directing and enhancing his career. It provides him with information he otherwise could not generate; and it gives him working partners he may never have found on his own.

At the same time, however, the network limits his activities to those dictated by the fence's needs and it restricts his associations to that particular range of thieves. The thief, then, is isolated in his own world by the network's boundaries. He is kept apart from many other segments of the theft microcosm by its restrictiveness. The rewards associated with the network may more than compensate for such isolation. Where they do not, the thief will attempt to join new networks or maintain separate affiliations with several of them. Although this latter situation appears frequently, information from the data site suggests that only the good burglar can do this successfully. Other thieves depend too greatly on the information provided by the fence to maintain a free-floating independence and will usually tend toward continual association with at most one or two fencing units.

THE NETWORK AND ITS IMPLICATIONS

The implications of the fencing network are several. First, the existence of continual network associations seriously calls into question the perception of fencing itself as a randomized, intermittent buying arrangement engaged in by the shady merchant. Instead it suggests an ongoing organizational structure taking steps necessary to its continued preservation, including the binding of supply sources to its destiny. Next, the ratiocination of theft accomplished through the fencing network begins to shed some light on what are now familiar crime statistics relating to theft—a high rate of occurrence accompanied by a disappointing rate of clearance and property recovery. Once the highly systematized behavior of individuals within networks is appreciated, the folly of attaching such statistics to the activities of lone thieves, more or less wandering about our cities spontaneously lifting whatever property meets their eyes, is made clear. It also suggests why the one thief most likely to engage in such behavior, the addict, is also the thief most often arrested (although not necessarily for theft). [35]

Finally, the careful linkage of groups and of individuals with specific theft tasks suggests why the network is so prominent on the theft scene. It is in effect the "personnel department" of the theft industry linking the right man to the right jobs and to the right working partners in the competent execution of those jobs. By assembling the skills of many, the network learns to minimize its personnel mistakes by including those who demonstrate the requisite abilities, while isolating those who do not. The network also fosters and encourages the theft behavior of the talented by rewarding and teaching the young thief and by reintegrating the ex-con. Unless the careful and selective linkages of the network are understood, neither the consistency of the thief's behavior nor the continuity of the theft industry itself can be explained or appreciated.

There may be a little larceny in the heart of every man, but it is unlikely to be acted upon without the help, encouragement, and reinforcement of like-minded individuals. Neither is it likely to be as systemized, as rational or as "safe" as that perpetrated by the fencing network.

6 | *The decreasing utility of the theft game*

We have described the fence as history has presented him to us, noting along the way the selective manner in which conventional wisdom has drawn on the past. In addition, we have sought and found a detailed picture of the contemporary criminal receiver as he is known to those detectives and burglars who monitor his operations and interact with him. Most startling has been the considerable incongruity existing between these two characterizations of the fence. What remains now is to appraise the implications of the present study not only for what it has told us about contemporary property theft but also for what it implies about the manner in which we as a society seek to control this form of criminal conduct.

In this chapter, then, we assess the operational effectiveness of the traditional approach to property theft as it is acted upon by most police departments in this country. We have called this approach the "conventional view of theft." Because this view has largely relied on the selective "wisdom" of the past as opposed to more current analyses of the present, we see it as one focusing primarily on the thief, to the exclusion of the criminal receiver. As we examine the "conventional view of theft," we will consider first the various sources of its practical effectiveness as an operating principle; and then we will attempt to evaluate its utility at the "margin," that is, the value of its *continued* acceptance as an organizing principle around which both our thoughts and our policies with regard to property theft are drawn.

In the present investigation we shall rely heavily on the analytical tools of the economist and the game theoretician. From the economist we have adopted the concept of "utility" as that amount of satisfaction derived from the expenditure of scarce resources upon an item.[1] It is the special property of utility that although it may in the main continue to increase as increasing amounts of a good are consumed, each additional dosage of said good can become *relatively* less satisfying than the one preceding it. Economists call this the law of diminishing marginal utility,[2] a principle which suggests that even where *total utility* continues to increase, a good should only continue to be consumed up to the point where its *marginal utility* can successfully compete with other goods. When the marginal utility of an item cannot compare favorably with the satisfaction to be derived from the same expenditure elsewhere, we should invest our resources in other areas.

The logic of the utility concept is simple. For even the hungriest of men, the total utility of food does not continually increase and at some point an extra unit of food becomes no longer as "satisfying" as an expenditure in other areas, on clothing for example. Similarly, with ideas and beliefs. We have all confronted ideas that have "outlived their usefulness"—not in their totality but in the marginal sense. But the marginality of a concept is somehow not so easily discerned as is the diminished satisfaction associated with a third helping of dessert, for example; neither is it as easy to discard a tired idea as it is to refuse that last piece of cake. Part of the difficulty with the former lies in the fact that it is often somewhat difficult to appreciate the need for and to find a suitable or immediately satisfying replacement for an outmoded concept. The pursuit of an outworn idea for its own sake appears to blind us to the need for new ideas and to the consideration of alternatives. Thus we tend to cling to beliefs long after they have stopped providing us with a level of marginal utility commensurate with our investment in them.

This situation, it is contended here, is exactly where we find ourselves with regard to the "conventional view of the theft." This traditional conceptualization of property theft counsels social control agencies concerned with property theft to concentrate exclusively on the thief. Because the general idea behind this view is so sensible (that is, it is the thief who steals property), it has come to be little questioned and its usefulness is rarely asked to be demonstrated. It is not the total utility of the concept with which we are concerned here, however; rather it is the marginal utility which a continued acceptance of this view is yielding that concerns us. How useful, in other words, is continued "consumption" of this view to the exclusion of others? Might not a conceptual investment placed elsewhere generate a more satisfying return on our expenditures of time, energy, and dollars with reference to property theft? Thus, notwithstanding the considerable value which the conventional view of theft seems to have, it must be investigated further. It must be challenged to prove that it deserves our continued support and acceptance.

The analytical tools of the game theoretician have been chosen to so test the "conventional view of theft." We have done so because game theory[3] is a very useful device for the description and analysis of situations in which opposing interests meet. The "game" is an abstraction of the conflict situation in which the opposing players are described, their relevant strategies are enumerated, and a determination is made as to each player's best course in the play of the game. As such the game concept conforms nicely to our conceptualization of property theft as a situation in which the opposing interests of violators of the laws relating to property theft (thieves) confront and oppose the police who must uphold these laws. Game theory analysis can, therefore, help us to objectively assess what we are doing in this conflict area as well as how well we are doing. It is this latter assessment that can aid in our evaluation of the conventional view of theft.

THE THEFT GAME

We shall begin by considering theft as a two-person, zero-sum game. In doing so we have conceptualized property theft as a conflict situation (game) in which two players (whom we are calling the police and the burglar) meet whose interests are so opposed that the success of one side requires the defeat of the other. This may seem intuitively obvious, but it must be realized that we were not limited to this choice for the game's parameters. We could, for example, have decided that theft is a three-person game and have included ourselves (property owners and citizens) as a player. Or, if we were to accept the notion that criminals processed by the criminal justice system receive rehabilitative help thereby, we might not call it a zero-sum game at all, since the burglar's arrest would not represent a "loss" to him but a boon. The simple description of our game provided above, then, already represents the fact that we have made some definite decisions about its structure. The decision with regard to its players requires some further explanation.

First, we said that we had chosen only two players (the police and the burglar), having excluded the citizen which to some might represent a significant omission. In answer, we could show that we really have included the citizen in our model, for in game theory the term "player" or "person" is not designed to represent an individual but an *interest*. The game model is parsimonious to the extent that it only seeks to consider those *relevant* interests which are truly opposed and which affect the play and/or structure of the game. Thus, while the citizen could be set apart as a third player, his interest is considered to be represented by the player we call the police. We assume here that the interests of both citizen and police are one and are equally oppositional to burglars. Further, we assume that in reflecting the world accurately, we can look on the citizen as having transferred to the police the responsibility of opposing the burglar in his behalf and in his stead. Therefore, the player we are calling the police can be looked on as a coalition between citizens and law enforcement.[4]

The next explanation we need to put forth is the manner in which the police player is represented. We shall consider the police to be a fairly homogeneous entity, although we know that in "real life" this is not always true. Not all police departments are the same, have the same amounts of resources, or attack crime with the same set of priorities. We will, for argument's sake (and because we feel it represents the concept we are testing) assume that all police agencies are similarly against theft and on that basis represent them as a single entity.[5]

Our final qualification with regard to players involves the burglar. We have already learned that it would be ludicrous to treat this interest as a single entity, since the spectrum of thieves is so varied. We will, therefore, delineate three separate models of the theft concept on the basis of three different types of thieves: the addict, the known burglar, and the good burglar.[6]

With our three explanations done, we are now ready to begin our game. The first task is to set down the strategies for each player and arrange them in a game matrix. Each cell in the matrix represents the face-off of two strategies and contains the sum of the payoffs to each player within it. Thus, in the game in Table 24 the upper left cell represents the intersection of Player A's strategy 1 and Player B's strategy 1 and the 4 within it means that the face-off of these two strategies would net 4 units (of whatever) to Player A. As a convention, positive numbers in the cells signify gains to Player A; negative numbers are gains to Player B (that is, losses to Player A).

Although we will be concerned with three separate theft games—the police versus the addict, the police versus the known burglar, and the police versus the good burglar—we can delineate at the outset the strategies used by the police player for they remain virtually the same in each situation. That is, the police are characterized by a distinct set of responses which vary only in their frequencies of use depending on the thief involved. These responses to property theft (here we call them strategies) can be divided into two broad areas: crime prevention activities (which include intelligence gathering and structured surveillance); and crime response activities (which include post hoc investigation and information acquisitions). The four strategies we have outlined for the police player in the game, therefore, represent both these types of activities. Under the crime prevention rubric we place:

Strategy 1: Surveillance of known hang-outs, meeting places, and associates of thieves.

Strategy 2: Target patrolling of areas where the incidence of the thief's crime is thought to be highest.

These strategies reflect the fact that much of the work of a detective level squad involves going around to bars and all-night restaurants that are "known hang-outs" for thieves, checking on who is with whom or who is missing from a group known to meet together. The following is a typical and frequently replicated item in police intelligence reports:

Item 1 (police file item):

Stopped in the —— Casino bar. (Names of six young burglars noted in the place.) This is a place where all the young hoods gather.

TABLE 24: MODEL OF THE GAME MATRIX

PLAYER B

PLAYER A	Strategy 1	Strategy 2
Strategy 1		
Strategy 2		

The practice known at the data site as the "suspicious car check" is both a harassment and an attempt to maintain a generalized surveillance over thieves and their current associates. Thus, a monthly (and often weekly) listing of the current cars and license plates used by active thieves is distributed throughout the police department with the result that such cars are stopped and their occupants noted by police. Witness the following, a representative example of this frequent strategy:

Item 2 (police activity report):

Suspicious car check on auto driven by John; Carl was with him at the time. Both men are active burglars.

The crime prevention logic behind these activities is admittedly subtle but detectives are convinced that if they can "keep up with" the varied associations in the theft microcosm, then they may find out about an emerging "score." For example:

Item 3 (police intelligence report):

Shortly after we arrived at work, received call from Patrolman —— that the cars of four of our good burglars were at —— house (home of a good burglar). Alerted crew to report to work as soon as possible. Checked 17th Precinct for house jobs or cars

this tour since due to Jewish New Year and the fact that syna-
gogues are full, assumed that homes of the participants might
be vulnerable to attack from thieves. This proved negative.

Less subtle is the kind of police activity found at the patrol level
which seeks to anticipate criminal events. There may be some question as to the "preventive" aspects of such activities but in cases such
as the following, the police, at least, believe that such is the nature of
their strategy.

Item 4 (author's observation at the data site):

I was taken one night to an intersection in the city at which were
parked an ambulance, two patrol cars and one K-9 squad truck.
My immediate response was to inquire into what had occurred.
"Nothing yet," was the reply, "but something *always* does!" It
was then that the criminological notoriety of the intersection
was described to me in detail and that I was told of the nightly
presence of said police vehicles, since "they're usually needed
before the night is out."

All of the above strategies or tactics, then, represent efforts by the
police player to anticipate or at least counter—by mere presence or by
intelligence gathering—*expected* criminal events.

Under the second category of police effort, the crime response category, we can place:

Strategy 3: Wait for the report of a crime.

Strategy 4: Rely on the information supplied by informants
(both known and anonymous).

Strategy 3 may not sound particularly responsive, but in the theft area
it is often all the police can do. Guarding every possible target of theft
in a city would be impossible and uneconomic, so the police must rely
on suspicious sights or sounds to arouse a neighbor or someone else to
call them, or on the gross mistakes of the thieves in committing the
offense. Sometimes thefts are cleared in this manner if the police
respond quickly (as when a burglar is caught breaking and entering
into or escaping from a residence), or if the victim is careful not to

disturb the scene (as when all the specific elements of a burglar's modus operandi are present). This strategy does result in apprehension of criminals as the following item reveals:

Item 5 (police activity report):

—— arrested for possession of burglar's tools. He was observed in rear of the —— Restaurant dropping a pitch bar and screwdriver. The door to the restaurant had been pried open.

Strategy 4 is perhaps even more valuable, however. It is unlikely that the most skilled burglar will belie his activities—while they are in progress—to anyone; neither will he leave behind anything incriminating. The police, then, usually hear of the crime some time after it is accomplished, and though they may have some ideas as to the identity of the thief, there may be no evidence to support their beliefs. They must in this situation rely on their ability to get information from the "theft element" (their term) itself. Surprisingly, there is a lot of gratuitous information floating around the theft microcosm in the form of anonymous tips and remarks as to who is spending freely of late, or who's been bragging about what. The following is an example of the not untypical information the police can receive.

Item 6 (police intelligence files):

Received information that Bob and Alan (known burglars) are working together out of Bob's cab. They are pulling house jobs, so if they are seen together in above cab, give them a car check.

Briefly, then, the four main police strategies in response to theft are: (1) surveillance, (2) target patrols, (3) quick response to crime report, and (4) use of informants. It remains now for us to oppose them to the strategies of each of the revelant thieves described below. As will be seen, the utility of each strategy is likely to depend on the nature of the thief involved so that the hierarchy of use and usefulness of the four strategies will differ in each case.

The Theft Game—Type A: Police versus Addict

To begin it is well to remember a few characteristics of the addict thief which we noted earlier, for they significantly influence the nature of his strategies. For example, the addict is typically a frequent theft offender, rarely making a score that will carry him beyond one day's need for drugs. This is because he usually stops stealing when he gets his quota, and next because more lucrative scores often demand some planning for which he neither has the time nor the inclination. His general strategy is the path of least resistance. He has a given amount of money to come up with before he can meet his supplier; and he will seize upon the first opportunity that presents itself. He is not completely undirected, of course, because he has some important mobility constraints. He must, for example, preserve his mobility at all costs since his physical well-being depends on that. Then too, his mobility is somewhat restricted with regard to where he can commit crimes, given his limited transportation resources. The addict thief, then, has three major characteristics: the frequency of his offense, his opportunistic/little planning nature, his limited geographic mobility. From the author's observations at the data site, from the numerous case histories in police files, and from discussions with police detectives, the addict appears on any given day to choose primarily from among the following four theft strategies. His actual choice is likely to depend upon his *familiarity* with the strategy as well as his perceptions of the *resistability* of its associated target. Given his substantial mobility constraints, each strategy is assumed to be plied within his own or an adjoining neighborhood.

Strategy 1: Popping (breaking into or stripping) cars. This is a preferable tactic because if successful it won't involve anyone who can recognize him. Also, it is unlikely that the crime will be reported for some time after it is accomplished.

Strategy 2: Trying the doors of houses or apartments. This strategy has the same qualities as strategy 1 except that it has the added risk that he will not find an empty residence at first try. He then risks a neighbor's remembering his coming to the door with little explanation for his presence.

Strategy 3: Boosting (shoplifting) in a store. This strategy has the

constraint of needing some amount of skill to perpe-
trate. (Some addicts are, of course, boosters by trade
so this will be their only strategy. We are more interested in the average addict, however.) If our addict
has some skill in this area, he may move to this
strategy, but it has significantly more risks with the
uncertain element of the store detective always
present.

Strategy 4: Purse snatching and mugging. This represents the
most risky, least preferred strategy to the addict
since the possibilities for identification are greatest.
Then too, depending on the victim's response, his
visibility and hence the discovery of the crime can be
most immediate indeed.

Before we place the police and the addict into a matrix format, we
can simplify somewhat the dimensions of their interaction, particularly with regard to the police. It is likely, for example, that police
strategies 3 and 4 can be eliminated from our consideration in this
game. Take strategy 4, for example. Given the frequency and opportunistic nature of the addict's offense, it would be impossible for even
his closest associates to know exactly what crime he committed, much
less where or when. Similarly with strategy 3, the report of an addict's
crimes is most likely to be some time after their occurrence so that
while its nature might suggest that an addict had committed the
crime, this information in and of itself would be of little value. The
number of addicts in a city, after all, while not being infinite, is certainly a large finite one; making the probability of matching the crime
to its perpetrator something like the proverbial haystack search.

This does not mean that the police will not respond to the report of
an addict-generated crime, but rather that the preferred way for
doing so will not be strategy 3. More likely is the use of target patrolling (strategy 2) for such purposes. We eliminate police strategies 3
and 4 since they are not likely to contribute to the solution of the
crime.

As a result we have derived the following 2 x 4 game, 2 refers to the
number of police strategies and 4 to the number of addict strategies.

In addition, we have noted in each cell (by means of a "+" or a "-") to which player the average advantage of the intersection of the two relevant strategies will go. Minus signs represent payoffs to the addict; plus signs are payoffs to the police. We propose that the Type A theft game looks like the matrix in Table 25.

The following rationales were used to assign the matrix payoffs in Table 25. If the police pursue strategy 1 against the addict, it is likely that by the time the addict thief arrives at his meeting place or hang-out, he will have already converted the property stolen to cash, or in the case of a mugging it will already be in that form. Thus, specific evidence of the theft will no longer be available. This is with the possible exception of a house burglary in which the goods may not be immediately negotiable and he may have them still in his possession. Hence, the only face-off of police strategy 1 which yields anything to the police is the case of a house burglary (addict strategy 2). It is reasoned that even if the addict is still carrying property yielded from his strategies 1 or 3, that it will be more easily concealable (particularly in strategy 3), so that the payoffs will go to the addict.

Clearly strategy 2 is the better choice for the police, since it can be said to *dominate* strategy 1. In game theory, the concept of dominance is important because it calls for the elimination of unworkable or un-

TABLE 25: THE THEFT GAME - TYPE A: POLICE VERSUS ADDICT

ADDICT

POLICE	S_1 Pop cars	S_2 Try houses	S_3 Shoplift	S_4 Mug
S_1 Hang-out surveillance	-	+	-	-
S_2 Target patrols	+	+	breakeven	+

usable strategies. To check for dominance the two strategies are compared cell for cell and if one is inferior across the board it is eliminated. This is the situation here. Cell for cell police strategy 2 dominates police strategy 1 because each of its payoffs is at least equal to or higher than those of strategy 1. This dominance allows us to assume that regardless of what the precise solution to the game might be, it will not include the use of strategy 1 by the police.

The reasoning behind assigning payoffs to police strategy 2 is that by patrolling areas in which a high incidence of addict theft occurs, the police are likely to observe and be able to interdict some of that crime. The greatest likelihood of this is in the case of a mugging which will potentially cause some disturbance, but it is also likely that an addict's activity around a residence will alert a police patrol. Add to this the addict's lack of planning particularly with reference to his exit from the crime as well as his visibility to the police because of frequent arrests, and the prospect of his behavior's being detected is very good. We have given the police a lower payoff against the addict's popping cars strategy (addict strategy 1) only because activity around cars may not appear to be as suspicious (at least initially) as that around residences. It is also likely to provide a better set of excuses for the individual's presence. Thus, people are known to misplace their cars in large parking lots, but are less likely to forget where they live. The police then must proceed cautiously since to interdict an innocent citizen getting into his own auto would definitely represent a negative payoff to them.

The lowest payoff at strategy 2 for the police is found in the situation where the addict shoplifts. Here we have evaluated the police and the addict as breaking even, because the exact payoff to each is really determined by a fairly unpredictable and certainly uncontrollable element, the store detective. Depending, then, on that individual's competence, we have estimated that the payoffs in that cell will average half the time to the police and half the time to the addict, hence the notation break even in that cell.

It should be emphasized that each of the notations in the cells is actually an *average*, and that at each play of the game the payoffs to each player may in effect be quite different. The game model, however, is not so interested in individual plays in the game, but in what the position of each of the players will be in the long run using the strategies they find at their disposal. Were we to assign specific numeric values to each of the players' strategies, we could derive a mathematical solution to the game. Instead we have merely indicated to whom, on the average, the gains for each intersection of strategies are thought to accrue. Even with the format employed here, however, we can indicate the solution to this game. It is based upon the *minimax* premise central to all game analysis, which states that a player's best course of action is to so arrange his behavior so as to minimize his losses and maximize his gains and he must do this assuming that his opponent is both rational and intelligent, that is, ready to capitalize upon his mistakes.

In looking at the matrix in Table 25, the minimax principle suggests that each of the players should employ a pure strategy. For the police, strategy 2 (target patrols) is preferred; for the addict, strategy 3 (shoplift). This is because by so doing neither can do worse than break even with his opponent. The "rational" solution to this game becomes very interesting indeed when we confront what we know to be the "actual" behaviors of the two players. Addicts, for example, do not employ the shoplifting tactic exclusively, primarily because not all are so skilled in that technique. In addition, the opportunistic nature of the addict's thefts makes his response to the game a more mixed strategy, moving intermittently between the strategies indicated for him. This may suggest that the game is somewhat favorable to the police since the matrix indicates that should the addict stray from his strategy 3, the advantage accrues to them. This is only true, however, where the police pursue strategy 2.

What do we know about the actual behavior of the police? Interestingly enough, the strategy most often employed by the police against the addict is strategy 1; the very tactic that allows the addict to reap rewards in the game. Thus, police are busy keeping surveillance over known drug exchange areas and "shooting galleries" to which an addict migrates *after* he has completed his thefts. This is because enforcement emphasis on the addict is concerned more with criminal activities relating directly to his addiction—the possession and sale of narcotics—rather than with his theft activities. The game between the addict and the police that is generally played, then, has very little to do with theft. In fact, it is unlikely that the game we have described is played very much at all. And that is just the point.

It is the lack of fit of the Type A theft game to reality that is its greatest and most revealing lesson. It tells us first, that for one significant area of theft (the addict's), the "conventional view of theft" is of little value, erring in trying to conceptualize an unlikely set of circumstances. Next it tells us that even where the set of circumstances above described were more actively pursued, the police would be unlikely to do very well against the addict. For the Type A theft game, then, the "conventional view of theft" does not suggest that its continued acceptance is warranted.

The Theft Game—Type B: Police versus Known Burglar

In this game we must first recognize that the police face a burglar somewhat different from the addict. Perhaps the best description that can be given of the known burglar is the account of such a group's activities at the data site.

Item 7 (author's summary from district attorney's investigative files; known burglar's statement):

The group noted here committed a rash of burglaries in the warehouse district of the city studied, using always approximately the same MO. It went something like this: someone's girl friend would drive them to a location near their target and let them off. They then would proceed on foot to the warehouse and on arrival would gain entry by forcing a door, breaking a window or hacking (literally) through the roof or side of the building. Once inside, they would gather together the items they wanted (in this series of thefts, the property stolen consisted mostly of metals and alloys); one of the group would meanwhile have searched the premises for a vehicle, crossed the wires, and backed it up near the building (a loading dock if one was available). Next they would load the loot onto the vehicle and proceed out through the front gate.

Not all known burglars, of course, limit themselves to warehouses; some are equally likely to steal from residences and business establishments. But the above example gives a fairly clear idea of how they work. First of all, it is obvious that semiskilled burglars have a greater geographic mobility in selecting targets than does the addict. Their target selection is, however, somewhat restricted by the degree of finesse with which they execute a crime. Thus, they must choose targets that can withstand their rather messy, often brutal, and ungracious means of entry. In other words, they must select places whose security is either minimal or easily neutralized, or premises with a degree of isolation so their activities will be unnoticed or not arouse suspicion. If a selected target does not fulfill these qualifications, it often becomes the known burglar's undoing. Thus, some burglars often are caught inside premises, in the act of entering or as they are executing an escape. This is what makes items like number 5 (see page 154) prevalent in police files with regard to the known burglar.

This also belies a final characteristic of the known burglar. Although his crimes are less frequent and more planned than the addict's, the known thief does not exhibit extraordinary planning capabilities. Rather, his planning is minimal; ordinarily it does not extend much beyond the selection of a target and the decision as to how many crowbars he will need. The determination of an orderly exit or of a contingent plan of action (should the need arise) appear to be activities for which the known burglar has little time or aptitude. Nevertheless, this type of thief represents a sizable proportion of the theft population, displaying varying degrees of skill, success, and just plain luck.

Now that we have reviewed the characteristics of the known burglar, we can talk about his strategies:

Strategy 1: The decision to enter a residence.
Strategy 2: The decision to enter a warehouse.
Strategy 3: The decision to enter a business establishment.

The semiskilled thief has, of course, a fourth strategy as well (one not open to the addict), and that is the decision *not* to steal. We will assume, however, that by proceeding with him to the game matrix, he has already decided against that strategy and will confine our attention to the three strategies listed.[7]

If we look at each of these targets closely, we will see that each of them offers an advantage in some area. With regard to security systems, for example, the residence is likely to have the least sophisticated set up (if it has one at all) and hence will be most attractive. If one looks at degree of isolation or the possibility of arousing suspicion, however, the warehouse emerges as most favorable. In terms of ease of approach, the business establishment with its delivery entrances, and so forth, is the best target. Depending on the known burglar's evaluations of the differing risks associated with each type of target *and* on his ability to deal with them, he will make a selection.[8] Beyond the inherent qualities of the targets he considers, however, he must also evaluate what the police will be doing.[9]

We delineated earlier four basic strategies for the police: two were related to crime prevention (surveillance and patrol activities) and two were related to crime response (investigative and information gathering activities following the report of a crime). In the addict-thief game we ultimately eliminated the latter two police strategies. Here we will retain all four, and slightly modify strategy 3. Instead of using strategy 3 to refer only to police responding to the discovery of a crime, we will enlarge it to include their response to alarm systems and phone calls that signal a crime is in progress. The response time of the police is very important for the known thief since many of his targets are likely to have security devices that alert law enforcement agencies. If, however, the police waited for the report of the crime by the owner, the theft would probably be hours old and the value of the on-the-scene information could be of little help. The following anecdote from the data site will give the reader some appreciation for the importance of security devices to the police when opposed to the known burglar.

Item 8 (author's observation at data site):

I remember being at police headquarters at a time when the detectives were investigating a break-in at a business establishment. In the corner of the office stood a pitchfork. "What," I asked, "is that for?" "Oh," said a detective, "that's what the guy used to get in. He just threw it through a plate glass window." My response was that that was pretty amazing and that certainly all the "class" had gone out of burglary. I was most interested in the detective's reply: "You're right! There was a time when you had to admire some of these guys. I mean, they were really talented. But now—a pitchfork through a window, you know *anybody* can do that!"

It is precisely because "anybody" can execute many of the known burglar's techniques, that if he makes a successful escape from the crime, it is often impossible to know whom to look for. Even though this type of burglar is likely to make some mistakes, being a fairly inept thief can easily lend him a sort of anonymity which hinders police investigation.

If we can oppose the police and the known burglar, we will find the 4 x 3 game shown in Table 26. The solution to this game indicates the need for players to use a mixed strategy, that is, varying their responses depending upon what they believe will be their opponent's choice of tactics. In this way each can get the most or lose the least in the situation. Both players are, of course, constrained to some extent in their abilities to mix strategies. The known burglar, for example, may not wish to steal from residences, fearing greatly the discovery by owners or neighbors. Hence his use of strategy 1 will be much less probable than the model would require or suggest.

It is the police, however, who are more affirmatively constrained in choosing among strategies. Strategy 3, for example, is rather an obligatory one for them. When an alarm sounds or a suspicious neighbor calls, they cannot ignore it. As long as resources permit, they cannot decide arbitrarily to answer only every third call or every third

TABLE 26: THE THEFT GAME - TYPE B:
POLICE versus KNOWN BURGLAR

KNOWN BURGLAR

POLICE	S_1 Residence theft	S_2 Business theft	S_3 Warehouse theft
S_1 Hang-out surveillance	-	-	-
S_2 Target patrols	+	+	breakeven
S_3 Alarm or call response	+	+	+
S_4 Use of informants	breakeven	+	+

alarm. Neither can they triple their patrol force for every one call received in order to achieve a strategy mix. This does not mean necessarily that there is something wrong with our game. It only tells us that the police, without the freedom to mix strategies as the game requires, probably are not doing as well against the known burglar as the game suggests. Just how well they are doing we do not know for sure; theft rates may tell us more about that. All in all, however, the conventional view of theft would seem to have come off moderately well vis-à-vis the semiskilled burglar. Its next test is against the professional thief.

The Theft Game—Type C: Police versus Good Burglar

The skilled, professional thief presents a most challenging subject for law enforcement agencies. Here is an individual whose activities are characterized by a substantial amount of planning. His target, entry, and exit will be planned. He will also prepare a back-up plan should things go awry. His prime motivation is to ensure that he will be undisturbed as he goes about his work. The professional thief, therefore, will provide for the worst, only to prevent the worst from happening. (This, it should be noted, is a prerequisite for being a good game player, which, of course, he is.)

Both the frequency and the target of the skilled thief's offense are determined in large measure by expected payoffs. He does not want to expend effort unless it is likely to yield a suitable reward. He is, then, likely to ensure the value of his targets before attempting the offense. Thus, although the professional thief is extremely mobile, his targets are limited by what we might call his utility index. One final descriptor characterizes the professional thief, and that is his tendency toward specialization. This specialization may be in terms of technique, the safe artist for example; or in terms of property, the jewel or art thief for instance.

Greg, the major informant in the trials being prosecuted at the data site, provides a rare picture of the good burglar in operation:

Item 9 (interview with Greg, summarized in narrative form):

Greg is a jewelry and fur specialist who has taken a gemology course in order to evaluate and learn about the property he steals. He has jewelers' tools and removes stones from their settings to weigh and safely secure them. His main targets are the homes of wealthy persons who, he takes the pains to discover, have such property in their homes rather than in a bank vault. Greg spends considerable time, before contemplating a theft, researching possible victims in order to build a profile of them. He searches the social register, the social and financial pages of the newspapers, the city directory and the directories of corporate officials. He visits the neighborhoods of the wealthy at different times and days to get a feel for their living patterns. When satisfied that an individual not only is likely to possess property in which he might be interested, but also maintains a life style which includes substantial periods away from home, Greg will add him to a list of *possible* targets. This list includes the name, address and phone number of that individual as well as a notation about any item that he may have heard about or seen worn by one of the occupants (in a news photo, for example) that particularly interests him.

When he is ready to pull a job, he has a group of three or four other burglars with whom he works. They begin by calling individuals on Greg's list until they find a home with no one answering. Next they proceed toward the target, stopping at a phone booth to try the residence again. If still no one answers, the drama begins.

They are equipped with two police radios and a walkie-talkie. One of them is designated as the driver and he lets the others out of the car somewhere near the preferred approach to the house. The driver then proceeds to a phone booth and giving his cohorts approximately 10 minutes he calls the home once more. If no one or someone unfamiliar answers, he proceeds immediately to a predetermined pick-up point. If his friends answer, he gives them his number and begins waiting at the booth monitoring police calls and phoning them intermittently to be advised of their progress.

In the house the thieves again divide the labors. One of them waits for the phone call and mans the walkie-talkie if it becomes necessary for them to be separated on different floors of the house. The first step is to find the luggage owned by the occupants, for they will be using this to transport the property from the house. This done, they proceed to steal what they will, opening a safe if that is necessary or merely lifting what is around of value. Their ease of operation will depend on what they have calculated to be the maximum time they will have to operate inside. Thus, if they know the occupants to be at a social function, they will use the luxury of several hours to do a thorough job. If, however, they have determined that their victims are out dining, they may allow themselves less time to complete the job and execute their exit.

When they have finished, they notify their driver with whom they have been in intermittent contact, and proceed to the arranged pick-up point, leaving as they came, through a side door or a back window with suitcases in hand. Anything that they decide is of little value, costume jewelry for example picked up by mistake, is put back in the suitcases and bag and baggage is taken to another predetermined safe place and disposed of. (Their preference was for a desolated wharf area from which they would drop the merchandise they didn't want into a swift-flowing channel.)

If we look next at police strategies versus the good burglar, it should not be hard to understand why the game we derive will be highly unfavorable to the police. Strategy 1 (hang-out surveillance), for example, yields a slight advantage to the police only because the class of professional thieves is a finite group over which some degree of surveillance is not impossible. It may even be possible to gain some significant information from some of the movements within this group as, for example, when thieves are considering a particular business target and someone with a specialized skill is needed. If this individual, not a usual cohort, is seen associating with this group, that information might later prove valuable. Generally, however, such surveillance efforts are most likely only to confirm suspicions already held by the police concerning who works with whom, and not provide evidence linking these individuals to specific crimes.

Similarly with police strategy 4 (reliance on informants). Once the crime is known to the police, it may be so characteristic or may exhibit such a skill level that certain suspects are immediately brought to the detective's mind. An informant may be able to confirm those suspicions, but his ability to provide evidence to support his "knowledge" and his willingness to come forward are likely to be remote.

Strategy 2 (patrolling target areas) is self-defeating for two reasons. To begin with, the professional thief goes to great lengths to ensure that his presence on a premises is far from apparent, making detection of this fact a matter of luck. Also the probable targets of the professional are numerous, and, in the example just discussed, at least somewhat indeterminate until just before the offense is committed. Employment of this strategy would suggest trying to outguess the thief at his own game (the possibilities of error being great), or attempting to cover all the possibilities (a highly inefficient strategy). Left with strategy 3, it should be obvious that once the crime is reported, the trail is already cold and the damage is done; and although a suggestion of the culprits is clear, the professional thief generally leaves no specific calling card at the scene, such as fingerprints, to link him definitively to the crime. This strategy is also of little help.

We are faced in dealing with the good burglar with the 4 x 2 game shown in Table 27, pitting the four police strategies against two for the thief: the high-value residence and the high-value business. The solution to this game indicates that each side can fare best by pursuing the pure strategies, number 1 for the police and number 1 for the thief. It is interesting to note that indeed these are the two most frequent strategies employed by these players at the data site. In doing so, the value of the game will be zero—they will break even with each other. This is thought to be an optimistic picture of this game, depending essentially on how one evaluates the efficiency with which the police use the intelligence information they gather in their surveillance efforts. In other words, the key to this game is how close the police can come to capitalizing on the potentialities of strategy 1. Here we have given them the benefit of the doubt (conservatively, however) of being able to, at least some of the time, put two and two together and get some payoff from their observations. If we had been more pessimistic on this point, the game would have a minus value indicating that payoffs would average to the good burglar most of the time. This is probably the more likely situation. For example, the trials in which Greg is now testifying are concerned with thefts from 1967 through 1969. By June 1971, none of them had been cleared and would most likely have remained so except that he agreed to testify. This situation, however, in which a thief is willing to inform against his cohorts is not so frequent that we can leave the police versus professional thief game with an optimistic feeling.

TABLE 27:   THE THEFT GAME - TYPE C:
            POLICE VERSUS GOOD BURGLAR

GOOD BURGLAR

POLICE	S_1 High-value residence	S_2 High-value business[a]
S_1 Hang-out surveillance	breakeven	+
S_2 Target patrols	-	-
S_3 Wait for crime report	-	-
S_4 Rely on informants	-	-

[a]The "rationality" of the good burglar makes only high value "scores" his target choices. Because he is also biased against volume theft, he is similarly unlikely to engage in warehouse or hijacking thefts.

Before undertaking a general evaluation of the conventional view of theft, it is necessary to consider one more game, which although not directly suggested by that conceptualization appears to flow from it. We call this the type D theft game or "we" versus "they." We intimated this game earlier when we said that we would consider the citizen to be represented in the theft game by the police. There has been a significant development in the past four or five years, however, that suggests that this may not indeed be the case.

Public-opinion surveys and magazine stories increasingly indicate that the average citizenry tends to view the police as fairly impotent in solving thefts and have opted instead to take their own measures against the thief.[10] Today citizen strategies are decidedly more passive than in the past. What citizens are doing generally is fortifying their homes with security alarms, sophisticated locks, guard dogs, and watchmen; when a crime does occur, personal property insurance acts as a buffer against losses due to theft. Increasingly, the police are being edged out of the theft game, notified only to allow the citizen to comply with the requirements necessary to file an insurance loss statement and be compensated. In some cases the police are more than ignored, often being subverted in their efforts by the crime victim. Witness the following:

Item 10 (police activity report):

Contacted Mr. Smith again re their recent burglary, wanted he and his wife to look at George's (suspect) van and some mug shots. Said they didn't have time, were leaving for Florida on vacation and didn't know when they'd return.

Such behavior has given the theft game a distinct "we versus they" connotation, whose effect on life styles is only beginning to be appreciated. We shall only present this game and dispense with solving it, because it has a terribly self-defeating quality some elements of which defy precise measurement. This game is set up in Table 28.

The idea of this game, of course, is for *us* to discourage *them* — deterrence, in the criminologist's vocabulary. Our real potential for success in this game, against an adversary who makes it his business

TABLE 28: THE THEFT GAME - TYPE D:
"WE" versus "THEY"

THEY

WE	S_1 Addict stealing	S_2 Semi-Skilled burglar stealing	S_3 Professional thief stealing
S_1 Lock systems			
S_2 Guard dogs			
S_3 Alarm systems			
S_4 Theft insurance			

to be informed on the latest security devices and other fortifications we might adopt, may be gleaned from the following police anecdote:

Item 11 (summarized by author):

A large apartment building had experienced a series of thefts. Because entry could only be had through the front door of the apartments (there being no fire escape possibilities), and because the doors entered showed no evidence of force, both the police and the residents suspected an inside key job, either by the superintendent or someone having access to his keys. They continued to maintain these suspicions until one of the residents, peaking through her peep hole, observed the true thief at work. She waited until he had made his entry and then called the police.

The culprit was a twelve year old boy who, armed with a knife, a dentist's mirror, and a coat hanger, had perfected a method for lifting the peephole slot, inserting the mirror and guiding the coat hanger to disengage the lock system.

The child was undoubtedly a prodigy, but it becomes fairly obvious that we will probably never devise a security system which the truly prodigious thief (or twelve year old) cannot learn to master. It should also be obvious that the marginal utility of such fortifying activities takes a definite plunge soon after they are initiated.[11] If this new wrinkle in the theft game must be evaluated, then, we must give it an even lower score than the more traditional manifestations of the conventional view of theft.

THE CONVENTIONAL VIEW OF THEFT: AN ASSESSMENT

We have seen the conventional view of theft pitted against the addict, in which it was deemed inappropriate; the known burglar, in which it drew a slight advantage; and against the professional thief in which it at best breaks even. That is not too distinguished a record, and yet it may not be entirely clear to the reader just how this seemingly useful concept is debilitated. We do not maintain that this view's consideration of the thief is unjustified, illogical, or erroneous.

What is argued here, however, is that *exclusive* concentration on the thief yields a myopic view of the process of theft, a view which draws the boundaries of the crime too tightly around that individual. It is a view that tends to consider each incident of theft as a unique event, determined and constrained by the motivations, needs, and skills of the perpetrator. The "conventional view of theft" prescribes a response to this crime which largely consists of a fairly sophisticated sorting process, linking one individual (or one group of individuals) with each event as it occurs.

It is the detective who becomes the main agent in this sorting procedure. Through his experience, knowledge of individual thieves, sources of information, and often "hunches" the detective can take the elements of a theft event and in most cases move toward the description of a set of suspects. He will do this by systematically excluding those portions of the theft population that for one reason or another could not have committed the crime. One further example, the case of the successful assault on the vaults of a large and well-protected fur storage firm, will perhaps best suggest the procedures and problems associated with the conventional view of theft.

Police investigation of the incident reveals that the firm's sophisticated alarm system was tampered with and neutralized by the perpetrators, that the vaults were entered by means of an acetylene torch, and that a large van was used to transport the stolen furs from the premises. The finesse of the original entry allows the detective to eliminate many persons in the theft population whose skills are not so sophisticated. That coupled with the technique used on the vaults suggests to him the combined skill levels of two very small groups of able thieves. The overall organization of the task continues to support his suspicion that the job was carried out by at least two very experienced and technically adroit thieves, perhaps acting in concert with others of lesser abilities. A quick check of those individuals competent in the neutralization of alarm systems yields, let us suppose, two good suspects since other individuals in this class can be accounted for either because they were observed elsewhere, are imprisoned, or for other reasons cannot be placed at the crime site. Similarly, of that small class of so-called "burn men" in the safe-cracking trade, all but three can be accounted for. The net begins to close in, drawing a circle around a much smaller group of suspects and their associates. Intelligence reports from the month preceding the incident further reveal that two members of the new suspect set had been observed together both in routine car checks and at various bars and night spots.[12] In addition, each had been seen in the company of two younger men later identified as burglars known to the police.

Within one or two weeks of the theft, rumors from the theft microcosm itself as well as information provided by informants indicates that these same four individuals have recently displayed new-found financial assets. The police pick up the two young burglars and under interrogation[13] one of them confesses to the theft and implicates his three accomplices. As it turns out the confessing thief does not know what happened to the furs nor is he aware of the origin or eventual destination of the truck. On the basis of his willingness to testify, however, his accomplices are persuaded by the district attorney to plead guilty and all are sentenced.

The above case is quite simply drawn. The police cannot ordinarily proceed with such ease. Rarely, for example, can so much of the theft population be immediately excluded on an initial sort; rarely can those individuals finally included in the suspect set be so easily and reliably accounted for; and rarely is the willing confessant so available. The utility of the above case is not in its approximation of the successfulness of the typical theft investigation, but rather in its portrayal of the elements of the responses to theft which the conventional view of theft considers essential.

For the conventional view of theft, the above case is "closed." The operating agencies of the criminal justice system have accomplished what this conceptualization of property theft requires of them: they have caught the thief. Our concern, however, is not so much with the capacity of the conventional view of theft to apprehend offenders (although our prior analysis questions whether it is generally as effective as the illustration above might suggest). Instead what becomes disconcerting is the realization that "catching thieves" is the major preoccupation of this view of property crime. Whether it is successful or not, we wonder if it really makes much difference. For behind the simple logic of the conventional view of theft, behind its seeming efficiency and apparent rationality, lie three major weaknesses for dealing with property crime.

1. The primary weakness of the conventional view of theft is its post hoc quality. Fully half of the time, the thrust of the con-

cept is not engaged in understanding a crime, but in responding to the fact of its occurrence. The investigation of theft, therefore, becomes a historical search—a search to link a "who" with a given set of circumstances, having little time or interest to determine the "why" or "how." Because so much time is spent looking back on an event, it cannot adequately interpret even the eventualities of that single event much less a more general future. The anticipatory capability (what we might designate as crime prevention capability) of this view is thereby greatly reduced. Each time there is a theft, a new cycle of search is begun but it does not involve any new undertaking. Instead more investigations of past events are recorded and the whole archeological bias of the process is reinforced. And, since no new information is ever really generated, the process continues to repeat itself, doggedly following the same procedures, over the same cold trails toward the same dead ends.

2. The second broad shortcoming of the conventional view of theft is its assumption that if and when the thief is caught, the game is over. In other words, one has solved the theft when one catches the thief. This tends only to reinforce and confirm the notion that each theft is a unique event and mitigates against its being interpreted in terms of a broad range of similar events. Merely attaching responsibility for a theft to an individual or group of individuals does not, after all, explain two important elements of the crime: opportunity and incentive. And if one has not understood these two elements, he will still not have "solved" that crime. Nor will he have made any headway in preventing similar acts in the future.

3. The final weakness of the conventional view of theft is its failure to consider the *system* of crime of which a theft is only a part. It sees theft essentially as a static situation, ignoring the dynamics of the stolen property marketplace. It considers only the fact that property was taken; it ponders not *where that property was taken to*. And, failing this, it misses the whole point.

An addict does not steal your stereo to listen to his records; he steals it for its negotiability—the means (money) he will get to acquire what he has better use for. The professional thief does not steal Renoirs to decorate his apartment but to satisfy the art pleasures of someone else. The theft is only the beginning of a very intricate system in which stolen property is acquired, converted, redistributed, and reintegrated into the legitimate property stream. This system involves not only "cops and robbers," but also several levels of marketers and customers. It requires a set of tasks (and their necessary functionaries) which the theft concept does not even begin to contemplate, much less appreciate. Because of this, it isn't hard to understand why, even when the conventional view of theft does its best, it doesn't do very much. It ignores most of the iceberg in favor of focusing on its most visible part.

The kinds of loose ends that were left in the case described above are typical of the operation of the conventional view of theft. Questions relating to the source and destination of the truck used in the theft, the destination of the furs, and even the choice of the theft target itself remain unanswered. For an explanation of these and similar other points, this view of theft relies on the idiosyncracies of the individual thief. It does this because it fails to follow the flow of the crime it is investigating. It concentrates on theft as an extraction event, ignoring completely its transfer function. In this sense, despite the apparent total utility of the conventional view of theft, its *continued acceptance* must be severely questioned. On the margin, then, this conceptualization can be seen to possess some major payoff limitations.

By clinging to its premises, without accepting a new concept of the stolen property world, we have, in effect, increasingly put ourselves in the situation that game theorists call "poor gambler's ruin." What this characterizes is the situation in which an individual has continually lost in a game to the point that it will take increasingly larger and larger investments in order to get back in the game as anything approaching an adequate adversary. For the player who has come to the table with limited assets, this is his demise. He cannot recoup his losses because he cannot get up enough capital to stay in the game.

We as a society are not nearly so poor as are many gamblers, but that does not mean that the investment which the traditional theft concept requires may not mean our ruin. It is time we stopped trying to escalate our resources and began looking for a new game.

PROPERTY THEFT: AN ALTERNATIVE VIEW

Having rejected the conventional view of theft as unsuitable for con-

tinued acceptance, we offer an alternative. It will come as little sur-
prise that the alternative conceptualization of property theft will place
greater emphasis on the fence of stolen goods than on the thief. This is
not only because the fence has been the subject of attention but also
because in so doing it is believed that the above-noted shortcomings of
the conventional view of theft can be diminished.

As we have seen, the fence is an important figure in the criminal life
of the thief. At minimum, he has an implicit influence over what the
thief will steal by mediating the rewards received for theft activities.
Because the fence will tend to specialize in certain lines or types of
products, the thief's targets will tend to reflect the preferences of the
fence(s) he knows. By providing the thief with information and assistance in committing a theft, the fence's influence can become quite
explicit and directive. This is particularly true where the fence sets up
a victim for theft, or in the case of the so-called hijack where the fence
has orchestrated the participation of many marginal persons in the
successful diversion of property.[14] While the fence is either implicitly
or explicitly influencing the type of property stolen by the thief, he is
providing that individual with a critical service, that of allowing the
thief to divest himself of stolen property in a timely fashion. For this
service the fence is himself duly rewarded, as reflected in the low
prices he pays for the stolen goods.

The network mechanism demonstrated how the fence exerts power
in contemporary property theft and shapes a thief's criminal career by
either limiting or expanding his access to crime partners or to the
acquisition of new skills. The fence, then, is the controlling influence
over both the thief and his theft activities. As such, the fence of stolen
goods emerges as the prime mover in property theft.

In order to accommodate the central role played by the fence both
literally and functionally in property theft, the new conceptualization
of this crime area is called the stolen property system (hereafter SPS)
view of theft. The SPS is defined as that set of individuals *and* their
interactions which locate, plan, facilitate, and execute the extraction
of property from a rightful owner *and* its transfer to a new owner.[15]
By definition, then, the SPS view of theft is broader in scope than the
conventional view, since it considers not merely one individual or one
type of individual (the thief) but rather a set of individuals performing
various roles in interaction with each other. In addition, the SPS view
of theft concerns how the activities of these individuals relate not only

to the extraction event but also to the transfer function of property crime. The comprehensive perspective of the SPS view of property theft, therefore, overcomes the weaknesses associated with more traditional views. Figure 2 (introduced earlier as Figure 1)[16] demonstrates why this is true and usefully distinguishes the conventional from the SPS view of property theft.

With regard to Figure 2, the conventional view of property theft considers only the extreme left portion of the schematic—the actions of the thief taken against a piece of property in the extraction event. In doing so, this view counsels the criminal justice system to focus exclusively on that event in order to probe for a solution to the crime. This becomes fateful indeed since the crime itself continues to move through the schematic with little pursuit by official agencies. In addition, some of the more critical interactions and elements of the crime follow the extraction event but remain virtually ignored by the conventional view.

The SPS view of property theft on the other hand encompasses the full schematic of Figure 2. Since it seeks to describe the interactive situation through which property theft is successfully perpetrated, it moves beyond the extraction event to the exchange process. In this way, the SPS view gives greater shape and meaning to the original extraction itself by accounting for the incentive system supporting it. But the SPS view does not stop here. It continues to follow the crime to its intended resolution, to the transfer of stolen property to a new owner(s). Thus, it considers the marketing and redistribution events over which the fence maintains control and direction.

Because the SPS view of property theft accounts for the totality of events (and individuals involved in them) that make up a property theft, it mitigates the post hoc bias of the conventional view; it encompasses the structures of incentive and opportunity surrounding the crime and it focuses on the dynamic nature of the system through which property is successfully stolen and redistributed. Leaving behind the static parameters of the extraction event, it demonstrates the degree to which property theft is less dependent on the random preferences or idiosyncracies of the individual thief than it is upon the direction and influence provided by the forces of demand and supply in the stolen property marketplace. Once this perspective is taken, the central role of the fence as marketing manager in property theft is appreciated and the complex system of individuals and their inter-

THE STOLEN PROPERTY SYSTEM VIEW OF PROPERTY THEFT

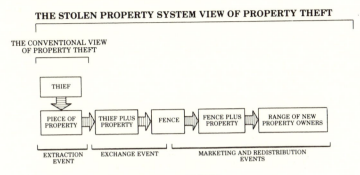

FIGURE 2. A SCHEMATIC OF PROPERTY THEFT EVENTS

actions through which property theft is accomplished and rewarded is revealed.

The stolen property system as a conceptualization counsels two important shifts in our reaction to property theft. First, it counsels a heightened awareness of the importance of *property* itself as the critical element shaping the activities of theft principals. In other words, we realize that property, not an individual, creates markets, engenders distribution channels, determines pricing policies, and influences the content of theft statistics. Second, the stolen property system concept demands that greater attention be given the key mechanism through which virtually all property-related decisions are made—the fence of stolen goods. In this way, the SPS view identifies the fence as the more strategic target for official intervention in the stolen property market-place.

We have a long way to go before sound strategies for such intervention can be achieved. We have centuries of misguided folklore and conventional wisdom to overcome, decades of traditional but ineffective policing practices to refocus and redirect, and much more to learn about the potent adversary we face. The simplicity and internal consistency of the thief-centered view of theft will not be easily discarded, nor will the design of operationally effective programs reflecting the realities of the stolen property system be readily accomplished.

Both the fence and the stolen property system through which he manages theft pose significant challenges not only to the criminologist but also to those police and theft offenders who know him well. These challenges must, however, be met. As a society, we cannot afford to do otherwise.

Epilog

A new look at the world of property theft and beyond

We began by stating our goal was to take a "new look" at property theft and by indicating that the main strategy to be adopted in reaching that goal would be a "search for the contemporary receiver." We believe these have been done. We found the contemporary fence, albeit in one metropolitan area of the United States, and that has caused us to take a new look at how to view and understand property theft. The fence we found, and the way we discovered him also revealed some important considerations about the course and conduct of criminological research.

First, we learned that it is not only feasible but also valuable to pursue basic crime research through official agencies. In particular, the police detective was found to be a worthy and highly informative data source. The character of the fence, being more an operational reality for than an official statistic of, the criminal justice system, surely influenced the value of the official sources used, but it remains clear that the "able (or uncaught) criminal," as John Mack has told us, is more easily found with the aid of the police than without such assistance.

Second, we learned that analytical tools not traditionally associated with the criminologist can be extremely useful in describing and understanding criminal activities. As a corollary to this, we learned that the perspective taken by the student of crime will in large measure determine the relevance and value attached to various analytical tools. Thus, the researcher who wants to describe the individual criminal will choose far different techniques from one who wants to describe the crime itself. And he who goes in search of the cause of crime will proceed somewhat differently from the researcher interested in how the crime is accomplished and what mechanisms support and encourage it.

Finally, the fence himself has amply demonstrated a point Sutherland tried to make some time ago: that the poor, the maladjusted, the uneducated, and the unfranchised have no monopoly on criminal conduct. Indeed, the powerful, the franchised, and the well-respected businessman is equally capable of criminal activity in his own right, not to mention the support he may give to significant criminal conduct by others. In this sense Radzinowicz's admonition that those "factors and circumstances associated with crime . . . can also be associated . . . with behavior accepted as normal" (or well respected) rings very true. If we have learned nothing else, then, we should begin to understand that supporting elements, factors, and circumstances in crime are as easily derived from stable and well-regarded social and economic institutions as from deprivations associated with the ghetto; and that crime, rather than being an aberration from accepted values and norms, may in fact constitute a striking manifestation of these values and norms and of the social and economic institutions through which they are represented.

Beyond these general lessons relating to the study of crime itself, if any specific implications are believed to potentially flow from this study, they would be these; that we shall have acquired a new perspective from which to view theft, the most frequently perpetrated crime in this society; that we may better understand the course of theft as it relates to the structures of incentive and opportunity surrounding it; that we may be able to refocus enforcement efforts and redesign legislative proscriptions in the area of property crime that better reflect the dynamics of contemporary receiving and thieving; and perhaps most important, that we shall at long last have brought to light the criminal receiver of stolen property, a crime figure who has been cast in shadows for more than two hundred years.

Appendix
The data: some
notes and caveats

Because the research strategy and data used in this study are not those frequently employed by criminologists, the reader is given an opportunity to judge each separately from the research findings and analysis. What follows is a detailed description of the data made available to the author, a discussion of the caveats attached to these data, and how any inherent shortcomings were resolved and/or rationalized.

It should be reemphasized first, that the primary sources of information used in this research were "official" in nature, that is, obtained from official agents and agencies of the criminal justice system; second, that the agencies contacted and utilized (the district attorney's office and the police department) are pre-adjudicatory bodies, and finally, that much of the information to which access was given was of an investigatory nature, that is, linked to ongoing or previously conducted intelligence-gathering and surveillance activities.

From the beginning some caveats regarding the nature of the data had to be confronted. Because the data were from "official" sources, for example, they were expected to reflect a specific slant toward the individuals mentioned and discussed. This was in spite of the fact that many of those persons may never have been arrested, and if so, may remain even now unconvicted of any crime. Similarly the investigative quality of the records meant that they contained information some of which could not be validated in any way, emerging from sources with whom the author could have no contact or based on the gratuitous assessments of the official agents collecting it. Given this situation, the researcher had two major problems to tackle. The first regarded the confidentiality of the accessible data. Confidentiality was maintained by using a coding procedure which substituted numerals for specific individuals in all notes except for a carefully guarded code book (now destroyed). Names used in the text do not correspond to the actual individuals studied. Any direct relationship of same to any persons, either living or dead, is unintended.

The second problem concerned the reliability of sources of information. It is doubtful that this issue can ever really be resolved to everyone's satisfaction (an issue limited not only to data of the kinds used here). The author resolved the reliability problem in the following manner. The data were considered to be reasonably reliable (that is, capable of supporting the present research) given certain structural constraints on the agencies involved. For example, the author was given access to information on which both the police and the district attorney's office either had acted or were presently acting; and upon which each agency could expect to be evaluated. Thus, the prosecutor would be expected to yield a reasonable number of convictions as a result of his three-year investigative effort and his convening of a special grand jury. Similarly, the police would be expected to make a reasonable number of arrests based on the quality of their investigative activities. Both of these structural, evaluative expectations were thought to mitigate the possibility of their having collected and included erroneous or clearly false information in their files.

In addition, whenever confusing or contradictory information emerged the researcher questioned the respondents with regard to its validity. Given the status of some of the persons involved, it was thought unlikely that the agency sources would have initiated and continued their investigative procedures with "shaky" or possibly unreliable information. Since the data used consisted of information on which official agencies had made or would make decisions an inherent control on that data's validity and potential usefulness was seen as operating. After having read, observed, and interacted with the agents and agencies involved, the researcher was certain that the agents and agencies assumed their information was credible and accurate. To what extent their information reflects "reality" relies on the trust one puts in their perceptions.

The author was and is prepared to trust the data sources first on the basis of their expertise, since they, after all, deal with the "reality" of crime full-time; and second, because it is believed that what a professional reports and files among peers will be at least as credible as what a respondent anonymously either tells the researcher or reports to higher sources of authority.

The actual data used must be described briefly. Data from the district attorney's office consisted of three kinds. The first was lengthy tape recorded transcripts of the statements given by the several informants in the cases presented to the special grand jury convened at the data site to investigate a series of major thefts. These statements (many were hundreds of pages long) were recounts by the burglar-informants of their theft activities and experiences with fences over approximately a three-year period. They were used to construct the cases presented to the grand jury which in turn handed down indictments on 44 persons for criminal receiving of stolen property and allied offenses.

The second data type consisted of the author's observation of four of the cases prosecuted by the district attorney in different stages of the adjudicatory proceedings, followed by a discussion with either the assistant prosecutor or an investigator. It should be mentioned that it was impossible to monitor all of the cases or even to see the four cases observed through conclusion. Other issues relating to the author's personal safety also somewhat diminished the utility of the case-observation strategy. However, the few observations made, in conjunction with the official discussions, proved valuable and interesting particularly in setting a tone rather than in providing substantive information.

The third and most valuable source of information from the district attorney's office was the access to interview the chief informant witness in the trials—the young, extremely professional burglar elsewhere identified as Greg. A highly intelligent and articulate individual, Greg became an important interview respondent, filling in many gaps and questions left by official records and giving a rare glimpse of the world of thievery and fencing from the good burglar's perspective.

The second, and most heavily relied on, primary source of information was the records and files of the Safe and Burglary Squad of the local police agency. This twelve-member squad consisted of detectives and detective sergeants, and was under the direct supervision of the Chief of Detectives. As a "headquarters squad" it was not limited within the city to any specifically defined bailiwick, as was the case with the four "district" detective squads. In addition, headquarters squads are assigned particular types of caseloads. Thus the squad at the data site was responsible for burglary and safe-job investigations.

The problem of investigative overlap between district and headquarters units was lessened during the research period. Departmental reorganization allocated all burglaries over $1,200 in value of goods stolen to the headquarters squad, leaving all others in the hands of the relevant district squads. In other words, the headquarters squad detectives were confined to investigations involving primarily the "better" or "good" burglar.

The standard operating procedures of the squad are as follows:

Each day consists of two tours of duty, the day crew and the night crew; each crew generally has four detectives split into two-man groups. Tours of duty and individual crew members are rotated although personal preferences for work partners seem to have emerged over time making certain pairs of detectives likely to work the same schedule.

After reporting to headquarters to check what has transpired or what instructions may have been left by the previous shift, the crew goes out on the street. If it is a day crew, its work generally will consist of continuing investigations, interviewing complainants, checking the scenes of burglaries, and sometimes responding to radio calls. Day crews may also have members detailed to courts for hearings or trials. Most of a day crew's efforts appear to be directed to either the initiation or continuation of investigations into specific crimes. This contrasts the night crew's activities which concentrate (unless otherwise directed) on structured surveillance of the good burglar and his haunts in order to gather intelligence information relating to the movements and associations of persons in the theft microcosm.

The different emphases of the crews reflect the hours of the "publics" they are responding to. Hence day crews respond to complainants and court matters during the business day, while night crews respond to the theft population. Interestingly enough, the flavor of these two publics is reflected as well in the reports written by detectives. Following each tour, the crews meet again in the squad room to file their "activity reports," complete accounts of the crew's activities during the tour of duty. Each item included carries the name or names of the detective(s) involved. For example,

Jan. 8, 1970 (Dets. Jones and Smith)
Continued investigation of break-in at home of —— etc.

These are typed (or phoned into a central typing pool to be typed) and entered into two monthly "books" of the squad's activities, one for the squad room and one filed with the chief of detectives. This is the "book" to which the next crew will refer before it goes out on the street. As might be expected the activity reports of day crews are for the most part terse and "official," recounting procedural duties required by theft investigations. It is in the activity reports of night crews that the personality of the detective as moralist, comedian, and, yes, as criminologist comes through. Here are found the anecdotes, the reproductions of actual dialogues with burglars, the asides and the conclusions about the "reality" out there. These reports tend to be lengthy and rich in detail, and often have a distinctive literary style.

There appear to be two reasons for differences in the tone and style of day versus night crew reports (even when written by the same detective). First, when engaged in responsive activities—such as the investigation of a crime scene, the interviewing of witnesses or complainants, the serving of warrants—the detective's activities seem justified and need little explanation. When engaged in surveillance, observation, or intelligence gathering for its own sake, however, the detective seems to feel the need to fully explain his activities, often hinting at his purposes and always including as much detail as possible. Apparently, detail is thought to connote "good" observation and therefore to be justificatory in and of itself. Second, it was obvious that detectives enjoy interacting with what they call the "theft element," sending ripples through it when possible or giving it something to think about. Similarly, the possibility of catching a good burglar off guard is positively delightful.

The items in the squad's "book" of activity reports eventually find their way to one of three destinations. First, items containing no information regarding any known or suspected criminal will remain in the book to be stored with previous monthly activity books. All other items revert to one of two files in the squad room. Items referring to arrests, warrants served, suspected involvements in crimes of specific persons will be reproduced in that individual's activity report file, if there is one. If he does not have a file, but is considered a likely offender, then a file is begun. If there has been a previous arrest, a mug photo (or its number) may be included. If several persons are noted in an activity report item, the same item is added to each file. With the exception of a print-out of prior arrests, when available, this will be the extent of information found in an individual's activity report file. It is estimated that the squad has several thousand persons recorded.

Once an individual's prominence in activity reports and/or his arrests become frequent, a separate personal file is begun on him. This is the third destination of activity report information that refers to the squad's best known clientele (the active and the skilled burglar). Though most information in these files is similar to that in the activity report files, it is always supplemented by prior arrest records and summary offender data. In addition, personal files are the repositories for special intelligence reports and summaries of what is "known" about the individual, his associates and his skills. Even activity report format data are different for these familiar offenders, generally being more detailed. Examples of detailed information are news clippings of the individual's arrests, phone numbers seized on his person, and legitimate news items such as his purchase of a home, a divorce, or otherwise. Whatever the detective can find out, observe, or glean about the subject of a personal file will be contained therein, in chronological order if possible, such that one begins to feel as though he knows the individual personally. These files, while fed by activity reports, remain intelligence files in the sense that they remain in the squad and contain the squad's thoughtful and detailed account of just what an individual thief is all about, is likely to do, or has probably done already. They are filled with the detective's certainties that he cannot prove and so with his frustrations and thwarted efforts as well.

It should be stressed once again that since the squad is a burglary detail its prime responsibility, caseload, and the majority of its files concern burglars. The author was, therefore, surprised to learn of and grateful to be granted access to its files related to fences. Files on fences are generated a little differently than are burglary files. First, criminal receivers are indexed separately and labeled "alleged fences." These separate cards contain either the names of persons, businesses, or both that the squad believes or has reason to believe are fences of stolen property. The information may vary from card to card depending on the nature of the initial entry. An informant's phone call, for example, may give only an address or a nickname and if the information has not been considered important it may not be followed up. Thus some cards in the fence file were totally uninterpretable; others, however, often contained a summary of information that was quite informative. Out of a possible 175 cards, however, after duplications arising from dual listings of a fence as well as his business and after little prospect of unraveling some of the barest of cards, some 25 or so names had to be immediately eliminated. From here, the individual names of persons or places were coded and the cross-file investigative research begun. Most of the remaining sample of fences were, upon checking, to be found in either activity report files or personal files, resting silently between burglars. Thus the information described above as being typical of these files on burglars is precisely the type of information existing on fences. Not all fences, of course, had personal files—just as not all burglars have—and the researcher had to be somewhat ruthless in the rejection of some members of the sample for whom activity report files had been started but had never really amounted to anything. Generally, where information scarcity was confronted, the following rule of thumb was developed: if you can validate this piece of information in at least one other source include it; if not, reject it.

The sources used for such purposes and eventually to run checks on the whole of the data were: (1) files on burglars in which separate notations regarding the fence were included but not transferred to the fence's file (this occurred often enough to make it worthwhile to check), (2) the city directory (a virtual gold mine of information about the residences, occupations, locations, and business ownership of persons in the city), and (3) the detectives themselves (especially when a potentially vital piece of information neared rejection for want of an explanation). When questioned detectives could supply information that had not yet been noted in recent activity reports. A sample of approximately 115 fences (depending upon the variable isolated) was generated.

The researcher was more than gratified by the quality and quantity of the information compiled by the detectives. Even though the fence is a sidelight for the squad officially, he is considered by detectives to be the key to property theft and so they collect information about him with something of a vengeance. It was the hypocritical "legitimacy" of the receiver that seemed to gnaw at the detective, making him the cynical observer of that individual. Often the level of animosity of the detective was more easily aroused by the fence than by the thief himself. It was obvious that the squad felt at once angered and powerless in the face of the fence whom they considered a wily and elusive criminal.

Whatever their motives, it was clear that detectives had collected a good deal of information about local fences. They brought a detail to their descriptions in some cases that was unexplainable, particularly since, with the exception of a few notorious individuals, receivers are not their main enforcement targets. It was concluded that, as in the case of the skilled burglar, the detectives tended to use detail and lengthy description of seemingly irrelevant (at least to them) facts in a justificatory manner and in order to become intimately familiar with the subject described. In any case, their fence files proved to be a most interesting, revealing, and highly substantive source of information about the contemporary fence.

A few further limitations to the data can be summarized as follows:

1. The information relied upon was of a current (or recent past) investigative nature and hence conclusions reached by its authors or the researcher may never have been demonstrated or proven in the judicial setting.

2. The information used relates to that part of the fencing in-industry *known to the authorities studied* and that neither its relationship to the total population "out there" nor its degree of representativeness of that population is known.

3. The data used describe criminal receiving and property theft relationships in one metropolitan area of the United States which, though not considered necessarily unique, may limit its generalizability.

Notes

INTRODUCTION

1. Sir John Fielding, testimony before the Committee of 1770, English Parliament (Commons), *House of Commons Journal*, 32: 784, 798, 874, 878-883.

2. Patrick Colquhoun, *A Treatise on the Police of the Metropolis*, 7th ed., (1806), reprint. (Patterson Smith, 1969), p. 289. Emphasis added.

3. Association of Grand Jurors of New York County, *The Criminal Receiver of Stolen Goods - Source of Organized Crime and Creator of Criminals*, p. vii.

4. President's Commission on Law Enforcement and Administration of Justice, *The Challenge of Crime in a Free Society*, Report of the Commission, p. 46.

5. Jerome Hall, "Theft, Law and Society—1968," *American Bar Association Journal*, 54 (October 1968): 962. Emphasis added.

6. This definition is a representative composite of receiving laws found in the United States.

7. Jerome Hall, *Theft, Law and Society*, p. 155.

8. Ibid.

9. Carl Klockars, "The Fence: Caveat Emptor, Caveat Vendor," (Paper delivered at the American Society of Criminology meetings, November 1970, Caracas, Venezuela), p. 8.

10. U.S., Congress, Senate, Select Committee on Small Business, *Criminal Redistribution Systems and Their Economic Impact on Small Business, Hearings*, 93rd Cong., 1st sess., 1 and 2 May 1973, p. 8.

11. Ibid.

12. John Mack, "The Able Criminal" (Paper delivered to the Current Research Seminar, VIth World Criminological Congress, Madrid, Spain, 1970), p. 10.

13. Ibid.

14. Ibid., pp. 9-10.

15. In addition, some investigative files of the prosecutor were utilized and judicial proceedings attended. As explained in the Appendix, however, this information was helpful primarily in setting a tone rather than in yielding substantive data.

16. This was primarily true because of confidential information about the informants known to the author.

17. Donald R. Cressey, *Criminal Organization: Its Elementary Forms*, p. 19. Emphasis added.

18. Ibid., p. 12.

19. Ibid.

20. Mary McIntosh, "Changes in the Organization of Thieving," in *Images of Deviance*, ed., Stanley Cohen, (Baltimore: Penguin, 1971), pp. 98-133.

21. Ibid., p. 114.

22. Ibid., p. 100.

23. Ibid., p. 111.

24. Ibid., p. 126. Emphasis added.

25. Cressey, *Criminal Organization*, p. 62, fn2.

26. McIntosh, "Changes in Organization of Thieving," pp. 127-128.

27. Cressey, *Criminal Organization*, p. 18.

28. Jerome Hall was the stimulus behind the adoption of a functional perspective.

29. Colquhoun, *A Treatise on the Police of the Metropolis*, p. 155.

30. Fielding testimony before the Committee of 1770, English Parliament, *House of Commons Journal*, (1770) 32: 784-798, 874, 878-883.

31. Association of Grand Jurors of New York County, *The Criminal Receiver of Stolen Goods - Source of Organized Crime and Creator of Criminals*, p. vii. Emphasis added.

32. Michael Lewis, Structural Deviance and Normative Conformity: The 'Hustle' and the 'Gang'," in *Crime in the City*, ed., Daniel Glaser, (New York: Harper and Row, 1970), pp. 179-180.

33. Sir Leon Radzinowicz, "Economic Pressures," in *The Criminal in Society*, eds., Leon Radzinowicz and Marvin Wolfgang (New York: Basic Books, 1971), pp. 420-442. Emphasis added.

34. See Chapter 2, Tables 3, 4, 5, and 6.

CHAPTER 1

1. Although the English common law recognized the taking of property as a specific crime as early as the tenth century, criminal receiving was considered an offense ancillary to theft, with the receiver punished as an accessory after the fact until 1827.

2. See, for example: Patrick Colquhoun, *A Treatise on the Police of the Metropolis*, 7th ed., reprint (London: Patterson Smith, 1969), pp. 288-309; Association of Grand Jurors of New York County, *The Criminal Receiver of Stolen Goods - Source of Organized Crime and Creator of Criminals*; and Jerome Hall, "Theft, Law and Society—1968," *American Bar Association Journal*, 54 (October 1968): 960-967.

3. This is with the possible exception of the following: Hall, *Theft, Law and Society*;

and Mary McIntosh, "Changes in the Organization of Thieving," in *Images of Deviance*, ed., Stanley Cohen, pp. 98-133.

4. Details regarding the life and actions of Jonathan Wild are taken from Daniel Defoe, *The King of the Pirates*; William MacAdoo *The Procession to Tyburn*; and Gerald Howson, *Thief-Taker General. The Rise and Fall of Jonathan Wild*. The Howson source is most relied on since he must be credited with the most exhaustive and least value-ridden account of Wild's life. In addition, much of the discussion is based in substance on the author's contribution to a paper coauthored with Duncan Chappell entitled, "'No Questions Asked': A Consideration of the Crime of Criminal Receiving," *Crime and Delinquency*, 20, No. 2 (April 1974): 157-168.

5. A place of confinement for London's debtors in the seventeenth and eighteenth centuries.

6. Howson, *Thief-Taker General*, p. 42.

7. Ibid., p. 37.

8. Ibid., p. 10.

9. Howson's explanation is that Wild was actually quite ill by 1725, suffering from some of the advanced stages of syphilis. He concludes that Wild had really lost touch with reality and by the time of his trial was fairly incoherent. Wild's contemporaries chose not to deal with his probable medical condition, preferring instead to attribute his peculiar behavior during the trial and execution to the sheer evil of the man.

10. These three elements were initially conceived and developed by the author in Chappell and Walsh, "'No Questions Asked': A Consideration of the Crime of Criminal Receiving." pp. 165-168.

11. Hall, *Theft, Law and Society*, p. 195.

12. The prevalent business combines of the time were the trading companies which existed not only through public subscription, but with government support and assistance.

13. Howson, *Thief-Taker General*, p. 283.

14. It finally happened in 1827 under the statutes 7 and 8, George IV, C. 29.

15. Defoe, *King of the Pirates* (New York: Jenson Society 1901), p. 231.

16. Ibid., p. 243.

17. Ibid., p. 274.

18. Commentators differ on the date of the first staging of the play. We have used the chronology and history of the work as described by the editors of the Regents' Restoration Series at the University of Nebraska whose version of the play was used as the source document. John Gay, *The Beggar's Opera*, Regents' Restoration Series (Lincoln, Nebraska, 1969).

19. At one point MacHeath stresses his similarity to high men of state as follows:

Since laws were made for every degree,
To curb vice in others, as well as me,
I wonder we han't better company upon Tyburn tree!
But gold from law can take out the sting
And if rich men, like us, were to swing,
'Twould thin the land, such numbers to string upon Tyburn tree!

As found in Gay, *The Beggar's Opera*, p. 79.

20. One of Peachum's stinging references to the legal profession is found in Gay, *The Beggar's Opera*, at p. 7:

> A lawyer is an honest employment; so is mine. Like me too he acts in a double capacity, both against rogues and for 'em. For 'tis but fitting that we should protect and encourage cheats, since we live by them.

21. Gay, *The Beggar's Opera*, p. 23.

22. William Robert Irwin, *The Making of "Jonathan Wild"*, p. 27.

23. Ibid., p. 37; see also Gay, *The Beggar's Opera*, p. xxiv.

24. Henry Fielding, *History of the Life of the Late Mr. Jonathan Wild*.

25. Charles Dickens, *Oliver Twist* (London: Oxford University 1949).

26. Ibid., p. xi, as noted by Humphrey House in his introduction to the edition of Dickens' work used here.

27. Ibid., p. xiv, as quoted by Humphrey House.

28. Sir William Holdsworth, *A History of English Law*, 5th ed., reprint (London: Methuen, 1966), 5:72.

29. Holdsworth, *A History of English Law*, 15:198. This law required pawnbrokers to record the names and addresses of their customers as well as of all goods accepted and to detain those persons who appeared to be in suspicious possession of property.

30. Colquhoun, *Police of the Metropolis*, p. 301.

31. Ibid., p. 115.

32. Ibid., p. 116.

33. Ibid., p. 120.

34. Ibid., p. 292.

35. Ibid., p. 321.

36. "The Report of the Society for the Suppression of Mendicity," *The Quarterly Review*, 64 (1839): 360.

37. Ibid., pp. 358-359.

38. Bertolt Brecht and Kurt Weill, *The Three-Penny Opera* (New York: Grove Press, 1964).

39. Sentencing hearing attended by the author at the data site, January 1972.

40. For a good summary of many such views, see Marvin Wolfgang and Franco Ferracuti, *The Subculture of Violence*, pp. 47-51.

CHAPTER 2

1. This census category was thought to most closely approximate the functional role of the criminal receiver with a legitimate occupational endeavor. Since the use of census data is for broad rather than specific comparisons, a more precise status clarification was not thought needed. The statistics used are taken from U.S., Department of Commerce, Bureau of the Census, *Characteristics of the Population*, vol. 1, New York, part 34, section 2, (Washington, D.C.: Department of Commerce, March 1973), Table 174; and refer specifically to the Standard Metropolitan Statistical Area of the data site.

2. Ibid., the actual census figures for the data site are as follows:

White female managers and administrators (except farm)	5390
Black Female managers and administrators (except farm)	228
Black male managers and administrators (except farm)	423

3. This phenomenon finds excellent and detailed treatment in Alan R. Andreasen, *Inner City Business*, see particularly, p. 9.

4. Betty C. Churchill, "Rise in the Business Population," *Survey of Current Business*, May 1959, pp. 17-18.

5. Each of these subgroups finds fuller treatment at Chapter 4.

CHAPTER 3

1. See Chapter 2, Table 5.

2. Ibid.

3. We use Hall's distinction between the lay receiver and the professional receiver, the former being one who buys stolen property for personal use and the latter who buys it for the purpose of resale to others. This distinction might be extended to the fence and his customers with the latter being considered lay receivers. See Jerome Hall, *Theft, Law and Society*, p. 155.

4. We have not here accepted the premise that the fence's activities enjoy significant social support or tolerance. The position taken here is that this is an assumption that to date has not been adequately or systematically tested and hence of arguable validity.

5. See particularly the crime typology introduced in Marshall Clinard and Richard Quinney, *Criminal Behavior Systems: A Typology*, pp. 16-17.

6. For some understanding of the range of debate on the subject, see, Edwin H. Sutherland, "Is 'White Collar Crime' Crime?" *American Sociological Review*, 10 (1945): 132-139; also E. H. Sutherland, "White Collar, Criminality," *American Sociological Review*, 5 (1940): 1-12; also Paul W. Tappan, "Who is the Criminal?" *American Sociological Review*, 12 (1947): 96-102. For a general reference, see Gilbert Geis, *White Collar Criminal*.

7. Neil H. Borden, "The Concept of the Marketing Mix," *Journal of Advertising Research*, 4, no. 2, (1964): 2-7.

8. Borden's concept is particularly important in its stress of the *interdependence* which must exist in the formulation of policy in the four areas of product, place, price, and promotion. Even the best of products will fail if policies relating to its pricing, promotion, and distribution are not consonant with its "image." Similarly, the best promotional program in the world will not succeed in selling a poorly-conceived product or one whose mode of distribution is inappropriate.

9. The sale of goods can of course carry with it certain service obligations, such as the extension of warranties, credit, and repair facilities but since this transaction is centered on the sale of a product(s) the relationship must be characterized as goods-oriented rather than services-oriented. On the other hand, the customers of the fence might be construed as individuals providing "services" to him but this interpretation is

rarely used in business or marketing literature. In order to so interpret the relationship between fence and customer, one would need to establish not only a completely knowledgeable relationship but also a close and continuing commercial association. Even then it would remain somewhat moot as to who was providing whom with what "service."

10. The fence does of course respond to and benefit from the new product innovations of others. Thus when five- and ten-speed bicycles became popular consumer goods in the early 1970s they became popular targets for theft. The fence in this sense does not incur the costs of new product research and development or marketing program development but rather must decide his response to those products and programs paid for and made successful by others.

11. It should be remembered that the discussion here refers only to the stolen property product line of the fence and does not consider the legitimate lines he may also carry through the business he operates.

12. It was remarkable to the author to discover as much product information about fences in police files. This appears to demonstrate that detectives see, at least, the potential importance of such data for enforcement purposes.

13. This was a surprising finding since the "generalist fence" appears to be the one most often characterized as representative of the industry. That is why, undoubtedly, pawnbrokers are so often associated with criminal receiving, for their legitimate commercial generalism appears to imply an easy facilitation of illicit generalism.

14. The author attended this seminar on June 19, 1973, at the Federal Court Building in Albany, New York. The goods listing presented at the seminar included both products and product lines.

15. Two items in Table 11 which may strike the reader as surprising, however, relate to the single individuals noted to handle automobiles and guns. It is believed that the reasons for this are as follows.

First, the situation in which only one member of the sample is known to deal in stolen autos does not reflect the industry, but rather the compartmentalization of theft enforcement efforts within a police department. Thus, there was a separate auto theft squad in the department at the data site and that squad is believed to have significant information regarding the fence of motor vehicles. Burglary detectives with whom the author studied apparently did not see such fences or their supply sources as within their enforcement bailiwick and thus omit files on them.

Second, guns are a frequently stolen item and the reason for their lack of prominence here is that many guns and gun collections are considered "antiques" and are to be found under this category, handled by persons in this trade.

16. It should also be noted that the inclusion of the particular set of fences referred to here followed the investigation of a specific set of thefts of copper and nickel alloy primarily from warehouses.

17. Similar arrays of products as those noted here as being handled by fences are reported by: R. Kenneth Keenan and Loraine S. Peterson, "On Fencing," draft copy, report on fences in Miami, Florida, prepared for the National Institute of Law Enforcement and Criminal Justice, Law Enforcement Assistance Administration, U.S. Department of Justice, (August 1973), p. 65; copy kindly supplied by authors; and by the Memphis Police Department, Memphis, Tennessee, information compiled during a

field project by the Department in 1971 in which police spent $12,000 to recover $150,000 worth of stolen goods. Author acquired information through personal correspondence.

18. A more detailed discussion of the social and personal relationships that contribute to fencing networks follows in Chapter 5.

19. See Edwin H. Sutherland, *The Professional Thief*; Mary Owen Cameron, *The Booster and the Switch: Department Store Shoplifting*; Neal Shover, "Burglary as an Occupation" (Ph.D. dissertation, University of Illinois at Urbana-Champaign, 1971); and David W. Maurer, *The Whiz Mob*.

20. See Clinard and Quinney, *Criminal Behavior Systems*, pp. 16-17, for a tabular representation of many of these individuals.

21. From the picture presented at the data site, "safe men" appear to be a dying breed. No young safe men could be found; most with such skills being in their early to mid-forties. It is hard to know why this is so, but it is thought that the few talented safe artists left are not sharing their skills with others in an attempt to remain "useful" to others in the theft industry (both fences and other thieves) for as long as possible. The retirement prospects and prosperity of the professional thief remain melancholy indeed.

22. The juvenile burglar comprises such a small part of the detective's files that he will not be included henceforth. He is reflected here to illustrate the full range of thief types described by detectives.

23. There are, of course, a few quite successful addict-thieves at the data site. One safe man, for example, is an addict and has been able to support that habit quite comfortably without degenerating into the perpetration of foolish and unplanned thefts. Most individuals, however, appear to let their addictions "manage" their theft careers rather than vice versa, making them somewhat careless thieves regardless of the skills they may possess.

24. Location is a critical factor not only in fencing but in any "service" industry. This is because of the four inherent characteristics of "services"; intangibility; inseparability (i.e., they are created and marketed simultaneously); heterogeneity (no standardization); and perishability and fluctuating demand, derived from an inability to "store" them. For a fuller discussion of "services" as a commodity, see William J. Stanton, *Fundamentals of Marketing*, 3rd ed., pp. 566-572.

25. It should be noted once again that police files contain surprising amounts of information relating to the products handled by fences and stolen by thieves. Detectives do not appear to use this information, in the sense of devising policing strategies around it, and may include it for the sake of detail as discussed in the Appendix.

26. This was a random sample selected from the personal files on thieves maintained by the detective squad, described in the Appendix. Demographic information for this sample is available in Tables 3 and 6 in Chapter 2.

27. Police relate that recent changes in the exchange rates for gold and silver by the ounce have been reflected in the theft microcosm. At one time, for example, monogrammed silver pieces were ignored or junked by the good burglar because only scrap rates would be paid by fences; they are now exchanged at a discount of the legitimate metals market rates. The same is true of the settings for gemstones. Once junked by

thieves since the outlet was mostly to dental supply houses, they are now being sold to jewelers at some wholesale percentage of weight.

28. These codes will usually include at minimum the pawnbroker but may be extended as well to all retail businesses that buy and sell second-hand goods.

29. The "knowledgeable victim" presents another precaution for the fence or even a legitimate second-hand merchant to contend with. Pawn squad detectives reported cases in which some victims, initially unable to give a complete description of their property, will proceed to a pawnbroker or a second-hand merchant and take identifying information from an analogous item in his store. Then they will call the police and say they have found their records identifying the property. They will also say that they think they've found their property with "Mr. so and so." And for the price of a pawn ticket or the merchant's fee they can get that piece of property. It is because of the fraud of such victims that even bona fide stolen property found in such merchants' possession must have the ticket paid before it can be repossessed.

30. Incidents of this type have been reported by, among others, the New York City Police Department. See the statement of Assistant District Attorney Franklin H. Smitow, County of New York in U.S., Congress, Senate, Select Committee on Small Business, *Criminal Redistribution Systems and Their Economic Impact on Small Business, Hearings*, 93rd Cong., 1st sess., 1 May 1973, pp. 44-45.

31. In general marketers divide goods into two broad categories: consumer goods destined for consumption by final consumers; and user goods destined for intermediate markets where they are to be used in the manufacture or preparation of consumer goods. Each of these categories is further subdivided with consumer goods divided to include convenience, shopping and specialty products, and user goods divided into operating supplies, accessory equipment and so forth. The subdivisions of industrial or user goods are not used here since the user segment of the sample is so small.

32. In general, the subclassifications of consumer goods are based upon the degree of special or comparative shopping effort consumers will invest to acquire a given product. Some individuals in marketing feel that these classifications are too dependent upon a monolithic view of the consumer market. They note that what is a convenience good for one socioeconomic group of consumers may be a shopping good for others. The definitions used here do not come from standard textbook usage but from one such critical article by Richard H. Holt, "The Distinction Between Convenience Goods, Shopping Goods, and Specialty Goods," *Journal of Marketing*, 23, no. 1 (July 1958): 53-56. What is particularly attractive about Holt's discussion of the classifications is his conceptualization of them as being on a continuum rather than in strictly separate categories.

33. This is in the situation where the fence is not willing to exchange drugs for merchandise, a fairly common practice in some parts of the United States although not in the area in which this study was undertaken.

34. These exchange rates are examples only and not intended to suggest invariable pricing arrangements.

35. The nature of the wholesale price structure for furs and antiques depends upon the quality of the merchandise involved. The exchange rates here may not look particularly attractive but one must remember that they are *wholesale* quotations and there-

fore represent a good investment return for the thief of between 33 percent and 50 percent of the wholesale price.

36. This individual, a good burglar specializing in residential jewelry and fur thefts, is discussed further in the Appendix.

37. The particular relationship between the fence and the young thief is amplified in Chapter 5.

38. See Chapter 5.

39. One specific characteristic of the known burglar is the immobile status he achieves in the theft population. He usually cannot progress to the status of the good burglar since he has been "passed over," as it were, as a potential partner or associate for that individual. Hence his greater association with the fence than with other thieves exclusively.

40. What was particularly ironic about the case is that after it was purchased and its serial number recorded for inventory purposes, the analyzer was found to be the identical machine purchased new two years earlier by the university. A further check revealed that the item had been "missing" for more than a year but the theft (or loss) had never been reported.

41. Another interesting aspect of the trade in clothing was the prominent use of the private residence as a "store." Typically a basement or spare room was used to house racks of the stolen articles. Property handled in these situations did not appear to be stolen to order. Rather the individuals involved merely maintained an ample assortment suitable for their customers, and the clothing moved quickly. The cheapness of prices in these "stores" evidently made the goods move, for even if one cannot wear a $7 sports coat (because of size), he usually knows someone who can—especially at that price!

42. See particularly Benson P. Shapiro, "The Psychology of Pricing," *Harvard Business Review*, 46 (July-August 1968): 14-16; Harold J. Leavitt, "A Note on Some Experimental Findings about the Meanings of Price," *Journal of Business*, (July 1954): 205-210; Douglas J. McConnell, "The Price-Quality Relationship in an Experimental Setting," *Journal of Marketing Research*, 5, no. 3 (August 1968): 331-334; and James E. Stafford and Bea M. Enis, "The Price-Quality Relationship: An Extension," *Journal of Marketing Research*, 6, No. 4 (November 1969): 456-458.

43. Probably the hustle of this type demonstrating the greatest finesse was found at the data site perpetrated by a peddlar fence working the bar scene. He managed to sell for $100 to a "knowledgeable" bar patron, a television set which did not even exist.

44. Mary McIntosh, "Changes in the Organization of Thieving," in *Images of Deviance*, ed. Stanley Cohen, pp. 98-133.

45. J. Edgar Hoover, *Crime in the United States, Uniform Crime Reports 1970*, Federal Bureau of Investigation, p. 4.

46. The fact that legitimate marketers are beginning to appreciate the possible diminishing returns of their expensive promotional budgets was illustrated at a national meeting on cargo theft attended by the author in Chicago in September 1974. There, the president of Zenith Radio Corporation, Mr. John J. Nevin, related incidents in which thieves had rummaged through boxcars of entertainment equipment to find and take only Zenith products.

47. This individual was earlier described in Chapter 2.

48. A fuller discussion of the potentialities of this fence is reserved for Chapter 4 when the functional-facilitating front is described.

49. This is a situation frequently noted by law enforcement in relationship to cargo theft operations, where, because of labor racketeering and/or loan sharking practices in transport centers many marginal persons are corrupted or threatened into "giving-up" goods under their control or responsibility. See the discussion of the "ten-percenter" in Vincent Teresa, *My Life in the Mafia*, pp. 134-140.

CHAPTER 4

1. It is interesting that skepticism is apparently being generated from two sources: revelations of shenanigans in many respected American industries, such as in the case of the great electrical company conspiracy disclosures; and the findings of Congressional investigative committees regarding the entrenchment of "organized crime" in the legitimate business world. Recent Watergate-related disclosures regarding the dairy industry and the contributions of individual industrialists to political campaigns both here and abroad have also served to point up some of the seamier sides of American business practice.

2. Carl Klockars, "The Fence: Caveat Emptor, Caveat Vendor" (Paper delivered at the American Criminological Society meetings, Caracas, Venezuela, November 1972), kindly supplied by the author, p. 8.

3. See Chapter 2, Table 5.

4. This is with the exception of three of the antique dealers and three of the second-hand merchants in this segment whose trade appears to be mostly illicit.

5. Police departments who have recently begun programs setting themselves up as fences have found little difficulty in so establishing themselves. The Memphis Police Department, for example, merely advertised in the paper and received all the trade they wanted. (Information received through personal communication.)

6. Neal Shover, "Burglary as an Occupation," (Ph.d. dissertation, University of Illinois at Urbana-Champaign, 1971), p. 159. Shover contends that fences are good theft targets for thieves because they cannot report losses to the police, but he fails to take into account the legitimate losses that can be claimed. Instances of fences at the data site being ripped off by their clients were almost nonexistent, except for revenge purposes. Even then, the "fall-out" from such an escapade appeared to be serious enough to one's future career as a thief as to question the wisdom of such a move.

7. This is apparently a typical array regarding minority business endeavors where unequal access to capital limits most entrepreneurship to small, service-type trades rather than allowing for manufacturing and larger retailing endeavors to be undertaken. Even so the failure rate of inner city, minority businesses remains high. See Alan R. Andreasen, *Inner City Business*, p. 53.

8. That is, direct distribution under other than suspicious circumstances. The functional-facilitating front can only distribute goods *directly* to knowledgeable or sympathetic customers.

9. See Note 24 for Chapter 3.

10. Theft of services can of course be a crime, but such statutes are related to the failure to recompense merchants for services rendered rather than the "removal" of a service from another.

11. Had such arrangements been discovered, they would have been classified as integrative fronts.

12. Carpentry was the most popular extracurricular trade of the good burglar, for example. Three good burglars were known to maintain membership in building trades unions for the purpose of "casing" homes; and three known burglars have worked in construction jobs on state highways. The prevalence of labor racketeering at the data site appears to account for these individuals' ease of entry into such jobs. Further detail regarding the occupational affiliations of a random sample of burglars at the data site was found in Chapter 2, Table 6.

13. The abbreviation used by marketers to refer to businesses in the areas of construction, manufacturing, transportation, and wholesaling.

14. Further amplified in Chapter 5.

15. A breakdown of businessmen-fences relative to respectability versus marginality is found in Chapter 2, Table 2.

16. Tangential associations with the private charter club, discussed further in Chapter 5, seemed to form the basis for initial contacts between these individuals. It should also be noted that telephone communications are brief and cryptic when used.

17. That is, the art school is not distributing stolen art through its gallery, thereby meshing it with legitimate art. Instead its illicit business lies completely apart from its teaching and displaying of art works legitimately. In most cases this art school has been used in a contactual and intermediary role of evaluating stolen art for others and getting a cut of the final exchange price for those services.

18. The legitimate marketing system contains so much variability relating to each of these indicators that a full-blown theoretical framework through which to describe channels of distribution has largely eluded marketers. Relied on extensively here to describe the kinds of functions necessary in a channel of distribution have been the work of the following: Louis P. Bucklin, *A Theory of Distribution Channel Structure*; and Reavis Cox, Charles C. Goodman, and Thomas C. Fichandler, *Distribution in a High-Level Economy.*

19. The postponed inventory system which does not initiate "production" until an order is received allows for the careful coordination of transit functions to be preplanned. The hijacking is a good example of preplanning for distribution found in the theft industry. A truck is not diverted until the final destination(s) of its merchandise has been determined. Thus hijacked goods have often already been resold before their loss is reported to authorities.

20. As noted earlier this was a rare situation at the data site although occurring with more frequency in other parts of the country.

21. The information from this interview conducted in 1973 by the author is summarized in narrative form here.

22. The thief is generally not an affiliated member of a criminal superstructure although he can develop quasi-permanent ties with it as noted in Chapter 5.

23. The need for a front in the "blinding," deceptive sense is quite important where

the burglar is concerned since he generally has considerable visibility with police and has developed a reputation of notoriety which puts him under considerable suspicion and surveillance.

24. The "illusiveness" of these endeavors is likely to be more perceptual than real, but the detective is no less guilty than the criminologist in assuming magical talents on the part of organized crime figures.

CHAPTER 5

1. This is with the notable exception of John Mack. See John Mack, "Full Time Miscreants, Delinquent Neighborhoods and Criminal Networks," *British Journal of Sociology*, 15, no. 1 (March 1964): 38-53.

2. For a complete review of the conceptual development related to the term "network" see Lawrence W. Crissman, "On Networks," *Cornell Journal of Social Relations*, 4, no. 1 (Spring 1964): 72-81.

3. First introduced by J. A. Barnes, "Class and Committees in a Norwegian Island Parish," *Human Relations*, 7, no. 1 (1954): 39-58; then by Elizabeth Bott, *Family and Social Networks*.

4. Bott, *Family and Social Networks*, p. 57.

5. Robert A. Stebbins, "Social Network as a Subjective Construct: A New Application for an Old Idea," *Canadian Review of Sociology and Anthropology*, 6, no. 1 (February 1969): 1-14.

6. Ibid., p. 11.

7. For the most detailed development of the "subculture" concept as it relates to crime see Marvin Wolfgang and Franco Ferracuti, *The Subculture of Violence*, pp. 95-99.

8. Alvin W. Wolfe, "On Structural Comparisons of Networks," *Canadian Review of Sociology and Anthropology*, 7, no. 4 (November 1970): 226-244, at p. 229.

9. Ibid.

10. Mack, "Full Time Miscreants," p. 43. Emphasis added.

11. In one such situation at the data site, a fence who owned a television and appliance store and was receiving stolen home entertainment goods through it was much assisted by his brother who worked for a record album distributor as a truck driver. Thus the latter provided his brother with information on shipments of records that he could fence through the store.

12. It is hoped that the reader can avoid making the obvious popular associations with the term "godfather" as it has been used elsewhere.

13. For a fuller discussion of the intricacies of what anthropologists call compadrazgo ties, see George M. Foster, "Godparents and Social Networks in Tzintzuntzan," *Southwestern Journal of Anthropology*, 25, no. 3 (Autumn 1969): 261-278.

14. In this situation the family friend worked at a veterans' hospital and peddled watches and so forth received by Carl to patients at the hospital, and friends and relatives who came to visit them.

15. See Peter M. Blau and Otis Dudley Duncan, *The American Occupational Structure*, pp. 295-330.

16. Sharma really approximates the driving force behind the work-a-day network in his description of the resource network in a political context. "The resource network," says Sharma, "is one consisting almost entirely of instrumental relationships sustained by the continuity of obligations flowing from transactions subserving mutual interests." See K. N. Sharma, "Resource Networks and Resource Groups in the Social Structure," *Eastern Anthropologist*, 22, no. 1 (January-April 1969): 13-28, at p. 20. Here the relationship between fence and thief is instrumental in nature sustained by the obligation flowing from those transactions involving stolen property and job employment which subserve their mutual interests.

17. Where the good burglar is concerned, the interpretation of new work groups would be less clear since these thieves tend to float between crime partners much more frequently than do other types of thieves.

18. As quoted in Georg Simmel, *The Sociology of Georg Simmel*, edited, translated and with an introduction by Kurt H. Wolff, p. 50.

19. See Simmel, *The Sociology of Georg Simmel*, pp. 43-50. In addition, Theodore M. Mills of Yale University is probably the best known American sociologist-student of Simmel and the latter's theoretical work. The discussion here is based primarily on his contribution of "Some Hypotheses on Small Groups from Simmel," in *Georg Simmel*, ed. Lewis Coser, pp. 157-170.

20. Mills, "Some Hypotheses on Small Groups," p. 158.

21. Ibid., p. 160.

22. Ibid., p. 161.

23. John Mack, "The Able Criminal," (Paper presented to the Current Research Committee, VI World Criminological Congress, Madrid, Spain, 1970), p. 2.

24. This tendency related to a different occupational context is explained and research in support of it described in David G. Berger, "Status Attribution and Self-Perception Among Musical Specialties," *Sociological Quarterly*, 12, no. 2 (Spring 1971): 259-265.

25. Private charters in New York State for social clubs and associations must be submitted to and approved by a local judicial authority.

26. Mills, "Some Hypotheses on Small Groups," p. 160.

27. Mack, "Full Time Miscreants," p. 47.

28. Ake Bjerstedt, "Preparation, Process, and Product in Small Group Interaction," *Human Relations*, 14, no. 2 (May 1961): 183-189.

29. Bjerstedt's actual experiments were with children involved in a story telling task although he himself implies wider applications.

30. The addict is excepted because his frequent incarceration and physical problems make it difficult for him to establish any permanent relationships no matter how useful these might be.

31. Erving Goffman, *Stigma*, pp. 2-3.

32. Neal Shover, "Burglary as an Occupation," (Ph.D. dissertation, University of Illinois at Urbana-Champaign, 1971), pp. 92-94.

33. Michael A. Wallach, Nathan Kogan, and Daryl J. Ben, "Group Influence on Individual Risk Taking," *Journal of Abnormal Social Psychology*, 65, no. 2 (August 1962): 75-86.

34. The incident noted here from police files occurred in the late 1960s. This is a situation extremely unlikely to happen today given the value of silver metal which has caused an increase in thefts of dentists' offices to acquire even small amounts of the metal.

35. A situation to be elaborated in Chapter 6.

CHAPTER 6

1. Economics derives the utility concept from the pleasure-pain principle of Bentham, although the concept has received wide and continued support in most economic theories. See Paul A. Samuelson, *Economics*, 7th ed., pp. 414-434 for the popular, "modern" explanation of the concept.

2. Ibid., pp. 417-419.

3. Game theory was first introduced by John von Neumann and Oskar Morgenstern in *The Theory of Games and Economic Behavior*, (Princeton: Princeton University Press, 1953) and has seen many applications, mostly mathematical and experimental, since that time. The sources used here are simple and straightforward treatments of the basic theory and excellent references for the nonmathematician. See J. D. Williams, *The Compleat Strategyst*, rev., ed., (New York: McGraw-Hill, 1966); Morton D. Davis, *Game Theory*, (New York: Basic Books, 1970).

4. A more faithful representation of the citizen's role in the game is discussed later as the Type D Theft Game.

5. There are some reservations which we have about this last assumption which we will note as they arise, but these are problems which have more to do with the "real world" than with our model of it.

6. It should be noted that we doubt that the conventional view of theft even goes so far as to distinguish thieves in any manner, but we will give it the benefit of that doubt.

7. One might also posit that the known burglar also has the choice of committing a crime other than burglary, but evidence suggests that even this choice would remain in the theft area, robbery, for example, in which case many of the dimensions set down here would remain the same.

8. The known burglar may, of course, be greatly assisted in his decision-making by set-up information provided by the fence. In this case it is unlikely that the police will do very well against him since the fence will thereby have lowered the risks inherent in the crime.

9. It is somewhat unlikely that the known burglar will either accurately or diligently calculate opportunity costs as game theory suggests he must. This only makes our model of the game somewhat pessimistic vis-à-vis the police when they may be doing better given this thief's carelessness.

10. See, for example, M. Mandell, "May This House Be Safe from Burglars," *New York Magazine*, 17 April 1972; and "Moneysworth Report on Security Devices," *Moneysworth*, 17 May 1971.

11. That is, once a minimal level of security is established, each additional quantum of security yields relatively less and less to the consumer.

12. The concepts of the "suspect set" and of the detective's sorting function are

taken from the work of M.A.P. Willmer, *Crime and Information Theory*, pp. 13-14.

13. It will be assumed that the interrogation was conducted within the guidelines of permissible police conduct and hence would be admissable in court. One might also consider the possibility that the police were able to skillfully maneuver the two young suspects into a prisoner's dilemma situation, thereby insuring a confession.

14. While the activities of each individual remain highly determinate and inescapable, it is unlikely that any of them will know precisely the source of the direction they so keenly feel.

15. This view of property theft receives full discussion in Marilyn Walsh and Duncan Chappell, "Operational Parameters in the Stolen Property System," *Journal of Criminal Justice*, 2 (1974): 113-129.

16. In Introduction.

Bibliography

BOOKS

Andreasen, Alan R. *Inner City Business*. New York: Praeger, 1971.

Blau, Peter M. and Duncan, Otis Dudley. *The American Occupational Structure*. New York: Wiley, 1967.

Bott, Elizabeth. *Family and Social Networks*. London: Tavistock, 1957.

Brecht, Bertolt, and Weill, Kurt. *The Three-Penny Opera*. New York: Grove, 1964.

Bucklin, Louis P. *A Theory of Distribution Channel Structure*. Los Angeles and Berkeley: University of California Press, Institute of Business and Economic Research, 1966.

Cameron, Mary Owen. *The Booster and the Snitch*: *Department Store Shoplifting*. New York: Macmillan, 1964.

Clinard, Marshall, and Quinney, Richard. *Criminal Behavior Systems: A Typology*. New York: Holt, Rinehart, and Winston, 1967.

Colquhoun, Patrick. *A Treatise on the Police of the Metropolis*. 7th London ed., 1806. Reprint. Montclair, N.J.: Patterson Smith, 1969.

Cox, Reavis; Goodman, Charles C.; and Fichandler, Thomas C. *Distribution in a High-Level Economy*. Englewood Cliffs, N.J.: Prentice-Hall, 1956.

Cressey, Donald R. *Criminal Organization: Its Elementary Forms*. New York: Harper and Row (Harper Torchbooks), 1972.

Davis, Morton D. *Game Theory*. New York: Basic Books, 1970.

Defoe, Daniel. *The King of the Pirates*. New York: Jenson Society, 1901.

Dickens, Charles. *Oliver Twist*. London: Oxford University Press, 1949.

Fielding, Henry. *History of the Life of the Late Jonathan Wild. The Complete Works of Henry Fielding*, Vol. 2. New York: Barnes and Noble, 1967.

Gay, John. *The Beggar's Opera*. Lincoln, Neb.: University of Nebraska Press, Regents' Restoration Drama Series, 1969.

Geis, Gilbert. *White Collar Criminal.* New York: Atherton, 1968.

Goffman, Erving. *Stigma.* Englewood Cliffs, N.J.: Prentice-Hall, 1963.

Hall, Jerome. *Theft, Law and Society.* 2nd ed. Indianapolis: Bobbs-Merrill, 1952.

Holdsworth, Sr. William. *A History of English Law.* 5th ed. reprint, Vols. 5 and 15. London: Methuen, 1966.

Howson, Gerald. *Thief-Taker General: The Rise and Fall of Jonathan Wild.* London: Hutchinson, 1970.

Irwin, William Robert. *The Making of "Jonathan Wild": A Study in the Literary Method of Henry Fielding.* New York: Columbia University Press, 1941.

MacAdoo, William. *The Procession to Tyburn.* New York: Boni and Liveright, 1927.

Maurer, David W. *The Whiz Mob.* New Haven: College and University Press, 1964.

von Neumann, John, and Morgenstern, Oskar. *The Theory of Games and Economic Behavior.* Princeton, N.J.: Princeton University Press, 1953.

Samuelson, Paul A. *Economics.* 7th ed. New York: McGraw-Hill, 1967.

Simmel, Georg. *The Sociology of Georg Simmel.* Edited, translated and with an introduction by Kurt H. Wolff. Glencoe, Ill.: Free Press, 1950.

Stanton, William J. *Fundamentals of Marketing.* 3rd ed. New York: McGraw-Hill, 1971.

Sutherland, Edwin H. *The Professional Thief.* Chicago: University of Chicago Press, 1937.

Teresa, Vincent. *My Life in the Mafia.* Garden City, N.Y.: Doubleday, 1973.

Williams, J.D. *The Compleat Strategyst.* New York: McGraw-Hill, 1966.

Wilmer, M.A.P. *Crime and Information Theory.* Edinburgh: Edenburgh University Press, 1970.

Wolfgang, Marvin, and Ferracuti, Franco. *The Subculture of Violence.* London: Tavistock, 1967.

ARTICLES IN BOOKS, JOURNALS, AND PERIODICALS

Barnes, J.A. "Class and Committees in a Norwegian Island Parish." *Human Relations* 7 (1954): 39-58.

Berger, David G. "Status Attribution and Self-Perception Among Musical Specialities." *Sociological Quarterly* 12(1971): 259-265.

Bjerstedt, Ake. "Preparation, Process, and Product in Small Group Interaction." *Human Relations* 14(1961): 183-189.

Borden, Neil H. "The Concept of the Marketing Mix." *Journal of Advertising Research* 4(1964): 2-7.

Chappell, Duncan, and Walsh, Marilyn. "'No Questions Asked': A Consideration of the Crime of Criminal Receiving." *Crime and Delinquency* 20(1974): 157-168.

Churchill, Betty C. "Rise in the Business Population." *Survey of Current Business* (May 1959): 17-18.

Crissman, Lawrence W. "On Networks." *Cornell Journal of Social Relations* 4(1964): 72-81.

Foster, George M. "Godparents and Social Networks in Tzintzuntzan." *Southwestern Journal of Anthropology* 25(1969): 261-278.

Hall, Jerome. "Theft, Law and Society—1968." *American Bar Association Journal* 54(1968): 960-967.

Holt, Richard H. "The Distinction Between Convenience Goods, Shopping Goods, and Specialty Goods." *Journal of Marketing* 23 (1958): 53-56.

Leavitt, Harold J. "A Note on Some Experimental Findings About the Meanings of Price." *Journal of Business* (July 1954): 205-210.

Lewis, Michael. "Structural Deviance and Normative Conformity: The 'Hustle' and the 'Gang'." In *Crime in the City*, edited by Daniel Glaser, pp. 176-199. New York: Harper and Row, 1970.

Mack, John. "Full Time Miscreants, Delinquent Neighborhoods and Criminal Networks." *British Journal of Sociology* 15 (1964): 38-53.

Mandall, N. "May This House Be Safe from Burglary." *New York Magazine*, 17 April 1972.

McConnell, Douglas J. "The Price-Quality Relationship in an Experimental Setting." *Journal of Marketing Research* 5 (1968): 331-334.

McIntosh, Mary. "Changes in the Organization of Thieving." In *Images of Deviance*, edited by Stanley Cohen, pp. 98-133. Baltimore: Penquin, 1971.

Mills, Theodore M. "Some Hypotheses on Small Groups from Simmel." In *George Simmel*, edited by Lewis A. Coser, pp. 157-170. Englewood Cliffs, N.J.: Prentice-Hall, 1965.

Radzinowicz, Sir Leon. "Economic Pressures." In *The Criminal In Society*, Vol. 1 of 2 vols., *Crime and Justice*, edited by Sir Leon Radzinowicz and Marvin Wolfgang, pp. 420-442. New York: Basic Books, 1971.

Shapiro, Benson P. "The Psychology of Pricing." *Harvard Business Review* 46 (1968): 14-16.

Sharma, K.N. "Resource Networks and Resource Groups in the Social Structure." *Eastern Anthropologist* 22 (1969): 13-28.

Stafford, James E., and Enis, Bea M. "The Price-Quality Relationship: An Extension." *Journal of Marketing Research* 6 (1969): 456-458.

Stebbins, Robert A. "Social Network as a Subjective Construct: A New Application for an Old Idea." *Canadian Review of Sociology and Anthropology* 6 (1969): 1-14.

Sutherland, Edwin H. "Is 'White Collar Crime' Crime?" *American Sociological Review* 10 (1945): 132-139.

———. "White Collar Criminality." *American Sociological Review* 5 (1940): 1-12.

Tappan, Paul W. "Who Is the Criminal?" *American Sociological Review* 12 (1947): 96-102.

Wallach, Michael A.; Kogan, Nathan; and Ben, Daryl J. "Group Influence on Individual Risk Taking." *Journal of Abnormal Social Psychology* 65 (1962): 75-86.

Walsh, Marilyn, and Chappell, Duncan. "Operational Parameters in the Stolen Property System." *Journal of Criminal Justice* 2 (1974): 113-129.

Wolfe, Alvin W. "On Structural Comparisons of Networks." *Canadian Review of Sociology and Anthropology* 7(1970): 226-244.

MONOGRAPHS, REPORTS, GOVERNMENT DOCUMENTS, AND UNPUBLISHED MATERIALS

Association of Grand Jurors of New York County. *The Criminal Receiver of Stolen Goods—Source of Organized Crime and Creator of Criminals.* Report of the Prison Committee. New York: Putnam, 1928.

Great Britain, Minutes and Proceedings of the Committee of 1770. Parliament (Commons). *House of Commons Journal* 32: 784, 798, 874, 878-883.

Keenan, R. Kenneth and Peterson, Lorraine. "On Fencing." Report prepared for the National Institute of Law Enforcement and Criminal Justice, Law Enforcement Assistance Administration, August 1973. Mimeographed.

Kockars, Carl. "The Fence: Caveat Emptor, Caveat Vendor." Paper given at the American Criminological Society Meetings, November 1972, Caracas, Venezuela. Mimeographed.

Mack, John. "The Able Criminal." Paper delivered to the Current Research Seminar, VI World Criminological Congress, 1970, Madrid, Spain. Mimeographed.

"*Moneysworth* Report on Security Devices." *Moneysworth*, 17 May 1971.

President's Commission on Law Enforcement and the Administration of Justice. *The Challenge of Crime in a Free Society.* Report of the Commission. Washington, D.C.: Government Printing Office, 1967.

"The Report of the Society for the Suppression of Mendicity." *The Quarterly Review.* 64 (1839): 341-369.

Shover, Neal. "Burglary as an Occupation." Ph.D. dissertation, University of Illinois at Urbana-Champaign, 1971.

U.S., Congress, Senate, Select Committee on Small Business, *Criminal Redistribution Systems and Their Economic Impact on Small Business,* Hearings, 93rd Cong., 1st sess., 1 and 2 May 1973. Washington, D.C.: Government Printing Office.

U.S., Department of Commerce, Bureau of the Census. *Characteristics of the Population,* vol. 1, New York, Pt. 34, Sec. 2. Washington, D.C.: Department of Commerce, March 1973.

U.S., Department of Justice, Federal Bureau of Investigation. *Crime in the United States—Uniform Crime Reports, 1970.* Washington, D.C.: Government Printing Office.

Index

Able criminal, 8, 9

Action set: as exclusive contract, 126; fencing definition of, 125; as temporal monopoly, 126; and thief's risk perception, 140; Wolfe's definition of, 118; and young burglar, 127, 141

Addicts: as burglars, 46-47, 62-63, 155; enforcement emphasis on, 159-160; fences dealing with, 63-65, 89, 97, 107; and fencing networks, 138; lack of planning of, 155, 158; as lone thief, 146; number of, 64, 156; prices received by, 71-72; strategies of, 155-159; and theft game, 154-60; volume stolen by, 65, 155

American business, 85-86

Antiques, 67; mark-up on, 77; promotion of, 82

Association of Grand Jurors of New York County: Study of receiving made by, 4, 13

Beggar's Opera, 30-31, 35-36; and Three Penny Opera, 35; political use of characters in, 31

Bjerstedt, Ake, 131

Blind. See Front

Bookmakers. See Criminal entrepreneurs

Boosters, 62; fences dealing with, 63-64; fence's monopoly over, 74-75; and standard price, 72; volume stolen by, 66

Boosting, 155-56

Borden, Neil, 53

Brecht, Bertolt, 38

Burglars: acquisition of skills by, 143-44; ages of, 42-44; arrest history of, 46-49, 61-62; associations among, 139-40; composite of, 49, 51; drug-related offences of, 47-48, 62; employed by fence, 96, 123, 126; as fences, 110-11; occupational affiliations of, 45-46; and "scores" owed to fence, 96; social sanctuaries of, 96, 132; weapons' use of, 47-48, 61-62; work groups of, 123, 141, 145. See also Thief

"Burn men," 171

Busch, Joseph P., 8

Businessman-fences: creative bookkeeping of, 68; and criminal entrepreneur, 135-36; criminological significance of, 52-53; employment of thief by, 96, 123, 126; factors contributing to illicit trade of, 91, 95; and fronts, 87-88; and independent fence, 135; links between, 134; price structure of, 79-80; product choices of, 58-59, 103; promotion by, 82-83; "scores" owed to, 96; storage facilities of, 65-67; and work-a-day network, 123. *See also* Criminal receivers; Fences

Cameron, Mary Owen, 61, 62
Categorical set, 118; and play network, 129
Caught criminal, 8
Channel of distribution, 85; in dissonant fronts, 101-103; and fence's front, 88; in functional-facilitating fronts, 92-93
Clothing, 55; and "one-third principle," 78. *See also* Products (of fences)
Colquhoun, Patrick, 13; comments on Jews and pawnbrokers, 34; indictment of criminal receiver, 3; *A Treatise on the Police of the Metropolis*, 3, 34
Consumer goods: handled by fences, 69-70; in 20th century, 27; mass-owned and mass-produced, 27, 69; types of, 70n. *See also* Personal property
"Conventional view of theft": and addict, 160; archeological nature of, 173; assessment of, 160, 164, 167, 170, 174; definition of, 147; enforcement response of, 171, 172, 176; and good burglar, 167; and known burglar, 164; marginal utility of, 149, 159, 160, 175; and stolen property marketplace, 173; thief-oriented nature of, 148, 171, 172; weaknesses of, 172-173; and "we-they" game, 168-69
Conwell, Chic, 61
Court of Aldermen, 22
Craft crime, 11, 18; bonds of similarity in, 12
Craft criminal, 12
Cressey, Donald B., 10-12

Criminal behavior: analyses of, 116; causes of, 14, characterizations of, 28; collective, 116; factors and circumstances associated with, 14, 179; fence's reward of, 142; as individual maladjustment, 10, 179; organized, 10-11; shaped by legitimate settings, 87
Criminal characterizations, 28
Criminal entrepreneurs: and businessman-fences, 135-36; contactual services of, 111; extortion by, 84, 108; as fences, 42, 83, 106-11; as mediators, 131; and play network, 132; primary vocations of, 107; retaliatory power of, 138; status of, 109; table on, 108. *See also* Criminal superstructures
Criminal organization: rationality of, 10; role differentiation in, 11
Criminal possession: arrests for, 8; related to criminal receiving, 5, 8
Criminal receiver(s): activities of, 3, 4; affect on property theft, 12, 140, 142, 143; anonymity of, 6, 17, 179; colloquial term for, 4; commercial characteristics of, 53; contemporary picture of, 16, 38; critical ingredients of, 24; demographic characteristics of, 15, 39-47; Dickens' portrayal of, 33; as established economic participant, 6; financial means of, 24; historical picture of, 16; illusiveness of, 6, 15, 179; image-building of, 24-25; importance of control for, 26, 27; importance of property for, 27, 177; individual attributes of, 12, 15, 52; as intermediary, 6, 15, 77; lack of investigation of, 6; lawful enterprise of, 24; legal definition of, 4; legitimate fronts of, 87-88; literary references to 4, 33; and marketer-producer relationship, 13, 175; as market manager, 11-12, 14, 15, 39, 175-76; profits of, 91-92; as recruiter of thieves, 142; relationship with police, 7, 26;

relationship with thieves, 3, 4, 7, 13, 58, 60, 71, 99, 100, 133, 137-151, 175; role of, 12, 17, 53-54; services provided by, 4, 53, 71, 121, 142, 175; setting of, 12, 25, 27, 65, 79-80, 106-15; social services dimension of, 96; tacit immunity of, 26. *See also* Fence

Criminal receiving: careers in, 15, 43; competitive state of, 137-138; conceptual framework relating to, 6; and contact with thieves, 92; crime of, 5; as crime without criminal, 28; definition of, 6; factors and circumstances associated with, 14; folklore relating to, 6, 15, 18, 27-38, 177; importance of organization to, 24-25; importance of power to, 25-26; importance of property to, 26-27; and Jews, 34-35; and location, 91; low visibility of, 24; medium-sized firms in, 137; misleading statistics on, 8; as original offense, 17, 28; and performance of marketing functions, 13, 106; personification of, 28, 33; proscribed as possession statute, 5, 8; and racial biases, 41, 144; as "theft insurance," 91

Criminals: businessmen as, 86; community of, 119; illicit settings of, 86; individual maladjustment of, 10; organizational arrangements of, 10; relationships among, 10, 116

Criminal superstructure: and businessman-fences, 101; contactual services of, 111; moral entrepreneurship of, 133; and theft industry, 132-33, 137; transit services of, 111; violent elements of, 132. *See also* Criminal entrepreneurs

Criminologist: relationship with offenders, 9-10; relationship with police, 8, 9; tools of, 178-79

Criminology, 14

Customers: as consumption ends, 6; of fence, 54; knowledgeable, 80

Debtors: in 18th century London, 18
DeFoe, Daniel, 29
Demand forecasting, 69
Deterrence, 169
Dickens, Charles, 32-33, 36
Discount house, 79
Dissonant fronts, 100-103; channel of distribution in, 101, 104-5; characteristics of, 102-3; clientele of, 100, 104; marketing patterns of, 106; product line of, 100-1, 103-4; relationship with legitimate businesses, 100-1; table on, 102; underworld associations in, 101. *See also* Front

"Drop," 75

Employee fences, 113-115. *See also* Criminal receivers; Fences
Enforcers, 74, 107-9. *See also* Criminal entrepreneurs
English Poor Law, 32-33
"Expected price," 79

Fagin: as caricature, 33; contemporary uses of, 36; as corrupter of youth, 32, 37; Dickens' description of, 32-33, 36; as generic term, 36; as Jew, 32, 35

False Pretenses Act, 34

Fences: ages of, 42-44; arrest history of, 46-49; burglars as, 110-11; businesses of, 46, 58-59; clients of, 54, 89, 96-98, 100, 103-4; collusive practice of, 73, 138; compared with legitimate managers, 40, 43-44; composite of, 49-52; cooperation with researcher, 7; customers of, 54; demographic characteristics of 15, 39-47; as differentiated part of underworld, 11-12; extortion by, 84, 108; females as, 39-41; functional relationships of, 13, 16, 175; "groupness" of, 138; guidance provided to thief by, 72, 142, 143, 175; handling new goods, 68-69; handling used goods, 68; as hustler, 13; as illegal entrepreneur, 42, 106-11; and industry norms, 138; legitimate product line of, 60; legitimate status of, 15, 41, 44-46, 52, 58-59; links between, 133-34; as market manager, 11-12, 13, 14, 15, 176; monopoly of, 74-75, 126-27; nonwhite males as, 39-42; occupational affiliations of, 45-46; as police statistic, 9; as pricemaker, 71, 175; as prison statistic, 8; product specialization of, 56-57, 58-59, 142, 175; profits of, 91-92; promotional considerations of, 81-84; rationality of, 13; as recruiter of thieves, 142, 146; role of, 13, 16, 53-54, 175; selling price of, 76-81; sophistication of, 13; sources of supply of, 60, 65, 91, 124, 137; storage and transit facilities of, 65-66, 105; as structural "given," 15; territorial rights of, 74-75; types of, 115; as unknown crime figure, 5, 179; as viewed by thief, 7, 138-39; volume handled by, 65-67; white males as, 39, 42-43. See also Businessman-fences; Criminal receivers

Fencing. See Criminal receiving

Fencing Networks: and addict, 138; advantages of membership in, 138-45; and association, 139; criminological implications of, 145-46; and information dissemination, 144-45; and initiation of thief, 141-42; as insulator and isolator of thief, 145; as personnel department of theft industry, 146; and procedural ratiocination, 142-43; race as barrier to, 144; and recruitment, 141; relationship with theft industry, 138-45; and risk-taking, 139-41; and selective skill diffusion, 143-44; types of, 119. See also Kinship network; Play network; Work-a-day network

Fielding, Henry, 31, 35

Fielding, Sir John, 13; Parliamentary testimony of, 3, 34

Field set, 118

Front: as blind, 86-87, 101; and channel stability, 85; functions of, 87. See also Legitimate fronts

Functional-facilitating fronts, 92-100; advantages of, 98-99; channel of distribution in, 92, 99, 100, 104-05; characteristics of, 93, 100; clientele of, 96-98, 104; employment of thieves in, 96; information generated by, 100; marketing patterns in, 106; product line in, 92, 94, 99, 100, 103-04; product-service mesh in, 93, 98, 100; and relationship with legitimate businesses, 94-96, 99-100; tables on, 93, 95, 97; types of, 97

"Game": interests in, 150; theft as, 149-51; theoretical definition of, 149

Game matrix, 150-52

Game theory, 149; "dominance" in, 157; minimax principle in, 159; mixed strategy in, 163; payoffs in, 151, 158; "player" in, 150; "poor gambler's ruin" in, 174

Gay, John, 30-31, 35; Beggar's Opera, 30; Polly, 30

Goffman, Erving, 139

Good burglars, 61; bargaining power of, 130-31; collusion by fence against, 73; "employment" by fences, 126-27; fences dealing with, 63-65, 89; as good game player, 164; independence of, 130-31; planning of, 164; and play network, 130; prices received by, 72-73; proportion of, 63; specialization of, 164, 166; union membership of, 96; volume stolen by, 65-66; work partners of, 131-32; work style of, 163-65

Hall, Jerome, 14; analysis of criminal receiving, 4; approach to criminal receiver, 6; distinction between lay and professional receivers, 5; shrewdness of criminal receiver, 24

Hitchen, Charles, 18-19
"Hood," 110

Illegal entrepreneurs. *See* Criminal entre-
    preneurs
Independent fences, 111-113; and busi-
    nessman-fences, 135; as full-time
    fence, 113. *See also* Fences
Industrialization: and increased output,
    81; and project crime, 11; and rela-
    tionship to property theft, 11, 81
Inner city: business interests in, 41-42;
    and non-white fences, 41; subcul-
    tural definition of, 36-37
Integrative fronts, 88-92; channel of dis-
    tribution in, 88, 105; characteristics
    of, 88, 90-91, 92; clientele of, 103-4;
    factors contributing to illicit trade
    of, 91-92; marketing patterns of,
    106; pricing in, 91; product line in,
    92, 103; profit margins in, 90-91;
    and relationship with legitimate
    businesses, 90-91, 92; tables on
    89-90; transaction capacity of, 90
Inventory systems, 105

Jewelry, 26, 57, 58, 63, 76. *See also* Prod-
    ucts (of fences)
Jews: Colquhoun's comments on, 34; and
    criminal receiving, 34; as described
    by Society for Suppression of Mendi-
    city, 35; and Fagin, 35
"John Doe alibis," 68
"Jonathan Wild Act," 21, 23. *See also*
    Wild, Jonathan
Junk Businesses, 36-37
Junkie, 62-63. *See also* Addicts
Juvenile burglar, 62

Kinship network, 119-123; definition of,
    119; and exploitation of family ties,
    122; familiarity of, 120; and family-
    like ties, 121; origin of, 119-20;
    paternalism of, 122; as personal set,
    119; progressive nature of, 120; and
    young burglar, 120

Klockars, Carl, 86-87
Knowledge: legal requirement of, 5
Known burglar, 62; anonymity of, 162-
    63; fences dealing with, 63-65, 89,
    97; fence's monopoly over, 75-76;
    planning ability of, 161; strategies
    of, 161; target selection of, 160-61;
    union membership of, 96; volume
    stolen by, 66; and work-a-day net-
    work, 123; work style of, 160, 162

Lay receiver, 5
Legitimate fronts, 87-107; channels of
    distribution in, 104-6; character-
    istics of, 92-93, 100, 101-2; clienteles
    of, 104; contactual complexity of,
    106; marketing indicators in, 103-6;
    markets tapped by, 105; product
    lines of, 103-4; types of, 88
Lewis, Michael, 13
Limited networks, 118
Loansharks. *See* Criminal entrepreneurs
Lost Property Office, 19, 25. *See also*
    Wild Jonathan

MacHeath, 30-31
McIntosh, Mary, 11, 81
Mack, John: and network concept, 119;
    and professional criminal, 8, 129,
    130
Madison Avenue ethos, 25
Malthusian philosophy, 32-33
Marginal utility, 148-49
Marketing (field of), 14
Marketing mix, 53; "place" element of,
    85; "price" element of, 71; "prod-
    uct" element of, 54; "promotion"
    element of, 81
Marketplace (legitimate; pre-selling in,
    84; production and marketing in, 13
Mauer, David W., 61
Metals, 56. *See also* Products (of fences)
Mills, Theodore M., 128-30
Minimax principle, 159
Monopolistic fence, 74-75

Narcotics dealers. *See* Criminal entrepreneurs
Neighborhood fence, 63, 143-44
Network: definition based on John Mack, 119; use in criminology, 119; use in social sciences, 117. *See also* Fencing networks

Oliver Twist, 32-33
"One-third principle," 78
Organization: Cressey's definition of, 10-12; as fundamental part of property theft, 12-13; illicit forms of, 13
Outlaw(s): as societal isolate, 11; Fagin's boys as, 32

Pamphleteers (handiwork of), 29
Parliament (Great Britain): act of 1712 relieving debtors, 18; Committee of 1770 of, 34; False Pretenses Act of, 34; Fielding's testimony before, 3, 34; Receiving Stolen Goods Act of 1770, 34; regulation of peddlars by, 35; 1719 statute on "transportation," 21; 1693 statute on thief-taking, 18-19
Pawnbrokers: American legal treatment of, 35; associated with criminal receiving, 7, 15, 33-34, 36-37; by British Parliament, 35; Colquhoun's comments on, 34; and False Pretenses Act, 34; Fielding's comments on, 34; 16th and 17th century regulation of, 33; trade of, 33-34
Peachum, 30-31
Peddlars: American legal treatment of, 35; association with criminal receiving, 7, 15, 36; and "knowledgeable" customer, 80; on New York's Times Square, 37; promotion by, 83; regulation by British Parliament, 35; setting of, 79-80. *See also* Independent fence; Street fence
Personal set, 118; and kinship network, 119
Personal property: 18th century owner-
ship of, 26; insurance of, 168-69; most frequently stolen, 55-57; serialization of, 68; 20th century ownership of, 27
"Play," 128
Play networks, 128-33; and businessman-fences, 131; as a categorical set, 129; and criminal entrepreneur, 132; and criminal superstructure, 132-33; definition of, 128; elitism of, 129-30; and good burglar, 130; and private social club, 130; stability of, 133; status of members of, 129, 130; symbolic function of, 133
Police: access to materials of, 8; capacity to mix strategies, 164; designations of thief-types, 61-62; files of, 9; organized nature of, 26; provincialism of, 99; relationship with criminologist, 8, 9; reliance on informants, 153-54, 166; response to crime, 153-54, 162, 167; strategies against addict, 156-57, 159-60; strategies against good burglar, 166, 167; strategies against known burglar, 162-63; surveillance by, 151, 159, 166, 167; target patrolling by, 151, 152-53, 158, 167; theft enforcement strategies of, 151-54; and "theft game," 149-50; as untapped resource, 8; use of fence by, 26; and "we-they" game, 168
"Poor gambler's ruin," 174
Popping cars, 155, 157, 158
President's Commission on Law Enforcement and the Administration of Justice, 4
Price/quality relationship, 79
Pricing policy (of fences), 71-81; to beat competition, 73; determined by, 71-72; impact of setting on, 78-81; loyalty of others to, 74; monolithic view of, 71-81; monopolistic aspects of, 74-76; and "one-third principle," 78; with regard to customers, 76-81; with regard to thief, 71-76
"Product set," 58

Products (of fences), 54-70; brand assortment of, 55; demand as determinant of, 69; lines of, 55, 103; matching legal goods, 88; in new condition, 68-69; policies relating to, 54; related to type of theft, 64-65; restrictions on, 60; specialization in, 55, 57, 64; in used condition, 67-68; volume handled, 65-66
Professional receiver, 5. See also Criminal receiver; Fence
Professional thief. See Good Burglar
Project crime, 11-12, 81
Promotion (by fences), 81-84; via blackmail/extortion, 84; of an image, 83-84; and pre-selling in legitimate marketplace, 84; and type of goods handled, 82-83
Property theft: complexity of, 12, 176-77; as conflict situation, 149; as craft crime, 11; developmental context of, 11, 81; integrated nature of, 142; occupational specialties in, 11, 175; opportunity and incentive for, 173, 176; organization of, 12, 81, 142-43, 145-46; as organized crime, 10-11; as part of economy, 14; perspectives on, 17, 147, 176; police responses to, 153-54; precautions taken against, 11, 161, 169-80; principals of, 17; schematic of, 16, 177; and Stolen Property System, 176; and "we-they" game, 168-69. See also Theft industry
Purse snatching, 156

"Quality," the, 19; snobbishness of, 22; thieves' impersonation of, 20

Racketeers. See Criminal entrepreneurs
Radzinowicz, Sir Leon, 14, 179
Receiver. See Criminal receiver; Fence
Receiving Stolen Goods Act of 1770, 34
"Reihan-Phanomen," 131
Residential fence, 83, 113-14. See also Employee fence; Independent fence

Role System set, 118

Safe artist, 61
"Scores," 96, 123, 152
Second-hand dealers, 36-37
Security systems, 161-62, 168-70
"Services," 92n, 94, 95, 98
"Set-up," 98, 121, 131, 140
Sheppard, Jack, 35; career of, 22; execution of, 23; and Jonathan Wild, 22-23; as MacHeath, 30-31
Shopping goods, 69; pricing of, 77-79; promotion of, 81-83
Shover, Neal, 61, 140
Simmel, Georg, 128
"Skim-the-cream" pricing, 77
Small businesses (and fencing), 42
"Social game," 127-28
Social network, 117; holistic perspective on, 118; and subculture, 117
Society for the Suppression of Mendicity, 34-35
Specialty goods, 70; pricing of, 77-78; promotion of, 81-82
"Standard price," 72
Stebbins, Robert A., 117
Stolen property marketplace: and conventional view of theft, 173; demand and supply in, 176; enforcement intervention in, 177; fence-thief interaction in, 13
Stolen Property System, 175-77; and conventional view of theft, 176; definition of, 175; and enforcement responses, 177; schematic of, 177. See also Theft industry
Store detective, 158
Street fence, 67-68. See also Independent fence; Peddlar
Subculture, 37; as a field set, 118; and social network concept, 117; and taxonomy of Wolfe, 118
Suspect set, 171
Suspicious car check, 152
Sutherland, Edwin H., 61, 179

Television, 55, 57, 58-59. *See also* Products (of fences)

"Theft element," 154

Theft game: players in, 150-51; strategies of addict in, 155-56, 157-58; strategies of good burglar in, 167; strategies of known burglar in, 161, 163; strategies of police in, 151-55; "we-they" version of, 168-70

Theft industry: basic changes in, 48; competitive state of, 73-74, 136-37; and criminal superstructure, 132-33; fence as middleman in, 53; fence to fence linkages in, 134; groupings in, 116, 118-19, 145; growth rate of, 81; medium-sized firm in, 137; nature of demand in, 69; norms in, 138; personnel department of, 146; "production" of goods by, 54; "product set" in, 58; promotional component of, 87; rational arrangement of, 65, 145; stable state of, 137. *See also* Property theft; Stolen Property System

Thief or thieves: associations among, 139, 145; as supply source, 60, 124; career development of, 143-44; as craft criminal, 11; demographic characteristics of, 15; distinguished from criminal receiver, 5; fence as customer of, 53; as fences, 110-11; fence's influence on, 72, 142, 175; and Jonathan Wild, 19-21: meeting places of, 132, 151; mobility of, 62-63, 155; as productive source, 6, 14, 142; as project criminal, 11; relationship with criminal receiver, 7, 13, 58, 60, 71-72, 99, 100, 103-4, 175; relationship with police, 7; types of, 61-64; who steals and sells stolen goods, 12; who steals to convert, 15, 173-74; willingness to talk about fence, 7; women as, 41; work groups of, 123, 141, 145. *See also* Addicts; Boosters; Good burglar; Known burglar; Young burglar

Thief-Taker General. *See* Wild, Jonathan

Thief-taking: as used by Jonathan Wild, 20-21; definition of, 18; exploitation of, 20; in contemporary era, 26; involvement of public officials in, 19; lucrative aspects of, 20, 32; rewards for, 19, 20; 1693 statute prescribing, 19

Three Penny Opera, 38

"Transportation" procedure, 21

Treatise on the Police of the Metropolis, 3, 34

Tyburn tree, 23

Under-City Marshall. *See* Hitchen, Charles

Underworld, 12

United States Senate Select Committee on Small Business, 8

Urbanization: relationship to property theft, 11

User goods, 70n; pricing of, 78-79; promotion of, 82-83

Utility (concept of), 148

Walpole Government, 31

Weill, Kurt, 38

"We-they" game, 169-70

Wild, Jonathan, 6, 15, 81, 126; advertisements of, 19; arrest of, 23; aura of, 29; association with Charles Hitchen, 19; and *Beggar's Opera*, 30-31, 35; career of, 18-23; as classic case, 17; compared with Fagin, 33; "corporation" of, 25; decline of, 23; DeFoe's biography of, 29; as evil incarnate, 29; historical context of, 23; information control of, 26; and Jack Sheppard, 22-23; and "The Jonathan Wild Act," 21; lessons of, 27; literary treatments of, 30-32; Lost Property Office of, 19, 21-22; minute historical niche of, 27; notorious death of, 25, 28; organization of, 23-25; as Peachum, 30-31; petition for freeman status by, 22; posthumous transformation of, 29-32; power of,

25-26; property awareness of, 26-27; public image of, 19, 21-22, 24-25; relationship with the "Quality," 19; relationships with thieves, 20; smuggling trade of, 22; standardization of English thievery by, 20; successors of, 28; symbolic use of, 31-32; as Thief-taker General, 20, 21, 25; and "transportation" procedure, 21; as unique case, 25

Wolfe, Alvin W., 117; criminological concepts related to work of, 118, 119, 125, 129; limited networks of, 118; taxonomy of social networks of, 117-118

Women: as fences, 39-41; as thieves, 41

Wood Street Compter, 18

Work-a-day network, 123-127; as action set, 125; and businessman-fences, 123; definition of, 123; and Jonathan Wild, 127; and known burglar, 123, 124; and offender employment, 123, 126, 141; and young burglar, 127

Young burglar, 62; and action set, 127; fences dealing with, 63-64, 89, 97; fence's monopoly over, 74-75; and kinship network, 120; prices received by, 72; volume stolen by, 66

Zero-sum game, 149-50

About the Author

Marilyn E. Walsh is a research scientist at the Batelle Law and Justice Study Center in Seattle, Washington. She has written articles for such publications as *Criminology, Journal of Criminal Justice*, and the *Crime and Justice Annual*.